Primary Readings on the Eucharist

Edited by Thomas J. Fisch

PRIMARY READINGS ON THE EUCHARIST

A PUEBLO BOOK

Liturgical Press Collegeville, Minnesota

www.litpress.org

A Pueblo Book published by the Liturgical Press

Design by Frank Kacmarcik, Obl.S.B.

Library of Congress Cataloging-in-Publication Data

Primary readings on the Eucharist / edited by Thomas J. Fisch.
    p. cm.
  "A Pueblo book."
  Includes bibliographical references and index.
  ISBN 0-8146-6187-4 (pbk. : alk. paper)
  1. Lord's Supper. I. Fisch, Thomas, 1946–

BV825.3.P75 2004
264'.36—dc22

2004001770

To the memory
of my father

FERDINAND JOSEPH FISCH

and of

MICHAEL MARX, O.S.B.

one of my fathers in theology

Contents

Acknowledgments

I am grateful to the persons and publishers listed below for permission to reprint material for this volume.

To Brevard S. Childs for the final two chapters of his book, *Memory and Tradition in Israel*. Studies in Biblical Theology 37. London: SCM Press, 1962.

To Robert F. Taft, S.J., and to *Worship* and the Liturgical Press for the essays reprinted here as chapters 2, 8, and 9.

To Dominic E. Serra and *Ecclesia Orans*, Rome, for chapter 7.

To Bishop Kallistos (Ware) of Diokleia and *Sobornost*, Oxford, for chapter 10.

To OCP Publications, Portland, Oregon, for chapter 3.

To Brill Academic Publishers, Leiden, for chapter 4.

To Sheed and Ward, Lanham, Maryland, for chapter 5.

To The University of Notre Dame Press, Notre Dame, Indiana, for chapter 6.

From *The Eucharist* by Louis Bouyer. Trans. by Charles Underhill Quinn. © 1968 by The University of Notre Dame Press, Notre Dame, Indiana 46556. Used by permission.

To St. Vladimir's Seminary Press for chapter 11.

The respective publication from which each of these essays is reprinted is indicated at the beginning of each chapter.

Introduction

Because the Eucharist is the central and life-giving celebration at the heart of the Church's life—the summit and source of that life (*Sacrosanctum concilium* 10)—the theological study of the Eucharist must be based fundamentally on the history of the Sunday Ecclesial Eucharistic celebration over twenty centuries. Liturgical Studies is thus foundational for all sacramental theology of the Eucharist.

But, as important as liturgical history is, it is not alone sufficient. The insights and context provided by biblical studies, Patristics, historical theology, and the history of doctrine are also fundamental.

This volume collects a number of significant items representing fields such as the above—items not readily accessible to students because of being out of print, available only in foreign or limited scholarly editions or published in journals. This collection is intended to supplement standard texts such as Jasper and Cuming, *Prayers of the Eucharist: Early and Reformed* (New York: Pueblo, 1987).

My thanks to all the authors and publishers who have graciously granted permission to reprint these essays. I am particulary grateful to my professor at Notre Dame, Fr. Robert Taft, S.J., of the Pontifical Oriental Institute, Rome, for his permission to include three essays from his book, *Beyond East and West* (Rome: PIO, 1991). I am also grateful to His Grace, Bishop Kallistos (Ware) of Diokleia, recently retired from Oxford, and my colleague Fr. Dominic Serra, now of The Catholic University of America in Washington, D.C., for allowing their essays to be included in this volume.

Finally, thanks also to Dr. Jeanne McLean, my academic dean and Fr. Ronald Bowers, both of The Saint Paul Seminary School of Divinity, for their support. I am particularly grateful to Mr. Gerald Milske of our staff for his extremely capable and unflagging assistance in preparing the manuscript.

Thomas Fisch
The Saint Paul Seminary
School of Divinity,
University of St. Thomas,
St. Paul, Minnesota
October 20, 2003

Contributors

Louis Bouyer of the Oratory was for many years a member of the faculty of theology of the Institut Catholique of Paris. He also taught in the liturgy program at the University of Notre Dame, and is a prolific author and lecturer.

Brevard S. Childs recently retired from his position as the Sterling Professor of Divinity and Fellow of Davenport College, The Divinity School, Yale University. He is an internationally respected and influential biblical scholar.

Edward Schillebeeckx, O.P., is professor emeritus of theology and the history of theology at the University of Nijmegen. He has achieved an international reputation through his publications on topics in sacramental theology, christology, and ministry.

Dominic E. Serra is professor of liturgy at The Catholic University of America in Washington, D.C. Prior to 2000 he taught sacramental theology and liturgy at The Saint Paul Seminary School of Divinity at the University of St. Thomas, Saint Paul, Minnesota.

Godefridus J. C. Snoek has long taught medieval history at the Leiden Institute of Education. In 1989 he earned his doctorate at the Free University of Amsterdam and today serves as superintendent of high schools in The Netherlands.

William G. Storey (Ph.D., University of Notre Dame) and Niels Krogh Rasmussen, O.P., [1935–1987] (doctorate, Institut Supérieur de Liturgie, Paris) both taught in the graduate programs in liturgical studies at the University of Notre Dame.

Robert F. Taft, S.J., is professor of oriental liturgy at the Pontifical Oriental Institute in Rome and visiting professor of liturgy at the University of Notre Dame. He is also editor-in-chief of *Orientalia Christiana*

Analecta and liturgical consultor of the Vatican Congregation for the Oriental Churches. He is the author of over 250 scholarly publications.

Cyrille Vogel [1919–1982] was professor at the University of Strasbourg as successor to his mentor Michel Andrieu. He also taught at the Institut Supérieur de Liturgie of the Institut Catholique of Paris.

Bishop Kallistos (Ware), of Diokleia, recently retired from Oxford University, where he was the Spalding Lecturer in Eastern Orthodox Studies and a fellow of Pembroke College, has been active for many years in work for Christian unity.

John Zizioulas, metropolitan of Pergamon, is professor of systematic theology at the University of Glasgow and has lectured widely elsewhere, including Rome's Gregorian University and King's College, London. He has also been a major Orthodox contributor to ecumenical discussions.

Abbreviations

AAS	*Acta Apostolicae Sedis*
ALW	*Archiv für Liturgiewissenschaft*
An. Boll.	*Analecta Bollandiana*, Bruxelles
BELS	Bibliotheca *Ephemerides Liturgicae*, Subsidia
BKV	Bibliothek der Kirchenväter
BZ	*Biblische Zeitschrift*
CC	Corpus Christianorum
CCSL	Corpus Christianorum, Series Latinae, Turnhout
CF	*Cahiers de Fanjeaux*
CSCO	Corpus Scriptorum Christianorum Orientalium
CSEL	Corpus Scriptorum Ecclesiasticorum Latinorum
DACL	*Dictionnaire d'archéologie chrétienne et de liturgie*, Paris
DOP	Dumbarton Oaks Papers
DS	H. Denzinger and A. Schönmetzer eds. *Enchiridion Symbolorum Definitionum et Declarationum*, 33rd edition, Rome, 1965
EL	*Ephemerides liturgicae*
ET	English Translation
EvTh	*Evangelische Theologie*
GCS	Die griechischen christlichen Schriftsteller
GSAT	*Gesammelte Studien zum Alten Testament*
HBS	Henry Bradshaw Society

Iren	*Irenikon*
JBL	*Journal of Biblical Literature*
JLW	*Jahrbuch für Liturgiewissenschaft*
LJ	*Liturgisches Jahrbuch*
LMD	*La Maison-Dieu*
LQF	Liturgiewissenschaftliche Quellen und Forschungen
LW	*Liturgisch Woordenboek*
Mansi	J. D. Mansi, *Sacrorum conciliorum nova et amplissima collectio . . .*
MGH	*Monumenta Germaniae Historica*
	-AA *Auctores Antiquissimi*
	-Cap *Capitularia*
	-Conc *Concilia*
	-Const *Constitutiones*
	-Ep *Epistola*
	-NS *Nova Series*
	-SRM *Scriptores rerum Merovingicarum*
	-SS *Scriptores rerum Germanicarum*
NT	*Novum Testamentum*
OCA	*Orientalia Christiana Analecta*
OCP	*Orientalia Christiana Periodica*
PG	J. P. Migne, *Patrologia Graeca* (Paris, repr. Turnhout)
PIO	Pontificio Istituto Orientale, Rome
PL	J. P. Migne, *Patrologia Latina* (Paris, repr. Turnhout)
RED	Rerum ecclesiasticarum documenta
RQS	*Römische Quartalschrift für christliche Altertumskunde und für Kirchengeschichte*

RSR	*Revue des Sciences Réligieuses*
SC	Sources Chrétiennes
SE	*Sacris Erudiri*
SeT	Studi e Testi
ST	*Summa Theologiae*
TQ	*Theologische Quartalschrift*
TRE	*Theologische Realenzyclopädie*
Ts. v. Theol.	*Tijdschrift voor Theologie*
TuA	*Texte und Arbeiten*
TvT	*Tijdschrift voor Theologie*
TW	*Theologisch Woordenboek*
ZAW	*Zeitschrift für Altestamentisches Wissenschaft*
ZKT	*Zeitschrift für katholische Theologie*

Brevard S. Childs

1. Israel's Theology of Memory

[The following are the final two chapters of Brevard Childs' *Memory and Tradition in Israel.** The first five chapters comprise a thorough study of the use of the Hebrew word *zkr* in the Hebrew Scriptures.]

MEMORY AND CULT

The evidence which has appeared from our study of *zkr* must now be brought to bear on the problem of Israel's cult. Our analysis revealed that the phrase "God remembers" had its provenance *(Sitz im Leben)* within the cultic life, in the complaint and in the hymn. The complaint brought a plea for God to remember, the hymn praise that he had remembered. A common meaning was shared by both these forms. God's remembering issued in his intervention on Israel's behalf based on his previous commitment to Israel. The role of the cultic memorials *(zikkārôn)* was to bring Israel constantly to God's attention, which would result in his gracious aid.

It is important to recognize that this cultic understanding of God's memory is not an actualization of the past. The problem of making a past reality contemporary is not involved in God's memory. God is in no sense confined to the past within the barriers of time and space. He is always present. The question at issue in the cult is whether God will continue to act in Israel's behalf as he did in the past or withdraw his aid because of her disobedience.

Turning to the phrase "Israel remembers," our analysis revealed that the verb had no roots in one specific area of Israel's life, but arose out of the general sphere of human psychological behavior. In this general sense it was employed widely throughout all phases of Israel's life. To remember was to call to mind a past event or situation, with the purpose of evoking some action. The most significant result of our analysis was to discover that in certain instances the term lost its general psychological sense to take on a highly theological

---

*B. S. Childs, *Memory and Tradition in Israel,* Studies in Biblical Theology 37 (London: SCM Press, 1962) 74–89.

1

meaning. To remember was to actualize the past, to bridge the gap of time and to form a solidarity with the fathers. Israel's remembrance became a technical term to express the process by which later Israel made relevant the great redemptive acts which she recited in her tradition. The question of how to overcome the separation in time and space from the great events of the past became the paramount issue.

Although the same verb *zkr* is used to express both God's and Israel's remembering, the comparison makes evident that a totally different process is involved.[1] Only in terms of Israel's memory can we correctly speak of an actualization of a past event. Only in relation to Israel's memory is the problem to contemporize past tradition.

Recent Old Testament scholarship has been almost unanimous in pointing out that the chief function of the cult was to actualize the tradition.[2] Israel celebrated in her seasonal festivals the great redemptive acts of the past both to renew the tradition and to participate in its power. Noth summarizes this consensus when he writes: "There is in the Old Testament the legitimate phenomenon of an actualization of past events which occurs in the cultic, liturgical context."[3] Israel's tradition bears unmistakable signs of being transmitted in a cultic form.

However, the fact that Israel's cult served chiefly to actualize her tradition raises a serious problem in regard to memory. We have just emphasized that the verb "to remember," when used in respect to Israel, carried the intense theological connotation of actualization. How, then, are we to explain the fact that the verb when it comes to mean actualization is not intimately connected with the cult? How

[1] This distinction is blurred by those who seek a general cultic context for memory without sufficient differentiation. Cf. H. Gross, "Zur Wurzel ZKR," *BZ* 4 (1960) 227–37; M. Thurian, *The Eucharistic Memorial*, I (ET, London and Richmond, Virginia, 1960); and to some extent H. Haag, "Gedächtnis," *Lexikon für Theologie und Kirche*, 4 (1 Aufl., Freiburg, 1960) 570–72.

[2] In spite of precursors S. Mowickel's work was basic, *Psalmenstudien*, II (Kristinia, 1922) 16 ff. Cf. also *Le Décalogue* (Paris, 1927) 114 ff.; *Religion und Kultus* (Göttingen, 1953). The following have also made a contribution: M. Noth, *Das System der zwölf Stämme Israels* (Stuttgart, 1930) 61 ff.; A Weiser, *Glaube und Geschichte im Alten Testament* (Stuttgart, 1931) 35 ff.; A. Alt, "Die Ursprünge des israelitischen Rechts" (1934) in *Kleine Schriften zur Geschichte des Volkes Israel*, I (München, 1953) 320 ff.; G. von Rad, *Das formgeschichtliche Problem des Hexateuch* (Stuttgart, 1938) 28 ff. (also in *GSAT*); A. Alt, "Die Wallfahrt von Sichem nach Bethel" (1938) in *Kleine Schriften*, I, 79 ff.; M. Noth, "Die Vergegenwärtigung des Alten Testaments in der Verkündigung," *EvTh* 12 (1952/53) 6 ff.; G. E. Wright, *God Who Acts* (London, Chicago, 1952); H.-J. Kraus, *Gottesdienst in Israel* (München, 1954) 122 ff.

[3] Noth, "Die Vergegenwärtigung des Alten Testament," *EvTh* 12, 14.

can actualization take place both in the cult and in memory without there being some genuine relationship evidenced in the vocabulary?

Assuming that our previous analysis of the verb has been correct, there are several possible explanations:

(1) One could argue that Israel's cult never had the function of actualization of tradition which has been assigned to it. However, in the light of the overwhelming evidence to the contrary,[4] this explanation seems excluded.

(2) It would be possible for the verb *zkr* to be employed somewhat late in Israel's history merely to describe a process which had been functioning without interruption within the cult of Israel from its earliest history. However, there is no evidence to support such an hypothesis. Rather, the context within which the verb appears points to a break with the past in which a new element has entered. The word has been reinterpreted and given its new meaning precisely to express a new approach, not merely to describe the continuation of a traditional form.

(3) One could conceive of two different means of actualization which were quite independent of each other, one through the cult and one through memory. However, we saw that *zkr* is used in a theological sense by those circles deeply involved in the cultic life. Memory as a term for the actualization of tradition did not develop in a context which was removed from Israel's cultic institutions. The evidence does not confirm a parallel development but an interrelation.

(4) Finally, it is possible that the original function of the cult as the traditional means of actualizing the tradition entered a period of crisis. Out of this situation there emerged various attempts to relate Israel to her past in terms of memory. The role of actualization underwent a process of transformation. This is an hypothesis which must now be critically examined.

Our study of Israel's memory (ch. 4) indicated the emergence of a new theological meaning in respect to memory which was concentrated in the preaching of the Deuteronomist, in Deutero-Isaiah, Ezekiel, and the complaint psalms. Is there any evidence that these four witnesses were concerned with a reinterpretation of Israel's cult as a means of actualizing Israel's tradition?

We shall begin with the Deuteronomist. It is not our concern to offer a detailed exposition of the book, but to bring to bear on our immediate

[4] Cf. 75, n. 2.

problem the results of recent scholarship.[5] The Deuteronomist had as one of his central problems the reinterpretation of the traditions of Israel to a later generation which had not itself participated in the redemption from Egypt and the Sinai covenant, indeed, as we now know, to a generation separated by centuries from these events. Von Rad writes: "We have in Deuteronomy the most comprehensive example of a theological re-statement of old tradition in which later Israel contemporized the message of Yahweh."[6]

In spite of the tremendous variety which was inherited from the tradition, the Deuteronomist managed to fashion it into a unity with the central perspective being Yahweh's absolute claim on the whole people of Israel. In terms of the cult this involved a radical reinterpretation. This is not to imply that we have in Deuteronomy an anti-cultic polemic. Von Rad has convincingly demonstrated that even the framework of Deuteronomy reflects a liturgical pattern, and that the writer stands in the traditions of the old tribal league at Shechem.[7] Yet the preaching of the Deuteronomist breathes a different atmosphere from the cult-oriented tradition. His message has lost the sense of immediacy. The paranetic style directed to evoke a response reflects his concern in finding a basis upon which Israel can again be related to the past.

Along what lines has the reinterpretation of the cult taken place? The total claim of Yahweh on his people results in the severance of all connection with those areas of nature which offer opportunity for syncretistic infiltration. The cult is legitimate only "at the place where Yahweh reveals his name." The emphasis of the liturgy shifts from concern with ritual minutiae to center in a joyous expression of thankfulness for Yahweh's benefits which are attributed solely to his election love. The criterion for obedience to the law is established in terms of social responsibility to the weak and disinherited. In a real sense, the sacred traditions of the past have been secularized to accommodate them to a new age (cf., e.g., 14:22 ff.).

---

[5] The writer is chiefly indebted to the several works of G. von Rad: *Das Gottesvolk in Deuteronomium* (Stuttgart, 1929) 28 ff.; *Studies in Deuteronomy* (ET, London, 1953); *Theologie des Alten Testaments* I, 218 ff. (cf. ET with revisions, 219 ff.). The following have also been consulted with profit: A. C. Welch, *The Code of Deuteronomy* (London, 1924); A. R. Hulst, *Het Karakter van der Kultus in Deuteronomium* (Wageningen, 1938); F. Dumerluth, "Zur deuteronomischen Kulttheologie," *ZAW* 70 (1958) 59 ff.

[6] This translation differs slightly from D. Stalker's, *Studies in Deuteronomy, 71.*

[7] G. von Rad, *Das formgeschichtliche Problem des Hexateuch,* in *GSAT,* 33ff.

The Deuteronomist, however, is faced with an obvious dilemma. If he divorces the tradition from its old cultic forms, how does later Israel participate in her past? Has he fallen into the inescapable trap of being forced to reinterpret the cult to a new generation, but by his very interpretation severed all possible means of a return to the past? The Deuteronomist offers his answer in a theology of memory. The task of later Israel is not to try to return to the events of the past. The Deuteronomist has a clear sense of history and he recognized the challenge of the present moment. Yahweh's redemptive dealing with Israel is not confined to the past, but continues. Israel now stands in an analogous position with the Exodus generation and is called upon to respond obediently to his command. Yet later Israel cannot understand the immediate claims of God upon her except in terms of her tradition. The commandments of the law can only be properly interpreted as events in a redemptive history. To lose the historical perspective with the past is to fall into a sterile nominalism. Israel's memory reveals the continuity in the one purpose of God in history. When the son asks the meaning of the commandments, he is recited the historical tradition of Israel's redemption, and admonished to present obedience (6:20 ff.). Israel's memory reminds her that she is not cut off from the past, but the redemptive action of God continues.

There is a second function of memory in the theology of Deuteronomy. Israel is commanded to be obedient to the commandments *in order to* remember the redemptive history. Our exegesis has demonstrated that memory in this case assumes the meaning of actualization. By keeping the Sabbath holy, later Israel remembers or participates in the redemptive history of her past. The Deuteronomist relativized the cultic tradition in conceiving of it along with non-cultic material simply as a commandment *(miṣwāh)* on which obedience could be tested (5:15; 15:15; 16:12; 24:18, 22). The result is a thorough internalization of the tradition. We feel, therefore, justified in concluding that the concept of memory served a significant role in Deuteronomy's theology in meeting the crisis brought about by a reinterpretation of the cult.

The crisis in the religious life of Israel caused by the exile is reflected in both Deutero-Isaiah and Ezekiel. The Temple lay in ruins. God's people were separated from the holy land. This did not mean that the cult suddenly ceased in the exile. Von Waldow[8] has demonstrated in

---

[8] Hans-Eberhard von Waldow, *Anlass und Hintergrund der Verkündigung des Deuterojesaja* (Dissertation, Bonn, 1953) 63 ff.

a most convincing manner how deeply rooted Deutero-Isaiah's message was in Israel's cultic life. Nevertheless, his message shows a profound reinterpretation of Israel's tradition. Deutero-Isaiah reminds Israel that she has not been forgotten (44:21). Her sins have been forgiven (40:1 ff.) and she now stands upon the threshold of her redemption which parallels the Exodus from Egypt (51:9 ff.). In the light of this situation Israel's memory has a twofold function. First, memory of the past links Israel with the one great purpose of God in history which encompasses both past and future (44:21; 46:9 ff.). Even the exile is bracketed within the divine will. Secondly, Israel need not turn to the past for meaning. God is bringing into existence a new age in which Israel can participate (43:18 ff.; 65:17).

The message of Ezekiel concerns itself with Israel's failure to understand the nature of her sin (16:22, 43). However, the day will come when Israel will recognize her true condition. Then she will be overwhelmed with the memory of her sin and loathe her deeds. Israel's redemption takes place in the form of a remembering which issues in the knowledge of God. Her memory turns her both to a repentance for past evil and to a stretching out for God. Even in the exile she experiences anew the same divine reality to which her tradition witnessed.

We turn finally to the complaint psalms. What evidence is there that Israel's memory assumed a role in relation to some crisis which threatened the traditional function of the cult? The nature of the crisis is different from that found in the prophets because no single historical period is reflected in these psalms. The complaint extended from the beginning to the end of Israel's life. Nevertheless, a crisis is apparent. The psalmist is afflicted by a great variety of trouble. He suffers from bodily sickness, rejection, and exile. All these have in common the effect of separating him from the community of faith and from the God of the covenant. Memory became a key word in a tremendous process of internalization of the tradition. It became the means by which Israel found a new avenue to faith when the older cultic paths had become inaccessible. This was in no sense a conscious reaction against Israel's cult or part of a reform movement. A return to the older forms often remained the highest aspiration (cf. Pss 42–43). Nevertheless, even when the vocabulary of memory became a part of Israel's worship, the increased intensification associated with the word was carried over into the liturgy (cf. Ps 105, 1 ff.).

In conclusion, we feel that the evidence confirms our theory regarding the relation of memory to Israel's cult as a means of actualizing the past. In times of crisis, when the role of the cult was threatened, Israel's memory assumed a new significance in renewing her tradition.

MEMORY AND HISTORY

Although we have frequently used the term actualization (= *Vergegenwärtigung*) with regard to the tradition, we have not as yet entered into a detailed exposition of what is meant. This omission is due, by and large, to a general uncertainty as to its meaning which reflects itself in a wide divergence of scholarly opinion. On the basis of our study we now feel in a position to turn to this question.

We shall begin by discussing two rival theories of actualization in respect to the Old Testament which serve to raise the central issues at stake. The first theory, represented for example by S. Mowinckel,[9] interprets the concept of actualization not as a category indigenous to Israel, but one which arose out of the mythopoeic thought of the Ancient Near East. Of fundamental importance is the relation of cult to myth. The cult has as its function the renewing of the structure of the world by reenacting the sacred drama of the myth. In this dramatic recapitulation the content of the myth is renewed, and participants of the cultic rite experience its elemental power. Mowinckel feels that the content of the drama can be either mythical or historical. Within this framework this distinction is insignificant.[10]

This explanation has contributed a lasting service to Old Testament research by making clear the mythical roots lying at the base of the process of actualization. Nevertheless, this theory has a fundamental weakness which has become increasingly evident.[11] Mowinckel has not done justice to the radical alterations in Israel's cult which set her apart from the general Near-Eastern pattern. The fact that the myth was replaced by historical events is not of secondary importance, but effected a fundamental change in perspective. For Israel the structure of reality was historical in character and not mythical. These historical events could not be repeated; they were forever fixed in an his-

[9] *Psalmenstudien*, II, 21 ff.

[10] *Ibid.*, 25, 45.

[11] There have been many who have criticized Mowinckel's position. W. Eichrodt's consistent argument with theories of mythical pattern still remains trenchant, *Theologie des Alten Testaments*, I (6 Aufl., Stuttgart, 1959) 53 ff. [ET, 98 ff.] etc.; also M. Noth, "Gott, König, Volk im alten Testament," *GSAT* (München, 1957) 188 ff. On the general subject of Israel's conflict with natural religion cf. the excellent book of G. E. Wright, *The Old Testament against Its Environment* (London, Chicago, 1950).

torical sequence. It is highly questionable whether the cult of Ancient Israel ever had the character of a drama which was re-enacted. The process of historization destroyed this element in the cult along with the myth.[12] Rather, the cult actualized within Israel her solidarity with the forefathers, with those who had actually participated in the Exodus. Old Testament actualization of tradition cannot be identified with a mythical concept.

The second explanation stands at the opposite end of the spectrum and is a reaction against the mythical theory.[13] It understands the role of actualization to be the recital in the cult of the great historical acts of the past which established Israel's existence. These acts share the quality of genuine historical events and are, therefore, non-repeatable, once-for-all in character. Actualization occurs when the worshipper experiences an identification with the original events. This happens when he is transported back to the original historical events. He bridges the gap of historical time and participates in the original history.[14]

In our opinion, this hypothesis is basically correct in attempting to guard the once-for-all historical character of biblical events against the timeless quality of the myth. We would also agree that there is a participation in the original events. The disagreement turns about the question of how this participation occurs. In what sense is it a return to the past? Are the original events stationary? We feel that those who emphasize the historical element in the process of actualization have tended to ignore the dynamic quality of an historical event. It enters the world of time and space at a given moment, yet causes a continued reverberation beyond its original entry. The biblical events can never become static, lifeless beads which can be strung on a chronological chain. In direct analogy to the "history-creating" Word of God, the redemptive events of Israel's history do not come to rest, but continue to meet and are contemporary with each new genera-

[12] Cf. von Rad's discussion of the rise of the historical sense within Israel, *Theologie des Alten Testaments*, II (München, 1960) 112 ff.

[13] A representative of this view is M. Noth, "Die Vergegenwärtigung des Alten Testaments in der Verkündigung," *EvTh* 12 (1952/3) 6 ff.

[14] Kraus, *Gottesdienst in Israel*, 127: "Actualization takes place in Israel not in the manner that the original occasion of the encounter of God with Israel is brought near to the assembled congregation, but rather the congregation is placed within the original situation. The once-for-all character of the *heilsgeschichtliche* events is not dissolved into a kerygma. . . . The revelation of God in history is once-for-all."

tion.[15] We shall return to this point shortly. We conclude that Old Testament actualization cannot be correctly identified with a return to a former historical event.

To summarize: we are suggesting that neither the mythical nor the historical analysis of the process of actualization are adequate to describe the biblical category. This appears to be a concept which shares features of both yet exhibits a unique character of its own. We shall now attempt to penetrate into this category.

The Old Testament witnesses to a series of historical events by which God brought the people of Israel into existence. These events were placed in a chronological order within the tradition, and never recurred in Israel's history. There was one Exodus from Egypt, one period of wilderness wanderings, one conquest of the land. These events were determinative because they constituted Israel's redemption. In other words, they became the vehicle for a quality of existence, redemptive time and space.

These redemptive events of the Old Testament shared a genuine chronology. They appeared in history at a given moment, which entry can be dated. There is a once-for-all character to these events in the sense that they never repeated themselves in the same fashion. Yet this does not exhaust the biblical concept. These determinative events are by no means static; they function merely as a beginning. Our study of memory has indicated that each successive generation encountered anew these same determinative events. Redemptive history continues. What does this mean? It means more than that later generations wrestled with the meaning of the redemptive events, although this is certainly true. It means more than that the influence of a past event continued to be felt in successive generations, an obvious fact no one could possibly deny. Rather, there was an immediate encounter, an actual participation in the [past — ed.] great acts of redemption. The Old Testament maintained the dynamic, continuing character of past events without sacrificing their historical character as did the myth.

We saw that the Deuteronomist conceived of later Israel as standing in an analogous position with the Israel of the Exodus. God was working her redemption and Israel was challenged to participate. In the memory of the tradition later Israel continued to share in the redemptive events. This is to say, each new generation was challenged

---

[15] Cf. von Rad's discussion, "Typologische Auslegung des Alten Testaments," *EvTh*, 12 (1952/3) 25 ff.

9

to enter God's redemptive time, to participate itself in the Exodus. The dynamic quality of the Exodus event is seen in the event's becoming a vehicle for a reality which then continued throughout Israel's history. The chronological position of the Exodus in Israel's history remained fixed (1250 B.C.?), but its quality as redemptive event—not just meaning—continued to reverberate in the life of the people. We wish to emphasize that the redemptive content of the Exodus was never divorced from chronological history as such.[16] It was not a timeless idea or a non-historical ground-of-being. Rather, a quality of time entered at the Exodus and this content continued to transform the chronological time of each new generation into redemptive time. Redemptive history continued in the sense that each generation of Israel, living in a concrete situation within history, was challenged by God to obedient response through the medium of her tradition. Not a mere subjective reflection, but in the biblical category, a real event occurred as the moment of redemptive time from the past initiated a genuine encounter in the present.

Actualization is the process in which a past event is contemporized for a generation removed in time and space from the original event. When later Israel responded to the continuing imperative of her tradition through her memory, that moment in historical time likewise became an Exodus experience. Not in the sense that Israel again crossed the Red Sea. This was an irreversible, once-for-all event. Rather, Israel entered the same redemptive reality of the Exodus generation. Later Israel, removed in time and space from the original event, yet still in time and space, found in her tradition a means of transforming her history into redemptive history. Because the quality of time was the same, the barrier of chronological separation was overcome.

This explanation raises several fundamental questions. If Israel's redemptive history continues in the successive encounters with the challenge of her tradition, how do these remembered events relate to the original event? First of all, it is essential to formulate the question

---

[16] In his most recent book, *Biblical Words for Time* (London, 1962) 20 ff., James Barr has clearly established his point that the Greek terms *kairos* and *chronos* show a variety of usages in the New Testament and cannot therefore be correlated with two different concepts of time. His book is exceedingly valuable for its negative conclusions. However, it is doubtful whether the proposed method of procedure can make a positive contribution, since it tends to remain almost entirely on the level of descriptive semantics with little cognizance of the depth dimension which form-critical analysis has opened up in the study of words. Cf. the author's review of Barr's *Semantics of Biblical Language, JBL* 80 (1961) 374–77.

correctly. We do not have in the Old Testament "an original event." What we have are various witnesses to an event. Some of the witnesses are closer in chronological time to the original historical happening than other witnesses. Still, these are all witnesses which point beyond themselves. We are not in a position to ask how the interpreted event relates to the "objective event." Rather we are forced to ask: how do the successive interpretations of an event relate to the primary witness of that event? One cannot "get behind" the witness. There are no other avenues to this event except through the witness.

Of course, this point of view will not pass unchallenged. In the history of biblical interpretation there have been several major attacks upon it.

(1) The most effective and persistent has been posed by the scientific historians who stand in the tradition of the great German positivistic historians of the nineteenth century.[17] Their position is familiar: the methods of historical criticism, especially the science of archaeology, provide a legitimate avenue to the same events recounted in the Bible. The Old Testament account is only one among many of a given event which must be tested on the basis of objective evidence. A moment's perusal of Pritchard's *Ancient Near Eastern Texts Relating to the Old Testament* will dispel any doubts as to the many areas of secular history which overlap with the biblical. The goal of research is to recover the uninterpreted fact as it happened. Objective event can be separated from subjective interpretation.

Two criticisms can be made to this approach. The first arises from the side of the historian, especially in the works of men such as B. Croce[18] and R. G. Collingwood.[19] They have pointed out effectively that the analogy of natural science, when applied to the study of history, has severe limitations. History cannot be described as a sequence of events causally linked, but history has an "inner side" which is the process of thought. The interpretation is not something added to the event, but constitutes the real event. The "brute fact" theory is a distortion of the essence of history which is the expression of human thought.

There is a second objection from the side of the theologian. While it is true that the external side of the Old Testament witness often has a parallel in extra-biblical sources, the heart of the Old Testament

[17] Cf. the position of W. F. Albright, *From the Stone Age to Christianity* (2nd ed., New York, 1957) 25 ff., 82 ff.; *JBL* 77 (1958) 244–48.

[18] B. Croce, *History as the Story of Liberty* (London, 1941).

[19] R. G. Collingwood, *The Idea of History* (Oxford, 1946). Quotations are made from the reprint (New York, 1957).

message—how Yahweh redeemed a people—finds its witness only in the Bible. The message of the Bible speaks of the history of a divine redemption which Israel accepted in faith or rejected in unbelief. There is no direct line from a common, outward framework to the heart of this biblical testimony. The faith response, the interpretation, was not something added to the real event, but constituted the event itself. We maintain, therefore, that it is a fundamental error in interpretation to conceive of redemptive history as a series of scientifically verifiable, historical data to which a religious interpretation has been added.[20]

This is not to imply for a moment that the biblical exegete has no need for historical research. It must be employed with the utmost rigor. The point at issue is whether historical research has as its function to illumine the *interpreted* event, or to attempt to play the so-called "objective" event against its interpretation. We resist the effort to identify historical research with the philosophical presuppositions of historicism.

(2) Another attempt to get behind the witness has been put forth by the school of modern historiography. We shall concentrate our attention on R. G. Collingwood, whose brilliant book presents the most incisive analysis of recent years. We have already noted Collingwood's criticism of historicism in which he rejects a method drawn from the natural sciences as being valid for historical study. The task of the historian is to understand historical events by re-enacting the process of thought in his own mind. The distinction between subjective and objective is dissolved precisely because the historian must take his stand within, not outside of, the history which he is trying to understand. "For even when the events which the historian studies are events that happened in the distant past, the condition of their being historically known is that they should vibrate in the historian's mind, that is to say, that the evidence for them should be here and now before him and intelligible to him."[21]

The historian exercises his critical function by cross-examining his sources and securing information which he can use in his own reconstruction. The historian is his own authority and his thought is autonomous. He possesses a criterion to which his so-called authorities must conform and by reference to which they are criticized. This criterion is his *a priori* imagination, by which is meant the sense of a coherent and continuous picture of the past.[22]

[20] This is basically the issue between von Rad and F. Hesse (*Theologie des A. T.*, II, 8 ff.).
[21] Collingwood, *op. cit.*, 202.
[22] *Ibid.*, 236 ff.

A full-scale criticism of Collingwood's concept of history, which would include among other things a detailed examination of his category of *a priori* imagination, lies beyond the scope of our concern and competence. However, we would like to examine the theory in the area in which it impinges upon biblical criticism.

Collingwood properly rejects the attempt to isolate the uninterpreted event. The past can only be recovered by re-enacting the process of thought. On the basis of critical historical imagination the historian can penetrate the uncritical testimony and create his own interpretation of what really happened. But is this not the opposite extreme of historicism which attempts to separate the event from the interpretation? Now the interpretation is divorced from the event. Because the historian shares general human nature, a common mind with the past, he can re-create the real event, which lies only in fractured form in his witness.

While there are some areas within the Old Testament witness to which one might successfully apply Collingwood's method, we feel that the approach would only distort the center of the Old Testament's witness. The events testified to in the Bible cannot be reconstructed on the basis of an *a priori* category, whether general human nature, or universal experience of the past. Theologically speaking, one cannot measure the radically new with the canons of the old. Again, we maintain that there are no avenues to the history of which the Bible speaks except through Scripture's own testimony to these events.[23]

We return to our original question: How do the remembered events relate to the primary witness? We have concluded from our study that the act of remembrance is not a simple inner reflection, but involves an action, an encounter with historical events. Each successive generation in Israel witnessed in faith to a reality which it encountered

[23] The most recent attempt in New Testament research to get behind the witness is forcefully presented by J. M. Robinson, *A New Quest of the Historical Jesus* (London, Chicago, 1959). Robinson suggests that the new historiography provides another avenue to the historical Jesus which can be detached from the *kerygma*. Both avenues have in common an existential encounter with the historical Jesus. An adequate criticism of Robinson's position would involve a discussion of the hermeneutical principle underlying the exegetical method of R. Bultmann which is presupposed throughout the book. This lies beyond the scope of our present task. That the question can be approached from a wholly different point of view is seen in the following essays: D. Bonhoeffer, "Vergegenwärtigung neutestamentlicher Texte," *Gesammelte Schriften*, III (München, 1960) 303–24; P. Meyer, "The Problem of the Messianic Self-Consciousness of Jesus," *NT* 4 (1960) 122–38.

when remembering the tradition. The biblical events have the dynamic characteristic of refusing to be relegated to the past. The quality of this reality did not remain static, but emerged with new form and content because it identified itself with the changing historical situation of later Israel. The people of God heard his call to obedience not in the abstract, but through specific historical moments. Redemptive history is not merely a reflection of Israel's piety—a *Glaubensgeschichte*. Rather, each generation reinterpreted the same determinative events of the tradition in terms of its new encounter. This gives the biblical witness its peculiar character. It consists of layer upon layer of Israel's reinterpretation of the same period of her history, because each successive generation rewrites the past in terms of her own experience with the God who meets his people through the tradition.

In the light of our study of memory we suggest that these successive layers cannot be seen as subjective accretion covering the "real event." The remembered event is equally a valid witness to Israel's encounter with God as the first witness. Israel testified to the continuing nature of her redemptive history by the events of the past in the light of her ongoing experience with the covenant God.

Our word study was significant in pointing out that the same verb is used to describe God's redemptive action toward Israel as well as Israel's response in faith to this action. This would indicate that, for the Old Testament, redemptive history is conceived of as resulting from God's action and Israel's response. These elements cannot be separated, nor can they be analyzed into objective and subjective components. They form a unity. Because of the nature of Israel's response which we have outlined, an understanding of the redemptive history depends on hearing the witness of all the different layers which reflect Israel's response to the divine initiative. Only in this way can one appreciate the fullness of the redemption which revealed itself in Israel's history.[24]

---

[24] This study was almost completed when the dissertation of C. L. Kessler came to my attention: *The Memory Motif in the God-Man Relationship of the Old Testament* (Evanston: Northwestern University, 1956). Kessler offers many good insights, but because his approach differs so sharply from mine, little help was afforded. The recently announced book of P. A. H. de Boer *Gedenken und Gedächtness in der Welt des Alten Testaments* (Stuttgart, 1962), has not been seen.

Robert F. Taft, S.J.

2. Toward a Theology of the Christian Feast*

In his excellent study of the Gospel accounts of Jesus' earthly be-
ginnings,[1] as well as in his briefer summary of the same material,[2]
Raymond Brown demonstrates that the aim of the Infancy Narratives
is not biographical; they do not attempt to provide a history of Jesus'
earthly origins. Rather, they present a message, that of the whole
Gospel in miniature: the announcing of the Good News, its acceptance by the disciples but rejection by most of Israel, its extension to
the gentile world. It is not the story of baby Jesus in Bethlehem, but
the meaning of Christ for humankind in the era of the post-pentecostal
Church, that is behind the narratives.

Now I think one can apply an analogous hermeneutic to the feasts of
the Christian calendar as a means of uncovering its theological sense,
and hence its liturgical or pastoral purpose, while at the same time re-
solving the numerous antinomies that surface in any discussion of the
church year: eschatology vs. history, dominical cycle vs. yearly, *kairos*
vs. *chronos*. I do not wish to imply that these tensions are not real. But
I think they arose, in germ at least, not in fourth-century Jerusalem as
one usually hears, but in New Testament times. And I think that the
New Testament itself provides us with the elements of a balanced theology that can lead to their resolution. This brings us to our reflections.

The basic question on every level—historical, theological, pastoral—
is the problem of *meaning*: just what are we doing when we celebrate
a Christian feast? Since the problem of any feast rooted not in myth
but in sacred history is the problem of time and event, that is, the relationship between past unrepeatable event and present celebration,
much ink has been spilt trying to uncover some special Semitic

* R. Taft, *Beyond East and West: Problems in Liturgical Understanding* (Second
Revised and Enlarged Edition. Rome: Pontifical Oriental Institute, 1997) 15–29.

[1] *The Birth of the Messiah: A Commentary on the Infancy Narratives in Matthew and
Luke* (New York: Doubleday, 1977).

[2] *An Adult Christ at Christmas: Essays on the Three Biblical Christmas Stories*
(Collegeville: Liturgical Press, 1977).

philosophy of time at the root of the whole business. This has not been very fruitful. Recent studies of Greek and Hebrew semantics and the relevant Old Testament material have concluded that there is no firm evidence for positing a peculiar sense of time in Hebrew thought, and that nothing in New Testament statements about time and eternity provides an adequate basis for a distinct Christian concept of time.[3]

What is true, however, is (1) that the Bible presents an historical teleology, a strong sense of the sequence of historical events as purposeful movement toward a goal, (2) that it uses this sequence as a medium for presenting the story of an encounter with God,[4] and (3) that it presents later cultic memorial celebrations of this encounter as a means of overcoming the separation in time and space from the actual saving event.[5] The salvation manifested in the past lives now as an active force in our lives if we encounter it anew and respond to it in faith, and we cannot do that unless we remember it. In the Old Testament, cultic memorial is one of the ways in which Israel remembered, making present the past saving events as a means of encountering in every generation the saving work of God.

That *present* encounter is the point of it all. In memorial we do not take a mythic trip into the past, nor do we drag the past into the present by repeating the primordial event in mythic drama.[6] For the events we are dealing with are not myths but history. As such they are *ephapax*, once and for all. There was one exodus from Egypt and one resurrection of Christ, and we can neither repeat them nor return to them. But that is not to say they are dead, static, over and done with. They created and manifested and remain the bearers of a new and permanent quality of existence called salvation, initiating a permanent dialectic of call and response between God and his people. The events that began and first signaled this divine wooing of humankind may be past, but the reality is ever present, for the promises were made "to you and to your descendants forever" (Gen 13:15). The liturgy presents this challenge to each new generation, that it too may respond in faith and love to the call.

[3] J. Barr, *Biblical Words for Time* (Studies in Biblical Theology, London: SCM Press, 1962).

[4] *Ibid.*, 144.

[5] B. S. Childs, *Memory and Tradition in Israel* (Studies in Biblical Theology 37, Naperville, Ill.: A. R. Allenson, n. d.).

[6] *Ibid.*, 81 ff.

So in memorializing the past event we do not return to it nor re-create it in the present. The past event is the efficacious sign of God's eternal saving activity, and as past it is contingent. The reality it initiates and signifies, however, is neither past nor contingent but ever present in God, and through faith to us, at every moment of our lives. And if the past event is both permanent cause and contingent historical sign of salvation, the ritual memorial is the present efficacious sign of the same eternal reality. The ritual moment, then, is a synthesis of past, present, and future, as is always true in "God's time."

What the New Testament adds to this is the startling message that "God's time" has been fulfilled in Christ. So New Testament time is not some distinctive theory of time, but the fullness of time. What distinguishes it is its completeness, its *pleroma;* what is inaugurated is not some new philosophy of time, but a new quality of life. The eschaton is not so much a new age as a new existence. "New age" is but one of its metaphors, and it is important not to mistake the sign for the signified, not to be distracted from the work at hand by lofty disquisitions on kinds of time. Since our *pleroma* is in God, what we are confronted with is not the *past* made present, or even the *future* present, but the *end* present, not in the sense of the *finish* but of *completion:* God himself present to us.

This presence is fulfilled in Jesus, and that is what we mean by the "eschatological" nature of the New Age. Patrick Regan has said it better than I:

"The death and resurrection of Jesus are eschatological in that they bring the history of faith and the history of the divine presence to a close by bringing them to fulfillment. In the death of Jesus faith finds full expression; in his resurrection the divine presence is fully given. . . . But they come to a close as history only because they have reached that condition of fullness *(pleroma)* toward which their respective histories are ordered.

"The goal toward which all faith tended, and from which it derived its saving power, was the death of Christ. And the goal toward which all of God's gifts tended was the gift of himself to Christ in the Spirit. Thus the entire history of man's faith and God's self-gift are destined to find their eschatological perfection in the glorification of the crucified One. Consequently, neither faith nor the divine presence cease to exist. Rather do they remain everlastingly actual precisely because they have attained definitive and final form in the Spirit-filled Christ.

Hence the eschaton is really not a thing *(eschaton)*, but a person *(eschatos)*. It is the Lord Jesus himself—the last man, the spiritual man—the one in whom God and man have fully and finally met in the Spirit.

"The death and resurrection of Jesus bring to fulfillment not only history but creation as well. . . . In him, man and the world have, for the first time, come to be what they were meant to be. Hence the eschatological 'last days' join the protohistorical 'first days.' The kingdom is the garden. Christ is Adam. The eschaton is the Sabbath; the day on which God rests from his work and delights in its perfection."[7]

In other words the New Testament does two things. First, as Cullmann said, it divides time anew.[8] No longer do we await salvation. It is here in Christ, though the denouement of his parousia still lies ahead. Secondly, the New Testament recapitulates and "personalizes" all of salvation history in Christ. Nothing is clearer in the New Testament than the fact that everything in sacred history—event, object, sacred place, theophany, cult—has quite simply been assumed into the person of the incarnate Christ. He is God's eternal Word (John 1:1-14); his new creation (2 Cor 5:17, Gal 6:15, Rom 8:19 ff., Apoc 21–22) and the new Adam (1 Cor 15:45, Rom 5:14); the new Pasch and its lamb (1 Cor 5:7, John 1:29, 36, 19:36, 1 Pet 1:19, Apoc 5 ff. *passim*); the new covenant (Matt 26:28, Mark 14:24, Luke 22:20, Heb 8–13 *passim*); the new circumcision (Col 2:11-12) and the heavenly manna (John 6:30-58, Apoc 2:17); God's temple (John 2:19-27); the new sacrifice and its priest (Eph 5:2, Heb 2:17–3:2, 4:14–10:14); the fulfillment of the Sabbath rest (Col 2:16-17, Matt 11:28–12:8, Heb 3:7–4:11) and the Messianic Age that was to come (Luke 4:16-21, Acts 2:14-36). Neither the list nor the references are exhaustive. He is quite simply "all in all" (Col 3:11), "the alpha and the omega, the first and the last, the beginning and the end" (Apoc 1:8, 21:6, 22:13). All that went before is fulfilled in him: "For the law has but a shadow of the good things to come instead of the true form of these realities" (Heb 10:1); and that includes the cultic realities: "Let no one pass judgment on you in questions of food and drink or with regard to a festival or a new moon or a sabbath. These are only a shadow of what is to come; but the substance belongs to Christ" (Col 2:16-17).

[7] P. Regan, "Pneumatological and Eschatological Aspects of Liturgical Celebration," *Worship* 51 (1977) 346–47.

[8] O. Cullmann, *Christ and Time. The Primitive Christian Conception of Time and History* (Philadelphia: Westminster Press, 1950) 82 ff., esp. 84.

This is seminal for any understanding of Christian worship. The Old Testament temple and altar with their rituals and sacrifices are replaced not by a new set of rituals and shrines, but by the self-giving of a person, the very Son of God. Henceforth, true worship pleasing to the Father is none other than the saving life, death and resurrection of Christ: "iam Pascha nostrum Christus est, paschalis idem victima!"[9] And our worship is this same sacrificial existence in us.[10] Paul tells us, "Just as surely as we have borne the image of the man of dust, we shall also bear the image of the man of heaven" (1 Cor 15:49; cf. Phil 2:7-11, 3:20-21, Eph 4:22-24), the Risen Christ, "image of the invisible God, the first-born of all creation" (Col 1:15; cf. 2 Cor 4:4), who conforms us to his image through the gift of his Spirit (2 Cor 3:15, Rom 8:11 ff., 29). For St. Paul, "to live is Christ" (Phil 1:21), and to be saved is to be conformed to Christ by dying to self and rising to new life in him (2 Cor 4:10 ff.; 13:4, Rom 6:3 ff., Col 2:12-13, 20; 3:1-3, Gal 2:20; Eph 2:1ff., Phil 2:5 ff., 3:10-11, 18-21) who, as the "last Adam" (1 Cor 15:45), is the definitive form of redeemed human nature (1 Cor 15:21-22, Rom 5:12-21, Col 3:9-11, Eph 4:22-24). Until this pattern is so repeated in each of us so that Christ is indeed "all in all" (Col 3:11) we shall not yet have "filled up what is lacking in Christ's afflictions for the sake of his body, that is, the church" (Col 1:24). For we know "the power of his resurrection" only if we "share his sufferings, becoming like him in his death" (Phil 3:10).[11]

To express this spiritual identity, Paul uses several compound verbs that begin with the preposition *syn* (with): I suffer with Christ, am crucified with Christ, die with Christ, am buried with Christ, am

---

[9] From v. 4 of the seventh-century Ambrosian hymn *Ad regias Agni dapes* used in the Roman office at Sunday vespers in the Easter season.

[10] All four levels—Old Testament cult, fulfilled by Christ in the liturgy of his self-giving, a pattern we emulate in our lives and in our worship, as a gauge of the future fulfillment—are expressed in Heb 13:11-16: "For the bodies of those animals whose blood is brought into the sanctuary by the high priest as a sacrifice for sin are burned outside the camp. So Jesus also suffered outside the gate in order to sanctify the people through his own blood. Therefore, let us go forth to him outside the camp, bearing abuse for him. For here we have no lasting city, but seek the city which is to come. Through him then let us continually offer up a sacrifice of praise to God, that is, the fruit of lips that acknowledge his name. Do not neglect to do good and to share what you have, for such sacrifices are pleasing to God."

[11] In 1 John 3:14 we know this power through charity: "We know that we have passed out of death into life, because we love the brethren. He who does not love remains in death."

raised and live with Christ, am carried off to heaven and sit at the right hand of the Father with Christ (Rom 6:3-11, Gal 2:20, 2 Cor 1:5; 4:7 ff., Col 2:20, Eph 2:5-6).[12] This is one of Paul's ways of underscoring the necessity of my personal participation in redemption. I must "put on Christ" (Gal 13:27), assimilate him, somehow experience with God's grace and repeat in the pattern of my own life the principal events by which Christ has saved me, for by undergoing them he has transformed the basic human experiences into a new creation. How do I experience these events? In him, by so entering into the mystery of his life that I can affirm with Paul: "I have been crucified with Christ; it is no longer I who live, Christ who lives in me" (Gal 2:20).

This seems to be what Christian liturgy is for St. Paul. Never once does he use cultic nomenclature (liturgy, sacrifice, priest, offering) for anything but a life of self-giving, lived after the pattern of Christ.[13] When he does speak of what we call liturgy, as in 1 Corinthians 10-14, Ephesians 4, or Galatians 3:27-28, he makes it clear that its purpose is to contribute to this "liturgy of life," literally to edify, to build up the Body of Christ into that new temple and liturgy and priesthood in which sanctuary and offerer and offered are one. For it is in the liturgy of the Church, in the ministry of word and sacrament, that the biblical pattern of recapitulation of all in Christ is returned to the collectivity and applied to the community of faith that will live in him.

So to return to where we began and borrow a term from the biblical scholars, the liturgy is the ongoing *Sitz im Leben* of Christ's saving pattern in every age, and what we do in the liturgy is exactly what the New Testament itself did with Christ: it applied him and what he was and is to the present. For the *Sitz im Leben* of the Gospels is the historical setting not of the original event, but of its telling during the early years of the primitive Church. It is this, I think, that gives the lie to the notion that the celebration of any feast but Sunday and, perhaps, Easter, is "historicism." For if feasts "historicize," then so do the Gospels. Do not both the New Testament and liturgy tell us this holy history again and again as a perpetual anamnesis?

[12] Here and in the following paragraphs I have drawn considerable inspiration from David M. Stanley, *A Modern Scriptural Approach to the Spiritual Exercises* (Chicago: Loyola University, 1967). I could recommend no better book for one who wishes to learn what it means to meditate on the mysteries of Christ's life in the cycle of the church year.

[13] Cf. for example, Rom 1:9; 12:1; 15:16, Phil 2:17; 4:18, 2 Tim 4:6; also Heb 13:15-16 cited in n. 10.

"Therefore I intend always to *remind you* of these things, though you know them and are established in the truth that you have. I think it is right . . . to arouse you by way of *reminder*. . . . And I will see to it that after my departure you may be able at any time to *recall* these things. For we did not follow cleverly devised myths when we made known to you the power and coming of our Lord Jesus Christ, but we were eyewitnesses of his majesty (2 Pet 1:12-16)."

Note that this is not kerygma, as it is almost always mistakenly called, but anamnesis. Preaching the Good News to awaken the response of faith in the new message is kerygma. By the kerygma written down and proclaimed repeatedly in the liturgical assembly to recall us to our commitment to the Good News already heard and accepted in faith, even though "we know them and are established in the truth," is anamnesis, and that is what liturgy is all about.

Is the problem of sacred history in the Christian calendar so different from the problem of meditating on sacred history in the Bible and proclaiming it day in and day out in the liturgy of the word? But note well how the New Testament proclaims this message. What Brown says of the infancy accounts is true of the Gospels *tout court*. They are not just a history of what Jesus did, but a *post factum* theological interpretation, for the Apostolic Church, of the meaning of what he said and did and was in the light of the resurrection and post-resurrection events. So the Gospels, "passion stories with a long introduction" in the famous phrase of Kähler,[14] were written backwards, and their *Sitz im Leben* is the later life of the Church when the accounts were written.

Thus when the account of the mission of the twelve in Matthew 10:18 refers to being dragged before governors and kings, and witnessing before the gentiles, it is bending the account to a new situation that had nothing to do with the original historical setting.[15] The Acts of the Apostles show that it took the Apostolic Church a long time to realize there was to be a time of mission, a time of the Church between ascension and parousia. That is why there was such resistance to receiving outsiders into the Jewish-Christian Church (Acts 10–11, 15). But once it was understood, there was no hesitation in

[14] "Passionsgeschichten mit ausführlicher Einleitung," M. Kähler, *Der sogennante historische Jesu und der geschichtliche, biblische Christus* (Leipzig, 1896²; Eng. tr. Philadelphia: Fortress Press, 1964) 80.

[15] Stanley (note 12 above), 168–75.

rewriting the account of the call of the twelve to reflect this new situation. Just as the Book of Deuteronomy applied the early experience of the exodus to the later Israel, so too the New Testament applied Christ to its life-situation, its *Sitz im Leben*. And when we preach and meditate on the same apostolic call and mission, and apply it to the demands of our vocation and mission today, we are using the Gospels as the Apostolic Church did, as they were meant to be used: not as a history of the past, but as "the power of God unto salvation for everyone who has faith, first for the Jew, then for the Greek" (Rom 1:16).

The Gospel, then, is not a story but a power (Paul wrote this before the Gospel had become the Gospels). It is God's Spirit in us now, in the age of the Church, calling us to himself. And so Matthew is not "historicizing" when he recounts the call of the twelve, nor is St. Ignatius of Loyola when he proposes in his *Spiritual Exercises* meditations on the saving actions of Jesus in the Gospels, nor is the Church when it presents the same saving mysteries to us in word and rite and feast. For the focus is not on the story, not on the past, but on Paul's "power of God unto salvation, first for the Jew, then for the Greek," and right now for you and me.

This is what we do in liturgy. We make anamnesis, memorial, of this dynamic saving power in our lives, to make it penetrate ever more into the depths of our being, for the building up of the Body of Christ.

"That which was from the beginning, which we have heard, which we have seen with our eyes, which we have looked upon and touched with our hands, concerning the word of life—the life was made manifest and we saw it, and testify to it, and proclaim to you the eternal life which was with the Father and was made manifest to us—that which we have seen and heard we proclaim to you, so that you may have communion with us; and our communion is with the Father and with his son Jesus Christ. And we are writing this that our joy may be complete (1 John 1:1-4)."

It seems to me, then, that the eschatological/historical problem arose and was solved by the Apostolic Church. But it was not solved by abandoning New Testament eschatology, which sees Christ as inaugurating the age of salvation. What was abandoned was the mistaken belief that this implied an imminent parousia. But that does not modify the main point of Christian eschatology, that the endtime is not in the future but *now*. And it is operative now, though not exclusively, through the anamnesis in word and sacrament of the dynamic present reality of Emmanuel, "God-with-us," through the power of his Spirit in every age.

In the Gospels the transition to this new age of salvation history is portrayed in the accounts of the post-resurrection appearances of Jesus.[16] They introduce us to a new mode of his presence, a presence that is real and experienced, yet quite different from the former presence before his passover. When he appears he is not recognized immediately (Luke 24:16, 37, John 21:4, 7, 12). There is a strange aura about him; the disciples are uncertain, afraid; Jesus must reassure them (Luke 24:36 ff.). At Emmaus they recognize him only in the breaking of the bread—and then he vanishes (Luke 24:16, 30-31, 35). Like his presence among us now, it is accessible only through faith.

What these post-resurrection accounts seem to be telling us is that Jesus is with us, but not as he was before.[17] He is with us and not with us, real presence and real absence. He is the one whom "heaven must receive until the time for establishing all that God spoke by the mouth of his holy prophets from of old" (Acts 3:21), but who also said "I am with you always, until the close of the age" (Matt 28:20). It is simply this reality that we live in the liturgy, believing from Matthew 18:20 that "where two or three are gathered in my name, there am I in the midst of them,"[18] yet celebrating the Lord's Supper to "proclaim the Lord's death until he comes" (1 Cor 11:26) in the spirit of the early Christians, with their liturgical cry of hope: "Marana-tha! Amen. Come Lord Jesus!" (Apoc 22:20).

So the Jesus of the Apostolic Church is not the historical Jesus of the past, but the Heavenly Priest interceding for us constantly before the throne of the Father (Rom 8:34, Heb 9:11-28), and actively directing the life of his Church (Apoc 1:17–3:22 and *passim*).[19] The vision of the men that produced these documents was not directed backwards, to the "good old days" when Jesus was with them on earth. We see such nostalgia only after Jesus' death, before the resurrection appearances give birth to Christian faith.

[16] *Ibid.*, 278 ff.

[17] *Ibid.*, 280 ff.

[18] I am aware of the recent challenge to the liturgical interpretation of this pericope [J. Duncan M. Derrett, "'Where two or three are convened in my name . . .': a sad misunderstanding," *Expository Times* 91 no. 3 (December 1979) 83–86], but no matter; the liturgical application has become traditional regardless of the original *Sitz im Leben* of the text, and it is this traditional belief that interests us here.

[19] Stanley, *op.cit.*, 284–85.

The Church did keep a record of the historical events, but they were reinterpreted in the light of the resurrection, and were meant to assist Christians to grasp the significance of Jesus in their lives.[20] That this was the chief interest of the New Testament Church, the contemporary, active, risen Christ present in the Church through his Spirit, can be seen in the earliest writings, the epistles of St. Paul which say next to nothing about the historical details of Jesus' life.

It is this consciousness of Jesus as the Lord not of the past but of contemporary history that is the aim of all Christian preaching and spirituality and liturgical anamnesis. Christian vision is rooted in the gradually acquired realization of the Apostolic Church that the parousia was not imminent, and that the eschatological, definitive victory won by Christ must be repeated in each one of us, until the end of time. And since Christ is both model and source of this struggle, the New Testament presents both his victory and his cult of the Father as ours: just as we have died and risen with him (Rom 6:3-11, 2 Cor 4:10 ff., Gal 2:20, Col 2:12-13, 20; 3:1-3, Eph 2:5-6), so too it is we who have become a new creation (2 Cor 5:17, Eph 4:23-24), a new circumcision (Phil 3:3), a new temple (1 Cor 3:16-17; 6:19, 2 Cor 6:16, Eph 2:19-22), a new sacrifice (Eph 5:2), and a new priesthood (1 Pet 2:5-9, Apoc 1:6; 5:10; 20:5). This is why we meditate on the pattern of his life, proclaim it, preach it, celebrate it: to make it ever more deeply our own. This is why the Apostolic Church left us a book and a rite, word and sacrament, so that what Christ did and was, we too may do and be, in him. For this reason, sacred history is never finished. It continues in us, which is why in liturgy we fete the saints, and ourselves too, as well as Christ, for God's true glorification is Christ's life that he has implanted in us. So the "communion of Saints" is also a sign of sacred history, proof of the constant saving action of Christ in every age.

For Christian life, according to the several New Testament metaphors for it, is a process of conversion into Christ.[21] He is the *Ursakrament* which we have seen the New Testament present as the personalization of all that went before, and the recapitulation and completion and model and foretaste of all that will ever be. As such, he is not just the mystery of the Father's love for us, "the image of the unseen God" (Col 1:15); he is also the revelation of what we are to be (1 Cor

[20] *Ibid.*, 285.
[21] See M. Searle, "The Journey of Conversion," *Worship* 54 (1980) 48–49, and "Liturgy as Metaphor," *Worship* 55 (1981) esp. 112 ff.

15:49, 2 Cor 3:18, Rom 8:29). His life is the story of entering sinful humanity and returning it to the Father through the cross, a return that was accepted and crowned in Christ's deliverance and exaltation (Phil 2:5 ff.). And this same story, as we have seen, is also presented as the story of everyone, the archetype of our experience of returning to God through a life of death to self lived after the pattern Christ showed us: "He died for all, that those who live might live no longer for themselves but for him who for their sake died and was raised" (2 Cor 5:15).[22]

In the New Testament, the very process of its composition reveals the growing realization of this fact: that our final passage to the Father through death and resurrection was to be preceded by a life of death to sin and new life in Christ. The whole point of the New Testament rewrite of Christ's life is to make it speak to this new awareness: that the new age was to be not a quick end but a new holy history. As Patrick Regan said in the passage already cited, the eschaton is not a time or a thing, it is a person, the new Adam, Jesus Christ (1 Cor 5:20 ff., 42 ff.). And the new creation is life lived in him (2 Cor 5:13-19)—or rather, his life in us (Gal 2:20).

Liturgical feasts, therefore, have the same purpose as the Gospel: to present this new reality in "anamnesis" as a continual sign to us not of a past history, but of the present reality of our lives in him. "Behold *now* is the acceptable time; behold, *now* is the day of salvation" (2 Cor 6:2). It is this vision of the mysteries of Christ's life now that we see in the festal homilies of the golden age of the Fathers, such as those of St. Leo the Great (440–461), which always stress the present salvific reality of the liturgical commemoration.[23] For salvation history does go on, but not in the sense that at Christmas Christ's birth is somehow present again. For such events are historical, and they are past, and liturgy does not fete the past. What is present is our being born anew in Christ, *our* entrance into new life through this coming of God to us now.[24] For as St. Leo says in his famous aphorism that is an entire liturgical theology, what Christ did visibly during his earthly ministry

---

[22] See also 1 John 3:4 cited in n. 11.

[23] For example, *Sermo 63* (*De passione* 12) 6, *PL* 54, 356: "Omnia igitur quae Dei filius ad reconciliationem mundi et fecit, et docuit, non in historia tantum praeteritarum actionum novimus, sed etiam in praesentium operum virtute sentimus." On Leo's liturgical theology see M. B. de Soos, *Le mystère liturgique d'après s. Léon le grand* (LQF 34, Münster: Aschendorff, 1958).

[24] *Sermo 36* (*In epiph.* 6) 7, *PL* 54, 254.

has now passed over into sacrament: "Quod itaque Redemptoris nostri conspicuum fuit, in sacramenta transivit."[25]

One pastoral conclusion from all this should be obvious: there is no ideal model of Christian feast or calendar which we must "discover" and to which we must "return." Rather, it is up to each generation to do what the Apostolic Church did in the very composition of the New Testament: apply the mystery and meaning of Christ to the *Sitz im Leben* of today. A liturgy is successful not because of its fidelity to some past ideal, but because it builds up the body of Christ into a spiritual temple and priesthood by forwarding the aim of Christian life: the love and service of God and neighbor; death to self in order to live for others as did Christ.

And so Christmas is not just about the coming of Christ to Bethlehem, but about the coming of Christ to me, and about my going out to others. And Easter is not about the empty tomb in Jerusalem some 2,000 years ago, but about the reawakening here and now of my baptismal death and resurrection in Christ. We shall see this, I think, if we put aside the folklore of the past and the modern theories of time and leisure and play, and meditate on the texts of the word of God, and of the Fathers, and of the worship of the Church. There we shall find that the festal cycle is but one facet of the life of the church, one way of expressing and living the mystery of Christ that is radically one in all aspects of its Christian expression. As Jean Daniélou said,

"The Christian faith has only one object, the mystery of Christ dead and risen. But this unique mystery subsists under different modes: it is prefigured in the Old Testament, it is accomplished historically in the earthly life of Christ, it is contained in mystery in the sacraments, it is lived mystically in souls, it is accomplished socially in the Church, it is consummated eschatologically in the heavenly kingdom. Thus, the Christian has at hand several registers, a multi-dimensional symbolism, to express this unique reality. The whole of Christian culture consists in grasping the links that exist between Bible and liturgy, Gospel and eschatology, mysticism and liturgy. The application of this method to scripture is called exegesis; applied to liturgy it is called mystagogy. This consists in reading in the rites the mystery of Christ, and in contemplating beneath the symbols the invisible reality."[26]

That's what the church year, and indeed all of liturgy, is about.

[25] *Sermo 74 (De ascens. 2) 2 PL* 54, 398.
[26] "Le symbolisme des rites baptismaux," *Dieu vivant* 1 (1945) 17 (my trans.).

Cyrille Vogel
translated and revised by William G. Storey and Niels Krogh Rasmussen

3. The Development of the Private Mass[*]

The reduced version of the solemn Mass was the result of a number of factors that appeared at different times and places but eventually became almost universal in the Western Church. Some of the more important factors were the following:

1. The attempt to replicate the liturgy of the Roman basilicas and shrines with their manifold eucharistic celebrations in the local church(es) of an episcopal city or monastery;[1]

2. The establishment of daily Mass in cathedrals and monasteries and then several daily conventual and non-conventual Masses including the *missa matutinalis, missa maior,* and others, as well as the need to create more and more priest-monks;[2]

3. The view of the Mass as an *opus bonum* to be offered frequently in intercession, or as an act of subjective piety;[3]

---

[*] C. Vogel, *Medieval Liturgy: An Introduction to the Sources.* Translated and revised by W. G. Storey and N. K. Rasmussen (Washington, D.C.: The Pastoral Press, 1986) 156–59.

[1] This is the key to A. Häussling's theory as will be explained further on in this section. Vogel, on the other hand, makes bold to say that there is no connection between the small-group Masses of antiquity—the "house Masses," the shrine Masses at martyr's graves and the *refrigeria,* etc.—and the later "private" Mass. C. Vogel, "Une mutation cultuelle inexpliquée: le passage de l'Eucharistie communitaire à la messe privée," *RSR* 54 (1980) 231–50, esp. 234–35. Häussling's views on this are summarized in his *Mönchskonvent und Eucharistiefeier,* LQF 58 (Münster, 1972) 238–51.

[2] A. Häussling, *ibid.,* deals with *missa matutinalis* on 323–37, *missa maior* and the other Masses, *passim* and 315–23. C. Vogel, "Une mutation cultuelle," 240, argues that the private mass influenced the appearance of the monk-priest, while noting (note 12) that Nussbaum makes no allusion to this relationship in his "remarquable travail," i.e., O. Nussbaum, *Kloster, Priestermönch, und Privatmesse,* Theophaneia 14 (Bonn, 1961); the latter deals with *missae matutinalis et maior* on 124–32.

[3] On *opus bonum* see the study of R. Berger, *Die Wendung "offere pro" in der römishen Liturgie,* LQF 41 (Münster, 1965). The rise of the private Mass for Nussbaum is explained largely by the change in understanding of the Mass as an *opus bonum* and his entire theory concerning the frequency of Mass revolves around

4. The *redemptiones paenitentiales*, which advised the saying of impressive numbers of Masses (as commuted penances) which could only be accomplished if many monks and canons were henceforth ordained;[4]

5. Increasing devotion to the Blessed Virgin and to the faithful departed with the growing custom of having at least one Mass per day *de Beata* and *de requie* in communities;[5]

6. The endowment of more and more "chantries" in cathedrals and monasteries (and much later even parishes) and the resulting need for more priests;[6]

---

the notion of subjective piety; see Nussbaum, *Kloster, Priestermönch und Privatmesse*, 152–73. This has been challenged by Häussling throughout *Mönchskonvent*, esp. 243–58, 287–88, and 342–44. According to Häussling, the Eucharist was still considered an *actio ecclesiae* "and not of an isolated individual" even when celebrated by a single representative of the Church. On this see R. Schulte, *Die Messe als Opfer der Kirche. Die Lehre frühmittelalterlichen Autoren über das eucharistische Opfer*, LQF 35 (Münster, 1959). A. Franz describes the votive Masses for various needs in *Die Messe im deutschen Mittelalter*, 268–91; on the so-called Gregorian Masses, Franz, *ibid.*, 244 and C. V. Héris, "Théologie des suffrages pour les morts," *LMD* 44 (1955) 58–67, R. W. Pfaff, "The English Devotion to St. Gregory's Trental," *Speculum* 49 (1974) 75–90, and A. Angenendt, "*Missa specialis*. Zugliech ein Beitrag zur Entstehung der Privatmessen," *Frühmittelalterliche Studien* 17 (1983) 153–221.

[4] See C. Vogel, "Une mutation cultuelle," 242–46 and the detailed documentation in his "Composition légale et commutations dans le système de la pénitence tarifée," *Revue de Droit Canonique* 8 (1958) 289–318; 9 (1959) 1–38; 341–59.

[5] On the weekly votive Masses, see H. Barré–J. Deshusses, "À la recherche du missel d'Alcuin," *EL* 82 (1968) 3–44 and J. Deshusses, "Les Messes d'Alcuin," *ALW* 14 (1972) 7–41. On votive Masses in general, A. Franz, *Die Messe*, 115–54; Häussling, *Mönchskonvent* 243–46, 255, 283. On the rising cult of the virgin, see G. Frénaud, "Le Culte de Notre Dame dans l'ancienne liturgie latine," *Maria*, ed. H. Du Manoir, vol. 6 (Paris 1961) 157–211; H. Barré, *Prières anciennes de l'Occident à la mère du Sauveur, des origins à S. Anselme* (Paris, 1963). In the tenth century, Alcuin's *Missa Sanctae Mariae* came to be widely celebrated on free Saturdays but little by little a daily Mass known as the *Missa familiaris* or *De Domina* spread everywhere. Accompanied by the evermore popular *Officium parvum B. M. V.*, it soon required a Lady chapel of its own—usually east of the apse—in every monastery, cathedral, and large parish in Western Europe. On the development and spread of the additional Marian Office, see J. Leclercq, "Formes anciennes de l'office marial," *EL* 74 (1960) 89–102 and "Fragmenta Mariana," *EL* (1958) 292–305; J. M. Canal, "El oficio parvo de la Virgen," *Ephemerides Mariologicae* 15 (1965) 463–75; J. B. L. Tolhurst, *The Monastic Breviary of Hyde Abbey, Winchester*, vol. 6: *Introduction to the English Monastic Breviaries*, HBS 80 (London, 1942), 120–29; in addition to the Office of Our Lady, Tolhurst has a full discussion of all the devotional accretions to the medieval Office.

[6] This was related to the penances as well as the growing concern throughout the Middle Ages with "intercessory foundations" to pray for the dead, i.e., the

7. The stipend system itself which encouraged even slovenly priests to celebrate daily for their Mass-penny.[7]

Various approaches have been taken to explain these phenomena. Scholars such as Otto Nussbaum and Cyrille Vogel have stressed

founders and their relatives. On Masses for the dead, see K. J. Merk, *Die messliturgische Totenehrung in der römischen Kirche. Zugleich ein Beitrag zum mittelalterlicher Opferwesen* 1 (Stuttgart, 1926); R. Berger, *Die Wendung "offere pro" in der römischen Liturgie*, LQF 41 (Münster, 1965) 125–28, 162–67, 212–23. For the enormous proliferation of chantries, chantry priests and chantry chapels, see A. H. Thompson, *The Historical Growth of the Parish Church* (London, 1911) 24–50; F. Bond, *An Introduction to English Church Architecture from the Eleventh to the Sixteenth Century* (London, 1919) 102–12; J. R. H. Moorman, *Church Life in England in the Thirteenth Century* (Cambridge, 1946) 15–18; A. H. Thompson, "Chantries and Colleges of Chantry Priests," *The English Clergy and their Organization in the Later Middle Ages* (Oxford 1947; reprint 1966) ch. 5, 132–60, 247–91; E. E. Williams, *The Chantries of William Canynges in St. Mary Redcliffe, Bristol* (Bristol-Oxford, 1950); K. L. Wood-Legh, *Perpetual Chantries in Britain* (Cambridge, 1965); G. H. Cook, *The English Mediaeval Parish Church* (London, 1956) 47—123; A. Kreider, *English Chantries and the Road to Dissolution* (Cambridge, Mass.-London, 1979), esp. chaps. 1–3 on the intercessory institutions, their priests, and the chronological contours of the various foundations, 1–92. It must also be remembered that in addition to the cantarists proper, there were large numbers of unbeneficed priests and lesser clerics who constituted a kind of clerical underworld or proletariat, living off occasional stipends for attendance at funerals, the singing of obits, etc.; see Kreider, 19–21. For a perfect description of a chantry college and its intercessory obligations, see A. L. Gabriel, *Student Life in Ave Maria College, Mediaeval Paris* (Notre Dame, Ind., 1955) especially ch. 11, 199–212. On occasion, whole monasteries were conceived of as chantries, e.g., Sheen and Syon Abbeys, both founded by King Henry V (1413–1422) in reparation for the murder of Richard II. Shakespeare has Henry pray before the battle of Agincourt: "Five hundred poor I have in yearly pay, Who twice a day their withered hands hold up Toward heaven to pardon blood; And I have built Two chantries where the sad and solemn priests Sing still for Richard's soul" (Henry V, lines 317–21).

[7] K. J. Merk, *Abriss einer liturgiegeschichtlichen Darstellung des Mess-stipendiums* (Stuttgart, 1928), *Das Mess-stipendium. Geschichtlich, dogmatisch, rechtlich und aszetisch erklärt* (Stuttgart, 1929), "Das Mess-Stipendium," *Theologische Quartalschrift* 136 (Tübingen, 1956) 199–228; K. Mörsdorf, "Mess-Stipendium," *Lexikon für Theologie und Kirche* 7 (1962) 354 ff.; M. F. Mannion, "Stipends and Eucharistic Praxis," *Worship* 57 (1983) 194–214; C. F. Keller, *Mass Stipends* (St. Louis, 1926); C. E. Gilpatric, "Mass Stipends and Mass Intentions," *Worship* 38 (1964) 190–201; J. A. Jungmann, "Mass Intentions and Mass Stipends," *Unto the Altar: The Practice of Catholic Worship*, ed. A. Kirchgässner (New York, 1963) 23–31; E. Kilmartin, "Money and the Ministry of the Sacraments," *The Finances of the Church*, ed. W. Bassett-P. Huizing, *Concilium* 117 (New York, 1979) 103–11; K. Rahner-A. Häussling, *The Celebration of the Eucharist* (New York, 1968).

certain of these factors in order to explain the appearance of the so-called private Mass.[8]

To begin, these scholars consider *missa privata* to be synonymous with *missa lecta* and *missa solitaria*, i.e., a Mass wherein a single priest assumes the liturgical functions normally reserved to the other ministers (readings), choir (chants) and congregation (responses, etc.).[9] For Vogel in particular, this "sacerdotalization" of the entire Mass is due to a basic changeover in religious and liturgical psychology—radically different from that of the early Church. The Mass has become a good work, "which takes its place among the ascetical exercises through which the religious sanctify themselves."[10] The Mass is now celebrated out of personal devotion as a means of ensuring salvation.[11]

A different approach is taken by A. Häussling.[12] Basing his conclusions on much of the same historical data but seen from a different perspective, Häussling argues first of all that the use of the term "private" in the sense of "solitary" as used by Nussbaum, betrays a post-Tridentine understanding of the term. "Private" in the early Middle Ages did not refer to something done alone but more than likely something "privated" or deprived of the elaborate or special.

A *missa privata*[13] is one celebrated not with the entire community with all the ministers functioning as on Sundays and other "liturgi-

---

[8] Nussbaum and Vogel are cited *supra*, n. 1.

[9] This is the working definition of Vogel based on his own research in the area of evolving penitential discipline and its influence on the frequency of eucharistic celebrations (see n. 4 *supra*). This is also Nussbaum's definition of private mass in his *Kloster, Priestermönch und Privatemesse*, 136. See Vogel, "Une mutation cultuelle," 234–35.

[10] Vogel, "Une mutation cultuelle," 241.

[11] Vogel, "Une mutation cultuelle," 247: "[the notion of] the Eucharistic celebration as a communal act is reinforced by considering the Eucharist as a 'mystery' in the ancient sense of the term. Thus the notion of *mysterion* is proper to the Christian communities native to the Mediterranean region. One can well imagine that at the beginning of the seventh century, the new-comers to the faith from the North would have found it difficult to conceive of this sort of eucharistic process. . . . This resulted in a kind of degeneration of 'mystery': the cultic society began to consider liturgical activity as an ensemble of practices designed for individual salvation. One could say quite correctly that *mysterium* gradually became *officium quotidianum* or in other words, the progressive divinization of the Christian in and through the Eucharist gave way to a cultic act which is simply an instrument of salvation."

[12] *Mönchskonvent und Eucharistiefeier: Eine Studie über die Messe in der abendländischen Klosterliturgie des frühen Mittelalters und zur Geschichte der Messehäufigkeit*, LQF 58 (Münster, 1972).

[13] Häussling, *ibid.*, 246, nn. 336 and 285, n. 522 notes that in the Early Middle

cal" days, but on ordinary days (even daily) with a small group. *Privata* is opposed to *publica* as "secondary" or "subordinate" is opposed to "principal," "solemn," and "official." *Missae privatae* in this earlier sense included those celebrated at the Roman shrines/basilicas not on the Sundays or festivals when the entire community was scheduled to worship there, but whenever the need arose, e.g., when there were enough pilgrims present.[14]

These Masses, then, were not in origin celebrated by a priest alone, but were nonetheless subordinate to the liturgies of the entire community such as those of the stational system for Sundays and feasts.

The smaller groups who gathered at the shrines on ordinary days celebrated the Eucharist not only to honor the saints and martyrs, but

---

Ages the actual term *missae privatae* occurs only once: Walafrid Strabo, *De exordiis et incrementis rerum ecclesiasticarum* cap. 26; *MGH, Capitularia* 2, 506 line 26. The context of its occurrence supports Häussling's theory: referring to the Patriarch Paulinus of Aquileia (+802), Strabo says: *saepius et maxime in privatis missis circa immolationem sacramenti ymnos vel ab aliis vel a se compositus celebrasse.* It wouldn't have made much sense to have hymns sung if no one was present save patriarch and server . . . who would have sung the hymns? It is more likely that "even at private Masses" signifies the subordinate liturgies celebrated on nonliturgical days in the episcopal chapel attended by the members of his household and at least some who could sing.

[14] See the dissertation of J. Wagner, *Altchristliche Eucharistiefeiern im kleinen Kreis* (Bonn, 1949) referred to by Häussling, 229, n. 266; Vogel, "Une mutation," 235, n. 5; Nussbaum, *Kloster, Priestermönch und Privatmesse*, 134, n. 5. Häussling points to the distinction between community-Eucharists (Gemeindeeucharistie) and memorial-Eucharists (Gedächtniseucharistie) 229f. which was apparent already in Jerusalem at the time of Egeria's pilgrimage (late IV century); cf. *Itinerarium Egeriae* c. 43, 2-3; cc. 3:6f.; 4:2-4, 5, 7 = CC 175, 84 ff. and 40–43. From Rome, Leo I wrote to the Alexandrian patriarch Dioskorus (ca. 445) concerning the frequency of celebrating the Eucharist on feastdays: *Ut autem in omnibus observantia nostra concordet, illud quoque volumus custodiri, ut cum sollemnior quaeque festivitas conventum populi numerosioris indixerit, et ea fidelium multitudo convenerit quam recipere basilica simul una non possit, sacrificii oblatio indubitanter iteretur; ne his tantum admissis ad hanc devotionem, qui prima advenerint, videantur hi, qui postmodum confluxerint, non recepti, cum plenum pietatis atque rationis sit, ut quoties basilicam, in qua agitur, praesentia novae plebis impleverit, toties sacrificum subsequens offeratur.* Leo, *Epistolae* 9, 2; *PL* 54, 626–27. When the number of pilgrims to the shrines even on "private days" seemed to demand it, the Eucharist was celebrated for their benefit, as is reported by the anonymous Ambrosiaster (ca. 366–84): *Omni enim hebdomada offerendum est, etiam si non quotidie peregrinis, incolis tamen vel bis in hebdomada* (Wednesday and Friday, the most ancient "liturgical days" after Sunday); *In Tim 3:12 f.*, sect. 4 = CSEL 81, 3, 269.

took the opportunity to intensify the intercessory aspect of the celebration: to give thanks or praise for recovery from sickness, to ask for safe childbirth, to pray for the departed, etc. and to do so more intently (and effectively) at the very place where the martyr-patron "lived" as a guarantee that God hears and answers the prayers of the individual and the community.[15]

Of course there were festivals of the martyr-patrons in the stational system as well, when the entire community celebrated at the shrine and where the pressing needs of the entire community or of special members of the community were likewise included as *vota* in the celebration of the Eucharist. These were among the first "votive Masses" to be included in the earliest *libelli* and sacramentaries.[16]

As has already been shown, the spread of the Roman liturgy north of the Alps began very early and unsystematically—even before the VIII century. In order to use the Roman books, the Franks needed to modify their own cities and monasteries in order to carry out the prescriptions of the stational and non-stational liturgies in which they had participated while visiting Rome and/or found in the various books. This is not to say that stational liturgies are exclusively Roman in origin,[17] but there is ample evidence that in many places by the late eighth century, there was a conscious attempt to replicate the Roman liturgies as best they could in their own situations.[18]

It is undeniable that there is a difference in the theology of Church, Orders, and Eucharist between that of the early Church and that of the medieval Church. Häussling argues, however, that for the early Middle Ages when the frequency of the Eucharist increased dramatically, there is no complete break—there is a gradual change of emphasis until the intercessory aspect overshadows the building-up of the gathered community.[19]

[15] Häussling, 242–43; J. P. Kirsch, "Die *Memoria Apostolorum* an der Appischen Strasse und die liturgische Festfeier de 29. Juni," *JLW* 3 (1923) 33–50, esp. 49–50.

[16] E.g., the prefaces *post infirmitatem* in the midst of the *libelli* for Peter and Paul in the *Veronense*, ed. Mohlberg, nos. 308, 314, 334 and the reference to the prayers *servi tui Gregorii* in one of the many orations provided in the votive mass *pro sterilitate mulierum* in the *Gelasianum Vetus* (*Vat. Reg.* 316), ed. Mohlberg, no. 1466.

[17] See the introduction and notes in J. F. Baldovin, *The Urban Character of Christian Worship in Jerusalem, Rome, and Constantinople from the Fourth to the Tenth Centuries*. Ph.D. dissertation (Yale, 1982) 1–6.

[18] Adaptation of the Roman stational system, see Häussling, 201–13; for the relic-cult and the multiplication of shrines, see *Ibid.*, 214–28.

[19] On the change in eucharistic theology, see Häussling, 251–55 and the works

Without such a change in eucharistic understanding the actual practice of the early Middle Ages would be unthinkable—the piling up of Masses and the "offering of the sacrifice for" so many reasons. And yet, the actual *formulae* and the ritual itself does not change so drastically that nothing from the Church of late antiquity remains. In fact, the forms and *formulae* that developed during late antiquity and the early Middle Ages were left as a treasured inheritance in the liturgy, guarded as the tradition of the Apostles from the City of the Apostles.

Still, although the possibility of a Eucharist celebrated by a priest at a side altar or chapel existed as early as the sixth century[20] and was common in Frankish monasteries by the ninth,[21] it is important to understand these celebrations as part of a whole—not individual "private" affairs occasioned by personal option or piety.[22] Indeed, what eventually became a thoroughly "private" Mass in the post-Tridentine Church, kept intact all the structural features of the solemn Mass, but with some additions:

Various prayers of preparation and devotion were added (at the beginning, at the offertory, before and after communion) perhaps influenced by ancient Gallican usages. Such prayers are very diverse and vary from manuscript to manuscript. These various, adapted ordinaries of the Mass were gradually reabsorbed by the Roman structure, fixed in the thirteenth-century Missal of the Roman Curia and passed into the *editio princeps* of the *Missale Romanum* of 1474.[23] The Roman rite of the Mass was only imposed on the Western Church by the *Missale pianum* (Pius V) in 1570.[24]

---

cited in his footnotes on those pages. On the new self-conception of the cleric see *ibid.*, 268–71.

[20] Vogel, "Une mutation cultuelle," 238.

[21] Nussbaum, *op.cit.*, provides an overview of references from the IX century and following on 185–202.

[22] Häussling, 243–58, 287–88, 342–44.

[23] The presence and role of the congregation is still assumed even in the *Ordo servandus per sacerdotem in celebratione Missae sine cantu et sine ministris secundum ritum S. Romanae Ecclesiae* (1508) by J. Burchard. This *ordo* served as a model for the rubrics of the 1570 *Missale Romanum,* but lost most of its references to congregational presence/participation. See the excellent summary in B. Neunheuser, "The Relation of the Priest and Faithful in the Liturgies of Pius V and Paul VI," *Roles in the Liturgical Assembly,* Conférences Saint Serge 23, tr. M. O'Connor (New York, 1981) 207–19, esp. 208–9.

[24] The editions of the Roman Missal are the following: *Missale Romanum* (Milan, 1474); Milan, Bibl. Ambrosiana *Incunabulum* SQN III 14 = *editio princeps.* This was

The *Hadrianum* forwarded to Charlemagne by the pope in the late eighth century contained a short *ordo* suitable for both solemn and private Mass:

---

reissued by R. Lippe, *Missale Romanum Mediolani 1474,* HBS 17 (London, 1899) and *Missale Romanum Mediolani 1474. A Collation with other editions printed before 1570. Indices,* HBS 33 (London, 1907). See also A. P. Frutaz, "Due edizioni rare del Missale Romanum pubblicate a Milano nel 1482 e nel 1492," *Miscellanea Giulio Belvederi* (Rome, 1954/1955) 55–107. The Missal of 1474 was based on the type of Mass-book called the *Missale Curiae romanae* or *Ordo missalis secundum consuetudinem romanae Curiae* from the thirteenth century; cf. M. Andrieu, "Le Missel de la chapelle papale à la fin du XIII siècle," *Miscellanea F. Ehrle* 2, SeT 38 (Rome 1924) 348–76; S. J. P. Van Dijk-J. H. Walker, *The Origins of the Modern Roman Liturgy* (London, 1960); S. J. P. Van Dijk, "The Lateran Missal," *SE* 6 (1954) 125–79, "The Legend of 'the Missal of the Papal Chapel' and the Fact of Cardinal Orsini's Reform," *SE* 8 (1956) 76–142, and "The Authentic Missal of the Papal Chapel," *Scriptorium* 14 (1960) 257–314. For the formation of the missal, see. J. W. Legg, *Tracts on the Mass,* HBS 27 (London, 1904–1905) (London, 1905); H. Grisar, *Das Missale im Lichte römischer Stadtgeschichte* (Freiburg, 1925); J. Ferreres, *Historia del Missal Romano* (Barcelona, 1929) and especially, A. Dold, *Vom Sakramentar, Comes und Capitulare zum Missale,* TuA (Beuron, 1943). The extract from the *Missal of Constance,* which was printed before the *editio princeps* (Copinger dates it 1470, Misset argues for ca. 1450 and therefore before the edition of the Psalter of 1457) does not contain the *formulae* for Advent, Sundays after Epiphany, Lent, and the Sundays after Easter and Pentecost; it has been edited by O. Hupp, *Ein Missale speciale, Vorlaüfer des Psalteriums von 1457* (Munich, 1898); E. Misset, *Un missel spécial de Constance oeuvre de Gutenberg avant 1450* (Paris, 1899); H. Stein, *Une production inconnue de l'atelier de Gutenberg* (Paris, 1899); A. Stevenson, *The Problem of the Missale Speciale* (London, 1967); and G. Widman, (ed.), *Der gegenwärtige Stand der Gutenberg-Forschung,* Bibliothek des Buchwesens 1 (Stuttgart 1972, esp. articles by F. Geldner and S. Corsten). From 1570 up to 1970, the official edition of the Roman Missal was the *Missale romanum ex decreto sacrosancti concilii Tridentini restitutum, Pii V, P.M. iussu editum* (Rome, 1570). This *Missale Pianum* was, for all practical purposes, a repeat of the *editio principes* of 1474, and after it had been aligned with the *editio princeps* of the Breviary (1568), it was promulgated by the Bull *Quo primum tempore* of Pius V on July 14, 1570 [the missal was to be adopted within six months by all churches who had not had their own rite for at least two hundred years]. An *Ordo servandus* and *Rubricae generales* based on the work of J. Burchard were joined to this 1570 missal; see note 23 *supra,* and A. P. Frutaz, "Contributo alla Storia della Riforma del Messale Promulgato da San Pio V nel 1570," *Problemi di Vita Religiosa in Italia nel Cinquecento,* Italia Sacra 2 (Padua, 1960) 187–214. A bibliography of printed missals by W. H. J. Weale, *Bibliographia liturgica. Catalogus missalium ritus latini ab anno 1475 impressorum* (London, 1886) notes the 211 editions/printings of the Missal from 1475 until the official edition of 1570; an enlarged and revised edition is C. Bohatta-W. H. J. Weale (London, 1928).

QUALITER MISSA ROMANA CAELEBRATUR. Hoc est in primis *introitum* qualis fuerit statutis temporibus sive diebus festis seu cottidianis, deinde *kyriae eleison.* Item dicitur *gloria in excelsis deo,* si episcopus fuerit, tantummodo die dominico, sive diebus festis; a praesbyteris autem minime dicitur nisi solo in pascha. Quando vero laetania agitur, neque *gloria in excelsis deo* neque *alleluia* canitur. Postmodum dicitur *oratio,* deinde sequitur *apostolum.* Item *gradalem* seu *alleluia.* Postmodum legitur *evangelium,* deinde *offerturium* et *oblationem super oblatam.* Qua completa dicit sacerdos excelsa voce: *Per omnia saecula saeculorum. Amen. Dominus vobiscum,* etc. Then follows the *Canon missae:* initial dialogue, *praefatio, sanctus, Te igitur, Pater noster* and its embolism *pax* and *Agnus dei;* the *Hadrianum* terminates here without any further indications.[25]

The best commentaries on the structure of the Roman Mass are B. Botte-C. Mohrmann, *L'Ordinaire de la messe. Texte critique, traduction et études.* Études liturgiques 2 (Louvain/Paris, 1953); B. Botte, *Le canon de la messe romaine.* Textes et études liturgiques 2 (Louvain, 1935); L. Eizenhöfer, *Canon missae romanae, RED, Series minor 1: Traditio textus* (Rome, 1954) and 7; *Textus propinqui* (Rome, 1966) and the classic work of J. A. Jungman, *Missarum sollemnia. Eine genetische Erklärung der römischen Messe,* 2 vols., 6th ed., Vienna, 1966; ET F. A. Brunner, *The Mass of the Roman Rite,* 2 vols. (New York, 1951–1955, from the 2nd German ed., 1949). On the term *missa,* see C. Mohrmann, "Missa," *Vigiliae Christianae* 12 (1958) 67–92 (best critical synthesis and bibliography); see also C. Callewaert, "Histoire positive du canon romain," *SE* 2 (1949) 102–10 and A. Coppo, "Una nuova ipotesi sull'origine di *missa,*" *EL* 71 (1951) 225–67. In the time of Gregory the Great, Mass lasted two to three hours, Gregory I, *Registrum* 10, 14; *MGH, Epistolarum* 2, 248.[26]

---

[25] Ed. J. Deshusses, *Le Sacramentaire grégorien: Ses principales formes d'après les plus anciens manuscrits.* Spicilegium Friburgense 16 (Fribourg 1971) no. 1, 85–86. Cf. H. Lietzmann, *Das Sacramentarium Gregorianum nach dem Aachener Urexemplar,* LQF 3 (Münster, 1921) 1; and H. A. Wilson, *The Gregorian Sacramentary under Charles the Great,* HBS 49 (London, 1915).

[26] For a discussion of the evidence regarding the frequency of celebration, see R. Taft, "The Frequency of the Eucharist throughout History." *Can We Always Celebrate the Eucharist?,* ed. M. Collins-D. Power (New York, 1982) 13–24; reprint Taft, *Beyond East and West: Problems in Liturgical Understanding* (Washington, D.C. 1984) 61–80; (Rome, 1997) 87–100.

Godefridus J. C. Snoek

4. The Process of Independence of the Eucharist*

In the early Christian Church the celebration of the Eucharist implied a meal, an obvious activity since Jesus had instituted the Eucharist within the context of a Jewish Passover meal. In his first letter to the Corinthians (1 Cor 11:17-34) written in 55 A.D., the apostle Paul assumes this tradition and, with his disciple Luke, gives the most ancient description of the eucharistic meal. Central to it was the command given by Jesus: "Do this in memory of *Me*" (Luke 22:19; 1 Cor 24:25) or the pronouncement of the eucharistic blessing, transforming the bread and wine into signs of Christ and his saving act, followed by the eating of the bread and the drinking of the wine. This act of eating and drinking was an "active" form of participation, an "entry into the paschal mystery of the Lord."[1]

Over the centuries attention shifted increasingly from the *activities surrounding* the bread and wine within the Lord's supper to *reverence for* the bread and the wine themselves. Up to the tenth century this was still within the context of the Mass but subsequently was placed more and more outside its liturgical setting. This gradual uncoupling of the eucharistic gifts from their sacramental and liturgical context, the community celebration of the meal, is sometimes referred to as the process in which the Eucharist became "independent" or "disengaged."[2]

The seeds of this "process of independence" can be found in the early shift from community meal or *"agape"* to the ritual consumption of his body and blood alone. It was practically an automatic process whereby the emphasis came to be placed more on Christ's presence as food for the soul and less on his eschatological presence in the community nature of the ritual, which was centered on praise

---

* Chapter 2 of G. J. C. Snoek, *Medieval Piety from Relics to the Eucharist: A Process of Mutual Interaction* (New York: Brill, 1995) 31–64. Complete bibliographical references are found below beginning on page 71.

[1] Verheul (1974) 13, 70, 77–82; Dix (1945) 743–44.

[2] Mitchell (1982) 4: "How did the eucharistic action (. . .) give way to a pattern of devotion quite independent?"; *ibid.*, 20–29.

of God, repentance and forgiveness. Within this process of limitation, from real to merely sacramental meal—a phenomenon already apparent in apostolic times—the taking of the Eucharist to those prevented from being present at the ritual was a logical step. In this way they too were enabled to share in Jesus by receiving the food over which the community prayer of thanksgiving had been uttered. Justinus Martyr mentions this custom in his *Apologia* written around A.D. 150.[3]

Following logically from this development, and helped partly by the persecutions, it became the custom to preserve and receive the Eucharist at home during the week. Home communion as celebrated in early Christian times persisted until the seventh century, although it was less common from the fourth century onwards. Despite this tendency towards privatization, the Church remained attached to the link with the community celebration, something clearly seen in the practice of the *fermentum,* a piece of the eucharistic bread which, around the year 400, the pope caused to be sent to the other titular churches[4] of Rome as a symbol of unity with his celebration.

The customs of the *fermentum* and home communion during ancient Christian times show that the presence of Christ in the eucharistic bread was not a source of awe at the time. The Eucharist was seen primarily as the *anamnesis*—remembrance—which made actual Christ's work of salvation. It was about the real and continuing memorial of Christ in his salvific acts. The emphasis was not so much on the awe-inspiring and cultic reverence of the actual body and blood of Christ.[5] But it should be noted that as early as the third century a protecting and magical power was attributed to the Eucharist preserved at home, similar to the powers to affect everyday life believed to be exercised by house relics in the then still heathen structures. Hence the practice of taking the eucharistic

---

[3] Ed. Quasten (1936) 17 *Apologia,* 1, c. 65; 2 c. 67; BKV XII, 80, 82; ed. Bartelink (1986) 82, 83; ed. Wartelle (1987) 193, *Apologie,* 67, 5; "puis on fait à chacun la distribution et le partage de la nourriture eucharistique, et l'on envoie leur part aux absents, par le ministre des diacres."

[4] I.e., in early Christian practice these would have been private places of worship denoted by the name of the individual owner *(titulum);* later the term was applied to a basilica or to one of the Roman parish churches (*LW* II, 2678); Wegman (1991) 58: small regional churches in the city where the presbyters celebrated the liturgy in the pope's name.

[5] Browe (1938) 147: with reference to the sacrificial meal Browe remarks: "Dafür sagte man: das unblutige Opfer, das Fleisch und Blut Christi empfangen; der Ausdruck: Christus empfangen, gebrauchte man nur gelegentlich einmal, d. h. man sah die Sache, die Speise, nicht die Person, die sich darbot"; Betz (1955); Mitchell (1982) 15.

bread on a journey or having it buried along with a corpse. The way to this magical interpretation lay open once the emphasis was shifted from the Eucharist as community meal to the Eucharist as individual ritual food, designed to create communication between the communicant and Christ and his church. It became possible to regard the Eucharist as an individual guarantee of protection both at home and when traveling or as a means of confounding sinners, especially when it was kept within easy reach. Hippolytus (+235) speaks of the apotropaic or protecting force of the Eucharist in circumstances of mortal danger and in an exemplary anecdote Cyprian (+258) portrayed the Eucharist as unapproachable by sinners: it would seem that a certain woman had been made aware of her sins and, on arriving home, saw flames coming from the *arca,* or small box, where she kept the Eucharist.[6]

Trust in the somatic healing powers of the Eucharist through communion can be seen in the advice given by Cyril of Jerusalem (+386) who recommended that after drinking from the chalice the communicant should touch his wet lips with his hand, then his eyes, his forehead and other senses. Cyril is also the origin of the following recommendation for communion—once more practiced in the Catholic Church since Vatican II:[7] "Make of your left hand a throne for your right hand in order to receive the King in the latter; take care that your palm is hollow and there receive the body of Christ, saying: Amen."[8] This devout reverence shown at communion is reported by more authors from the fourth–fifth century onwards. The eucharistic gifts were not only consecrated and blessed but also treated with reverence. Thus Augustine (+430) underpinned the showing of reverence towards the Eucharist—provided that it was interpreted as "sacramental"—using the words of the psalm: "Exalt ye the Lord our God, and worship at his footstool; for he is holy" (Ps 99:5).[9] Another

[6] CSEL 3, 1, 256; SC 11 bis, 118.

[7] Second Vatican Council, Oct. 11, 1962 to Dec. 8, 1965.

[8] *PG* 33, 1126, *Catech.* XXIII, c. 22: "Tum vero post communionem corporis Christi accede et ad sanguinis poculum: non extendens manus, sed pronus, et adorationis ac venerationis in modum, dicens, *Amen,* sanctificeris, ex sanguine Christi quoque sumens. Et cum adhuc labiis tuis adhaeret ex eo mador, manibus attingens et oculos et frontem et reliquos sensus sanctifica"; *ibid.,* 1123–24, XXIII, c. 21: "sed sinistram velut thronum subiiciens dexterae, utpote Regem suscepturae: et concava manu suscipe corpus Christi, respondens: *Amen*".

[9] CCSL 39, 1384–85. *Enarrationes in Psalmis,* XCVII, 8, 9: "Exaltate Dominum nostrum. Et adorate scabellum pedum eius, quoniam sanctus est"; "Nemo autem illam carnem manducate, nisi prius adoraverit."

sign of reverence was the solemn showing of the Eucharist just before the communion.[10] Nonetheless, up to Carolingian times, the ninth century approximately, similar modest expression of reverence remained within the context of the liturgical celebration.

The accompanying increase in eucharistic ceremonial lent itself to allegorical interpretation. An early indication of this can be found in the Greek Church writer Theodore of Mopsuestia (+428). He saw the eucharistic liturgy as a ritual allegory designed to reactivate Christ's suffering, death, burial, and resurrection. When the deacon spreads the altar cloths on the altar, this is no longer the preparation of the community table for the Lord's supper but is seen rather as the dressing of a bier or tomb, on which the bread is laid as the [dead and later — ed.] risen body of Christ.[11] In the West an early symptom of the passion for allegory can be found in the *Expositio Antiquae Gallicanae* ascribed to Germanus of Paris (+576) where the tower-shaped container used to hold the Eucharist is seen as an analogy of Christ's tower-shaped rock tomb.[12]

The tendency towards allegorical explanations won a great deal of ground in Carolingian times. Amalarius of Metz (+c. 852) regarded the Mass as the life of Jesus, as a passion play whose interpretative cloak enfolded even the most ordinary gestures and actions. He regarded the Introit prayer as the prophets announcing the coming of the Messiah, and the Gloria was the song of the angels [at Bethlehem— ed.]. The subdeacon reading the epistle was given the significance of John the Baptist, which was why the subdeacon stood one step lower than the reader of the gospel, since the preaching of the "Precursor" was subordinate to that of the Messiah. In the same spirit he explained the ritual surrounding the *Sancta,* the bread remaining from the previous celebration which was placed in the chalice as a sign of the unity of the eucharistic continuity within the local church. It had the same significance as the *fermentum* which came into use later

---

[10] Mitchell (1982) 47–49.

[11] Ed. Tonneau (1966) 331–32, IIe homilie *sur le baptême,* par. 6: 485, Ve homilie *sur la messe,* par 15; 505, par 26: "Et quand ils l'ont apportée, c'est sur le saint autel qu'ils la placent pour le parfait achèvement de la passion. Ainsi croyons-nous à son sujet que c'est désormais dans une sorte de tombeau qu'il (le Christ) est placé sur l'autel et que déja il a subi la passion. C'est pourquoi certains des diacres qui étendent des nappes sur l'autel, présentent par cela la similitude des linges de l'ensevelissement"; ed. Mingana (1933) VI, 21, 79, 86.

[12] *PL* 72, 93.

when, in Rome, the Mass was celebrated simultaneously in more than one church. This originally simple action involving the *Sancta* grew into a rich ceremonial, described in the *Ordo Romanus Primus*, dating from the seventh–eighth century. The bishop, accompanied by other priests and acolytes bearing censers and candles, carried it solemnly into the church.[13] Unfortunately Amalarius ignored the original significance since he failed to see the mingling of the bread and wine as the continuity with the previous celebration, regarding it as symbolic for the return of Christ's soul into his body.[14]

Up to the time of Amalarius such allegorical interpretation had been incidental. Following him the allegorical bent continued right through the Middle Ages,[15] supported from the time of the Crusades by the devotion to the sufferings of Christ. According to Bernold of Konstanz (+1100) the priest with outstretched arms symbolized the shape of the cross.[16] The more than twenty signs of the cross made over the eucharistic offerings during the prayer of the canon were seen by Rupert of Deutz (+1135) to symbolize such things as the journey of Jesus to the Mount of Olives, the betrayal by Judas, the witness of the centurion, and the piercing of Christ's side.[17] Although while still a cardinal the future Pope Innocent III (+1216) did something to put a stop to the allegorical interpretations which occasionally showed great powers of imagination, his own explanation of the canon proves an exception to his efforts by presenting an even more refined numerological symbolism than his predecessors had been capable of.[18] The canonist William Durandus (+1296) was to take Innocent's vision as his model.

To the extent that these pious and pseudo-historical meanderings of the ecclesiastical mind affected the bread and wine, they did so by—at a very early stage—removing the community and sacramental significance of these symbols. As far as the sacramental significance is concerned, Christian antiquity always showed a more differentiated

[13] Andrieu (1931–61) II, 82; Mitchell (1982) 56–59; Wegman (1991) 230.

[14] Ed. Hanssens (1948–50) I, 275, *Codex Expositionis*, II, XIV: "Quoniam et in alio loco evangelii confessus est non se esse Christum, stat in inferiori gradu qui verba horum qui incipes Iohannis adnuntiat"; *ibid.*, 320, *Ordinis missae expositio* II, 15: "Quid enim est panem in vinum mittere? Animam Christi ad eius corpus redire."

[15] *LW* I, 95–98; II, 1627–34.

[16] PL 151, 987, *Micrologus de ecclesiasticis observationibus*, c. 16.

[17] CCSL 7, 32–61, *De divinis officiis*, lib. II; Meyer (1965) 238.

[18] PL 217, 773–916, *De sacro altaris mysterio*; Jungmann (1962) I, 147 sqq.

approach, depending on the metabolism of Ambrose (+397) or the symbolism of Augustine (+430).[19] Ambrose's basic assumption was the transformation of the nature of the bread and wine by the words of consecration, while Augustine emphasized the visible symbol—the sacramental character of the eucharistic gifts—as an expression of the invisible: the Christ whom we were to meet. In addition Augustine distinguished between the sacrament itself and its power or *virtus*, which brings piety, unity, and love into being.[20] This *virtus* unavoidably calls to mind the special power or *virtus* emanating from a relic which, however, was no symbol but a tangible remnant of the saint.

The tensions surrounding the question of the *praesentia realis* increased in the early Middle Ages. The sacred act, the eucharistic celebration within the community, the *anamnesis* of Christ's sacrifice in which he is made present—all this lost its dynamism in the manner in which the Eucharist was experienced. This symbolic realism was replaced by a reality regarded as exclusively historically tangible, whereby the way was closed off from an understanding of the Eucharist that would indicate the sacramental. The approach adopted meant that the symbol was no longer an independent and dynamic reality: there was room only for a remembrance in allegorical form.[21] This caused the bread and wine to be released from the community liturgical context and to start to play a role in the allegorical representation of Christ's suffering and death during the Mass. Even that symbol—the table—which called out for active community participation in praise and thanksgiving to the Father for our salvation lost its community significance and was transformed into an allegorical tomb. The community aspect of the Eucharist lost in significance and the "process of independence" increased.[22]

Meanwhile the intriguing question regarding the relationship between the sign and the sacramental reality kept minds busy and, in the ninth century, gave rise to the eucharistic controversy between Paschasius Radbertus (+859), recorded in the previous chapter, and his pupil Ratramnus, who was also a monk of Corbie in northern France. This was a controversy that can be regarded as an early part of the "process of independence" since both authors concentrated on

[19] *TRE* I, 89.
[20] Gerken (1973) 94–95.
[21] *TRE* I, 90.
[22] Gerken (1973) 65–74.

the Eucharist as object, which meant that it became, in their arguments, isolated from the invisible reality of God's mercy and from the eucharistic activity around the table.[23] They were concerned with the nature of the change wrought in the bread and wine and the manner of Christ's presence, which each described in two separate books with the same title: *De corpore et sanguine Domini*.

Pachasius insisted on strict eucharistic realism. He maintained complete identity between the sacramental body of Christ, present in a mystical, nonmeasurable, and nonmaterial way, under the appearances of bread and wine, and Christ's historical body, born of the Virgin Mary, crucified and risen.[24] The eucharistic gifts are, he stated, spiritual food and after consecration they hold within themselves a miraculous physical reality, a belief he regarded as supported by the realistic miracle legends of Christian antiquity.

Of these there were two classic examples taken from the *Vitae Patrum*, which were constantly re-copied, re-told, and added to throughout the Middle Ages. The first concerned St. Basil of Caesarea (+397). It tells of a Jew who pretended to be a Christian in order to get at the truth behind the Mass and communion. He saw how the Christ-child was slaughtered in the saint's hands, and when he went to communion with the rest of the faithful he ate real flesh and drank real blood from a full chalice.[25] The second tale tells of a miracle said to have been experienced by the desert father St. Arsenius (+450). This authority related how a particular old man was incapable of believing in the real presence until he saw with his own eyes an angel slaughter the infant Jesus during celebration of the Mass and the blood being caught in the chalice. To his amazement, when the old man went to receive communion he was given flesh soaked in blood to eat, and it only became bread and wine again when his faith in the real presence had been restored.[26]

[23] Mitchell (1982) 35, 54.

[24] CCSL 16, 27, c. 3; 30, c. 4: "Vera utique caro Christi quae crucifixa est et sepulta, vere illius carnis sacramentum quod per sacerdotem super altare in verbo Christi per Spiritum Sanctum divinitus consacratur. Unde ipse Dominus clamat: *Hoc est corpus meum*"; Ratramnus: ed. Bakhuizen van den Brink (1954).

[25] PG 29, CCCII, *Vita apocrypha*, c. 2; Paschasius, CCSL 16, 87–88, *De corpore et sanguine Domini*, XIV.

[26] PL 73, 301–302, *De vitis patrum*, lib. I; 979, lib. V; PL 72, 94, *s. Germani exp. brevis ep.* 1; CCSL 16, 88–89.

Hrabanus Maurus (+856), John Scotus (+877), and—particularly—Ratramnus (+ca. 868) opposed the excessively realistic Capharnaistic notions (John 6:52) exemplified in these stories. Ratramnus dealt with the question at the request of the emperor Charles the Bald (+877). He emphasized the real and the sacramental presence as distinct from a real and literal presence, the latter stating that a small-sized Christ was as it were contained in the Eucharist. His approach left no room for blood-soaked images, since the bread and wine were not literal but sacramental signs of Christ's body and blood. For the believer the bread and wine were changed in a spiritual manner, *in figura*, but this did not mean that this spiritual food was identical to the flesh that was crucified and the blood that was shed on Calvary.[27]

The ninth century eucharistic controversy did not, however, place a strong enough emphasis on the presence of Christ in the Eucharist to prevent the rise of the veneration of the Eucharist outside the liturgical context. The theological debate largely went over the heads of the parish clergy or it was neglected. In a document such as the ninth-century catechism, known as the *Disputatio Puerorum*, a pastoral guide for the laity, the question is ignored.[28] The progress of the conflict only became truly evident in the second eucharistic debate from the middle of the eleventh century and in general devotion at the beginning of the thirteenth century, when the official Church finally decided in favor of Radbertus's previous opinion.

However, there was a gradual growth in the split between priest and people relative to the Eucharist, partly because the people no longer understood Latin—which had already been the case for some time in the non-Romance countries. The Mass thus became exclusively a clerical ritual in which the people could scarcely share. The problems stemming from the use of Latin can be deduced from an instruction issued by the Council of Tours in 813, requesting that bishops should preach in (old) French *(rustica romana lingua)* or in German so that the people could at least understand.[29]

The granting of special status to the priest was partly encouraged by the anointing of the ordinand's hands, a ritual by which he was

[27] Neunhaeuser (1963) 18.

[28] *PL* 101, 1099–144; Mitchell (1982) 100–1.

[29] *MGH Conc* II, 288 can. XVII: "Et ut easdem omelias quisque aperte transferre studeat in rusticam Romanam linguam aut Thiosticam, quo facilius cuncti possint intellegere quae dicuntur"; Mitchell (1982) 69; Gy (1987) 533–539; Lauwers (1987) 228: literature dealing with the knowledge of Latin in the Middle Ages.

thought to gain the unique power to change the bread and wine into the body and blood of Christ—which, according to the followers of Radbertus, were the real, physically present body and blood of Jesus. The *Missale Francorum,* the Gallic sacramentary dating from the eighth century, contains two texts used at the anointing of the hands[30] and in a mid-ninth-century sacramentary of St. Denis we read: "O Lord, bless and consecrate these hands of your priest, so that they can consecrate the sacrificial gifts offered for the sins and omissions of your people."[31] At a later date, in the midst of the delicate questions surrounding the Investiture Controversy, Pope Urban II (+1099) is reported to have said that the priest's hands had the power "to create the Creator of all things and offer him to God for the salvation and healing of the world." Indeed, people kissed the priest's hands because they had touched the Divine Majesty, surrounded by angels.[32]

From Carolingian times, therefore, only the priest could understand the sacred texts and the Eucharist was increasingly regarded as belonging to the spiritual domain of the celebrant, who consecrated the bread and the wine. Because of this unique relationship with God the priest was alone given the right to touch the eucharistic offerings. This was the reason for the changeover in the ninth century from communion received in the hand to communion received in the mouth, though the fear of desecration also played a part here.[33] In addition to other ninth-century declarations issuing from Italy, Spain, and France, a council held in Rouen made matters crystal clear: "Do not place the Eucharist in the hand of a lay person, neither man nor woman, but only in the mouth."[34]

The laity was also gradually denied the right to handle the chalice. From the seventh century a custom came about in Rome whereby some of the consecrated wine was mixed with ordinary wine in a chalice and given to the faithful to drink. In the same period outside Rome a reed, or *fistula,*[35] was used to suck up the wine in order to prevent

[30] Ed. Mohlberg (1957) 10, n. 33 en 34.

[31] Ed. Assemanus (1749–66) t. VIII, 128: "Benedic Domine, et sanctifica has manus sacerdotis tui ad consecrandas hostias, quae pro delictis atque negligentiis populi offeruntur"; Angenendt (1982) 194; Mitchell (1982) 89.

[32] Southern (1975) 128; Delaruelle (1975) 71.

[33] Mitchell (1982) 90; Browe (1932a) 601; Nussbaum (1969) 27–28.

[34] Hardoin, VI, p. 1, 205, c. 2: "nulli autem laico aut feminae eucharistiam in manibus ponat, sed tantum in os eius (. . .) ponat" (anno ca. 878); Mitchell (1982) 597–98.

[35] The *fistula, pugillaris* or *calamus* was not made of natural material but of gold or silver (*LW* I, 754).

spillage. The third way of administering communion with the wine, and for long the most popular method, was the *intinctio*, where the host was dipped in the consecrated wine and handed to the communicant. The opponents of *intinctio* considered that this too closely resembled the gesture employed by Jesus during the Last Supper to identify Judas as the one who was to betray him.[36] This was, in fact, the argument used by Innocent III to put an end to the custom at the beginning of the thirteenth century.[37] In the meantime the theologians had advanced the opinion that Jesus was entirely present under each separate species, so that *intinctio* was superfluous. Depriving the laity of communion from the chalice contributed in no small way to eucharistic piety being directed almost exclusively towards the host. Outside the Mass eucharistic devotion became, in fact, devotion to the host.[38]

A practical reason for abolishing *intinctio* was the fear of spillage. The presence of Christ required extreme care that not a drop should be lost. This almost scrupulous piety was also applied to the host. Around the year 800 came the first prescriptions calling for the use of unleavened bread. This type of bread, which does not produce crumbs, came into general use from the eleventh century. The introduction of separate hosts did away with the breaking of the bread.[39] The hosts were prepared with the utmost care: the monks of Cluny washed themselves and combed their hair beforehand and picked out the wheat grains one by one and washed them. Even the millstone was cleansed. The monks were careful that neither their saliva nor their breath came into contact with the hosts.[40]

Once consecrated, the bread belonged in sacred vessels. In Carolingian times the custom arose of consecrating such vessels, a gesture again exclusively reserved to the priest. The first sacred formulae for this type of ritual are to be found in the Gallic sacramentaries. The *Missale Francorum*, for instance, contains prayers for the consecration of the paten,[41]

[36] *LW* II, 1466; Nussbaum (1969) 28–29, 48; Freestone (1917) 152–65.

[37] *PL* 217, 866, *De sacro altaris mysterii*, VI, 13.

[38] Devlin (1975) 189–190; Mitchell (1982) 159–63; *LW* I, 1078.

[39] Nussbaum (1979) 107; *LW* I, 328.

[40] d'Archery, I, 694, *Antiquiores consuetudines Cluniacensis monasterii, collectore s. Udalrico*, lib. III, c. 13; *PL* 149, 757–58, *De hostiis quomodo fiant*; Pijper (1907) 65; Jungmann (1962) II, 44–45.

[41] This was originally a large tray used for distributing the leavened bread. When unleavened bread was introduced in the 8th–9th century and small hosts became more common, the tray lost its original shape and turned into a small, flat dish on which the celebrant's host was placed (*LW* II, 2170).

the chalice, and the chrismale, the latter called allegorically by the *Missale* "a new tomb for the body of Christ."[42]

Not only the manner but also the time at which believers received communion served to lay increasing emphasis on the separation between priest and laity. A first indication is contained in the *Institutio* of Angilbert (+814), who had gone from the court of Charlemagne to take up residence in the Centula-Saint Ricquier monastery in the diocese of Amiens. He became abbot and prescribed that at Christmas and Easter communion should be distributed to the children and lay adults who had not yet received it only after the clergy had left. We have to imagine the following scenario: the celebrant gave communion to the monks while another priest did the same for the laity, assisted by a deacon and subdeacon. Once the celebrant was finished, distribution of communion was halted and the celebrant continued with the Mass in order not to make the service too long. Leaving aside a few indications dating from the ninth and tenth centuries, reports of communion after Mass date from the twelfth century and later. By the end of the thirteenth century the custom had become general on major feast days.[43]

The increasing liturgical independence of the priest relative to the laity in Carolingian times was further emphasized by his private prayers during Mass at the time of communion or at the Sanctus. The people meanwhile were kept occupied with singing. In a manuscript written at the time in Sarum (Salisbury), in which Radbertus's influence can be clearly felt, the priest prays: "God, Father (. . .) by your mercy your only Son came down to this earth for our sakes. According to your will he took on the flesh which I now hold in my hands." And leaning forward he then addresses the Host: "I adore you, I glorify you, from the depth of my heart I praise you (. . .)." The humble words spoken by the centurion "Lord, I am not worthy" (Luke 7:6) were part of these private prayers until the thirteenth century, after which they were said out loud, by priest and congregation together, just before the communion.[44] A similar personal prayer can also be found in the late ninth–century sacramentary of Amiens, the prayer being said while the people sang the Sanctus. Sometimes the priest even began the canon

[42] Ed. Mohlberg (1957) 19.

[43] Hallinger, I, 295–96; Heitz (1963) 27; Nussbaum (1979) 44–47; Mitchell (1982) 226–27.

[44] Martène (1788) I, 241; Browe (1935) 31–32; Dijk v. (1960) 49–51; Jungmann (1962) II, 428–30.

on his own, a practice opposed by Archbishop Heraldus of Tours. The celebrant, he stated, would do better to sing with the people.[45]

The communal aspect of the celebration of the Eucharist probably lost most ground by the increase in the practice of private Masses, which Theodulph of Orleans vainly tried to oppose with his statement that "a priest should never celebrate the Mass alone."[46] The private Mass was no longer a novelty in his time. The question as to how it came into being has not yet been given a satisfactory answer.[47] The source must lie in the sixth-century monasteries, where more and more monks were ordained priests. At the time of Gregory the Great the monks were going out on mission and it was desirable that they should be priests. The priest-monks felt the need within the monasteries to celebrate Mass more frequently than would have been the case simply by taking turns to be celebrant for the whole community. Moreover, ground was being gained by the idea that a greater share in the Church's treasury of mercy was obtained not only as regards personal sanctity but also for the dead if the Mass was celebrated more often. The desire to honor the relics contained in the many altars was also of some significance.[48]

A further factor was that the Masses—sometimes great numbers of them—came to be regarded as "re-payment" of the penances handed out in private confession, a practice originating in Ireland and which spread rapidly in the seventh century. The penitent was granted forgiveness or absolution immediately following the confession of his sins and then had to do some form of penance. This could consist of having Masses said, involving payment of a gift or *stipendium*. Usually the penitent did not attend the *missa specialis*, which was celebrated in complete privacy.[49]

[45] *PL* 121, *Capitula Heraldi*, XVI: "Et ut secreta presbyteri non inchoent antequam *sanctus* finiatur, sed cum populo *sanctus* cantent"; Leroquais (1927) 442.

[46] Mansi XIII, 996, capitulare Theodulfi, VII: "Sacerdos missam solus nequaquam celebret: quia sicut illa celebrari non potest sine salutatione sacerdotis, responsione nihilominus plebes, ita nimirum nequaquam ab uno debet celebrari. Esse enim debent qui ei circumstent quos ille salutet, a quibus ei respondeatur: et ad memoriam illi reducendum est illud dominicum: *Ubicumque fuerint vel tres in nomine meo congregati, et ego in medio eorum*."

[47] Häussling (1973) 357; Vogel (1980) 232: "Les raisons (. . .) nous échappent encore, en grande partie"; Angenendt (1983) 153.

[48] Nussbaum (1961) 136 sqq.; Klauser (1969) 103; Häussling (1973) 219, 223–25, 232 sqq.; Jungmann (1974).

[49] Angenendt (1982) 183–85; Mitchell (1982) 109–12.

In the eighth century the daily private Mass was a familiar phenomenon in monasteries, an example followed by the secular clergy in the ninth century[50] despite theological objections. Walahfrid Strabo (+849) criticized the opinion that the mercy of the Mass could be directed towards one single person, and Peter Damian (+1072) remarked: "Whereas the Lord on his cross suffered for the salvation of the whole world (. . .) now the sacrifice of salvation is offered for the benefit of one son of man."[51] This echoed the warning given by St. Ignatius of Antioch (+ca. 118): "Be sure to celebrate one supper of the Lord, for there is only one body of Our Lord Jesus Christ and only one chalice of unity in his blood; that is why there is only 'one altar' and one bishop together with his priests and deacons."[52]

Around the year 600 this principle had thus been laid aside in the monasteries. The Masses celebrated at the side altars, placed against the wall of the monastery church, implied that the priest stood with his back to any congregation present. The situation in which the priest stood between the altar and the faithful was already a fact in the East, in small churches in Syria in the fourth century and in Greece and Egypt in the fifth century. From the seventh century onwards it happened regularly in Palestine and Asia Minor.[53] In the West it was only North Africa that followed the example of the Eastern church, but in the parish churches the celebrant's position was, until the seventh or eighth century, *versus populum*, facing the congregation.

The origin of the change in the position adopted by the priest can be traced back to the fourth century. The edict of tolerance of 313 meant that Christian worship could be carried out in public. The liturgy became more and more ornate, borrowing elements from court ceremonial. The majestic portrayal of the teaching Christ, great and imposing among his disciples arranged around him like "courtiers," can still be seen in the mosaic in the apse of the fourth-century church

---

[50] Dijk v. (1960) 45 sqq.; up to the end of the 8th century the demarcation between regulars and seculars was not so sharply drawn: Semmler (1980) 78–111.

[51] *PL* 145, 501: "Sed cum passus sit Dominus in cruce pro salute mundi, nunc mactatur in altari pro unius commodo et facultate presbyteri. Tunc crucifixus est pro totius populi multitudine, nunc quasi pro unius homuncionis utilitate salutaris hostia videtu offerri," Angenendt (1983) 180.

[52] SC 10, 1969. 123, Philad. 4: "Ayez donc soin de ne participer qu'à une seule eucharistie, car il n'y a qu'une seule chair de notre Seigneur Jésus-Christ, et un seul calice pour nous unir en son sang, un seul autel, comme un seul évêque avec le presbytérium et les diacres"; Klauser (1969) 106.

[53] Nussbaum (1965) 408–21: *"Die Abwendung des Liturgen von der Gemeinde."*

of Santa Pudentiana in Rome or in the sixth-century mosaics of the churches of San Vitale and the San Apollinare Nuovo in Ravenna.[54]

Heaven and earth, the visible and invisible, were joined together; angels and archangels crowded round the altar wreathed in incense. The sacred was withdrawn from view; participation by the faithful began to take a back seat; choir and clergy took over their task. Less and less notice was taken of the congregation, so that it was almost a logical step for the celebrant to place himself between the people and the altar.[55] In the West, the *missa sine populo,* or private Mass, encouraged this development. The growing number of side altars in cathedrals and monastery churches were used exclusively for private Masses, the high altar being reserved for high Mass celebrated for the monastery or parish. There too, around the year 1000, the celebrant stood between the people and the altar. Soon there was no objection to the altar being placed against the wall of the apse. It was to remain there until the Second Vatican Council. The back of the altar table provided plenty of space for the relics on rich retables.

The situation thus came about that the priest celebrated Mass no longer with the faithful present but in their name. The Canon, recited out loud by the celebrant in the Roman church up to about the eighth century, was now whispered inaudibly.[56] After the change undergone by the Eucharist in early Christian times from liturgy to individual ritual food had detracted from the communal character of a meal, and subsequently the allegorical interpretation had deprived the symbols of their communal significance—the table became a tomb—the intensification of the priestly relationship to the Eucharist isolated the people even more from the liturgy of the Mass. The alienation was revealed in the descriptions given of how communion should be received, the failure any longer to understand the liturgical language, the private Mass, and the priest's private prayers uttered with his back to the people.

These symptoms, contributing to the "process of independence of the Eucharist," were up to this point manifested within the eucharistic liturgy. But in the tenth century we see the first signs of a cultic reverence outside the Mass itself, in the practice of communion for the sick. This custom had existed as long ago as in the second century, as can be seen in the allusion made by Justinus Martyr. There

[54] *Ibid.,* 415, n. 261: lit.; Hauser (1975) 92, illustr. 36–39.
[55] Nussbaum (1965) 419.
[56] Klauser (1969) 97–101; Jungmann (1941) 88.

was at the time no fixed ritual. No one objected to lay people giving one another communion at home.[57] From about 800, however, the pastoral aspect was clarified and normally speaking the practice of *viaticum* was reserved to the clergy.[58] According to Theodulph of Orleans (+821) the sick person was brought to the church[59] while St. Dunstan celebrated Mass in the home of a sick woman.[60] Around the year 970 Dunstan's disciple, bishop Ethelwold of Winchester, addressed to the English monasteries his *Regularis Concordia*, in which he describes a third form of communion of the sick, a form which was most usual and was accompanied by a certain degree of ceremonial: after the Mass the priest [along with the whole congregation — ed.] went with the Eucharist to the sick person's home, preceded by praying and psalm-singing acolytes and servers bearing incense and candles.[61]

Round about the same time the Eucharist began to take on a role in the Good Friday solemnities. At the end of the tenth century, Gerard, the cathedral provost of Augsburg, described in his *Vita* of bishop Ulrich (+973) that after the faithful had received communion it was the prelate's "normal custom" to carry the remaining eucharistic bread to the Church of St. Ambrose and there bury it symbolically by laying a stone on it. On Easter morning Ulrich celebrated Mass there, took out the Eucharist and carried both it and the book of the Gospels, surrounded by candles and incense, to the Church of John the Baptist in order to sing Terce, the second Office of the day. Then the procession continued on to the cathedral for the Easter Mass.[62]

[57] See above, n. 3.

[58] Hincmar of Rheims (+882): *PL* 125, 779, *Capit. synod.* II, c. 10: "Si ipse presbyter visitet infirmos et inungat oleo s. et communicet per se et non per quemlibet, et ille ipse communicet populum nec tradat communionem cuiquam laico ad deferendum in domum suam causa cuiuslibet infirmi"; Rush (1974) 31; Mitchell (1982) 113.

[59] *PL* 137, 427.

[60] *PL* 105, 220.

[61] Hallinger VII-3, 141, c. XIV, 98: "sacerdos casula exutus cum reliquis ministris illius missae eucharistiam ferentibus praecedentibus cereis et turibulo cum omni congregatione eant ad visitandum infirmum canentes psalmos penitentiales consequente laetania et orationibus"; *PL* 137, 500 c. 12; Nussbaum (1979) 96.

[62] *MGH SS* IV, 392–393, *Gerhardi vita s. Oudalrici ep.* c. 4 (21, 23): "Et sacro Dei ministerio perpetrato populoque sacro Christi corpore saginato, et consuetudinario more quod remanserat sepulto (. . .) Desiderantissimo atque sanctissimo paschali die adveniente, post primam intravit aecclesiam sancti Ambrosii, ubi die parasceve corpus Christi superposito lapide collocavit, ibique cum paucis clericis missam de sancta Trinitate explevit. Expleta autem missa, clerum interim congregatum in scena iuxta eandem aecclesiam sitam solemnibus vestibus indutum anteces–

This *depositio* and *elevatio* can also be found in Ethelwold's document, but he states that it was the cross and not the Eucharist that was placed in a grave next to the altar. This is probably the oldest form of the ritual. From about 1100 both cross and Eucharist were placed simultaneously in the holy sepulchre.[63]

There are approximately two hundred documents witnessing to these three manners of ritual burial on Good Friday. In most cases only the cross was buried, in fewer cases both cross and Eucharist, and relatively infrequently only the Eucharist. The three variants show, in the incidence with which they are reported, similarities to the custom which increased in frequency from the eighth century during the consecration of a church: the *depositio* of three particles of the host in the *sepulcrum* of the altar, either instead of or together with the relics. The oldest form, as we saw in the previous chapter, consisted of the placing of relics alone in the altar. From Carolingian times particles of the host were used, possibly—as stated—because of a lack of relics. In this way the altar was turned not only allegorically but also practically into a tomb, a tomb for the "relics" of Christ as well as for those of his saints.[64] However, wherever the sources mention the placing of the Eucharist in the altar, they usually state that this was done together with relics.

The Good Friday solemnities described in the life of St. Ulrich and in the *Regularis Concordia* represented an extension of the veneration of the Cross that had existed in the West since the seventh century. The *depositio* and *elevatio* were a dramatization of the burial and resurrection of Jesus. Host, cross, and the book of the Gospels represent Christ, who was also represented in the late Middle Ages by a life-size statue with a cavity in the chest designed to contain the Eucharist. As far as the faithful were concerned this holy sepulchre contained Christ himself in his "unique relic,"[65] just as since the tenth

---

sit, secum portato corpore Christi et evangelio et cereis et incenso, et cum congrua salutatione versuum, a pueris decantata, per atrium perrexit ad aecclesiam sancti Iohannis baptistae, ibique tertiam decantavit"; Young (1920) 17; Nussbaum (1979) 190.

[63] Hallinger VII-3, 118, c. VI, 74: "Depositaque cruce, ac si domini nostri Ihesu Christi corpore sepulto, dicant antiphonam"; *PL* 173, 493, c. 6; Gschwend (1965) esp. 59, 161 sqq.; Nussbaum (1979) 191–97.

[64] Young (1920); Brooks (1921); Browe (1931d) 100–7; Corbin (1960); Gschwend (1965).

[65] Brooks (1921) 38; Browe (1931d) 107; Beck (1978) 161–67, illustr. 17–27; Nussbaum (1979) 190, 99: "die kostbarste wirkmächtigste Reliquie des Herrn."

century the images and shrines had contained the relics of the saints behind little doors or windows.

The desire was to approach reality. In Ulrich's *vita* the solemnities of Palm Sunday are described: a wooden donkey with a statue of Christ[66] mounted upon it, arms held out in blessing, was led through the streets in procession, and in the *Roman-German Pontificale* dating from approximately 950 the processional cross was the focus of attention.[67] In the eleventh century the *decreta* of Lanfranc (+1098) reveals a transposition of this form of reverence: the new focus of the Palm Sunday procession is now a shrine containing the Eucharist, surrounded by candles and incenses and reverently greeted with genuflections.[68]

Lanfranc, who was later made archbishop of Canterbury thanks to William the Conqueror's influence, had entered into a controversy by correspondence with archdeacon Berengarius of Tours (+1088), whose theology was once more centered on the presence of Christ in the sacrament.

Berengarius was continuing the Augustinian line taken by Ratramnus. He characterized Radbertus and his followers as "carnal illiterates" and characterized some of the miracles quoted by Radbertus as

[66] *MGH SS* IV, 391, *Gerhardi Vita s. Oudalrici Ep.* c. 4: "evangelioque et crucibus et fanonibus, et cum effigie sedentis Domini super asinum, cum clericis et multitudine populi ramos palmarum in manibus portantis, et cum cantationibus ad honorem eiusdem diei compositis"; Nussbaum (1979) 199.

[67] Ed. Vogel (1963) II, 40–51, *Ordo de die palmarum,* 47: "Ut autem pervenerint cum palmis ubi statio est sanctae crucis, clerus populusque reverenter stant per turmas in ordine suo cum baiolis et reliquo ornatu."

[68] Hallinger, III/IV, 23: "Praecedant famuli cum vexilis sequatur conversus ferens situlam cum aqua benedicta; alii duo portantes duas cruces, item duo cum duobus candelabris, accensis desuper cereis, alii duo ferentes duo thuribula igne et thure referta"; 24: "Cantore autem incipiente antiphonam *Occurrunt turbae* exeant duo sacerdotes albis induti, qui portent feretrum, quod parum ante diem ab eisdem sacerdotibus illuc esse debet delatum, in quo et corpus Christ esse debet reconditum. Ad quod feretrum praecedant statim qui vexilla portant, et cruces, et caetera qui superius dicta sunt (. . .) Pueri vero accedentes stabunt versis vultibus ad ipsas reliquias (. . .) Finita antiphona *Occurrunt turbae,* incipient pueri (. . .) *Osanna filio David,* flectentes genua (. . .) Quibus transeuntibus flectant genua, non simul omnes sed cinguli hinc et inde, sicut feretrum transibit ante eos (. . .) Cum venerint ad portas civitatis stationem faciant separatis ad invicem prout locus patietur utriusque lateribus. Feretrum vero ante introitum portarum sic ponatur super mensam pallio coopertam"; see 260, n. 51; Stemmler (1970) 195; Mitchell (1982) 130–31, 137–50.

"fables" and "foolishness." In his opinion, bread remained bread after consecration and wine remained wine, precisely in order to be a sign of the holy one, of the mercy, a *sacramentum* of the body and blood of Christ, the risen one, the one who was present, the unassailable Lord. After consecration the eucharistic gifts were on a higher level of reality. They had become signs *(sacramenta)* of the invisible spiritual body of Christ. This *res sacramenti* had an enormous spiritual effect on the soul of the faithful receiving communion "as if it were the real body of Christ."[69]

The "Ambrosian," Lanfranc, differed by making a distinction between the form or appearance of bread and wine after consecration (the visible reality) and the essence that it concealed (the invisible reality), namely, the body and blood of the Lord.[70] He and his disciple Guitmund were the principal opponents of Berengarius, and the latter lost the argument. In 1059 the Synod of Rome obliged him to recognize that after consecration the body and blood of Christ were really, physically and not just sacramentally present on the altar and that this body of Christ was touched and bitten by the teeth of the believer.[71]

He recanted this declaration in his book *Regarding the sacred meal (De sacra coena)*,[72] but in 1079 he was again called to order. The future lay with realism and with a sensual interpretation of that realism. Long after his death Berengarius continued to make life difficult for his doctrinal opponents with the philosophical question as to whether, as seen from the realistic point of view of the Eucharist, the body and blood of Christ was subject to decay or burning and whether it could be consumed by animals. The question: "What does the mouse eat?" kept the theologians occupied for many subsequent centuries.[73]

---

[69] Browe (1938) 182; Beekenkamp (1940); Engels (1965) 375; Montclos (1971) 143; Devlin (1975) 42–43, 53.

[70] PL 150, 430, *Liber de corpore et sanguine Domini*.

[71] DS 690; Mitchell (1982) 137.

[72] Ed. Beekenkamp (1941).

[73] Guitmund: *PL* 149, 1418, *De corporis et sanguinis Domini veritate*, lib. II: "Mihi equidem sacramenta haec nequaquam a muribus vel aliquibus brutis animalibus videntur posse corrodi"; Peter Lombardus (+ 1160): ed. *Bibliotheca franciscana scholastica* (1951–57) IV, 204, *Sent.* IV, 8: "Quaestio est propter, quod si corpus Christi ibi est, non sumitur a brutis animalibus"; Inn. III (+1216): *PL* 217, 863, "De sacro altaris mysterio," IV, c. 11: "si vero quaeratur quid a mure comeditur, cumsacramentum corroditur, vel quid incineratur cum sacramentum crematur"; *TW* III, 4593–99, esp. n. 4.

The supporters of substantial change and the real presence had difficulty in providing further formulation and description of these concepts. The process of theological reflection resulted in the doctrine of change of essence or transubstantiation, a distinction being made between *accidentia* and *substantia,* for which Lanfranc had laid the foundations. The doctrine was formulated at the Fourth Lateran Council in 1215. By formulating this dogma the Church took a stand against the heresy of the Albigenses, who regarded the eucharistic bread as mere bread, indistinguishable from other types of bread.[74]

After the victory over Berengarius, transubstantiation was given due emphasis by miracles involving blood and hosts, all of which served as the confirming evidence at synods, in scholastic works, and in sermons. The miracle stories detailed by Radbertus and dating from the time of Gregory the Great—or even earlier—supported the doctrine, but even more so did the growing number of miracles of change reported after the end of the eleventh century. Almost all of them referred to the mystery of the consecration, convincing doubters or rewarding believers.

Not infrequently miraculous hosts were conserved as objects of reverence, a phenomenon unknown in ancient times and the early Middle Ages. Browe provides a list of eucharistic miracles which caused a place of pilgrimage to spring up: eight in the eleventh century, nineteen in the twelfth, fifty in the thirteenth, sixty-five in the fourteenth, forty in the fifteenth, five in the sixteenth, and one in the seventeenth. The end of the thirteenth century and the whole of the fourteenth century were the high points. Desecrations of the host, blamed on the Jews, were also reported in the same period. The desecrated hosts all began to bleed.[75]

St. Thomas Aquinas (+1274) says of all of this: "Whatever that blood may be, one thing is sure: it is not the blood of Christ." For he rejected vigorously the bilocation or multilocation of Christ in his own appearance. The risen Lord was present in his bodily form in one place only, and that was heaven. Moreover, Thomas regarded the preservation of his so-called "flesh and blood" behind glass objectionable and unbecoming. And not only that: one could no longer speak of his sacramental presence once the *accidentia* or appearances—the smell and taste of bread and wine—had disappeared. Nor

[74] *TRE* I, 92–93; Nussbaum (1979) 128.
[75] Browe (1927); (1929e); (1938) 2, 128–46, 182–83.

could he agree with the realistic view of things that made Christ a prisoner in his tabernacle where, he states, only consecrated hosts are to be found, or sacramental forms, which realize the bodily presence of Christ in a sacramental manner. Albertus Magnus (+1280) and Bonaventure (+1274) supported his critical views regarding the excessive formula of 1059 to which Berengarius had had to subscribe. This thirteenth-century university reaction to the sensualist opinion failed, however, to win general approval and passed over the heads of the faithful. The collective consciousness remained captive to the realistic notion of the Eucharist.[76]

Within the liturgy the host was accorded a dominant position and, in the mind of the people, even became a source of power with the same kinds of miraculous effect that the relics had been believed to produce. Parallel to this, there was a move towards using the host for private ends such as during sickness or when fire broke out, or when the host was carried about to afford protection against natural disasters or to ensure a good harvest. Sometimes such activities descended to the level of magic. It was not unknown for women to keep the host in their mouth until after the end of the service in order to win the love of a partner with a kiss, as recounted by Peter Damian (+1071) and Caesarius of Heisterbach (+ca. 1240). According to Herbert of Clairvaux (+ca. 1180) the host was scattered over the fields to increase fertility or sewn into garments to ensure the acquisition of money and goods.[77] This sort of behavior was one of the reasons why the Fourth Lateran Council required the host to be preserved behind locked doors. Safety precautions were taken with regard to relics at the same time.[78]

Within the context of the "process of independence of the Eucharist" there is another important decision taken by the same council.

---

[76] Browe (1929d) 312 sqq.; Schillebeeckx (1967) 8 n. 2; *Summa Theol.* III, q. 76, art 8, 2 and 2: "Sed caro aut sanguis miraculose apparens non sunt consecrata, nec conversa in verum corpus et sanguinem Christi. Non ergo sub his speciebus est corpus vel sanguis Christi"; ed. Blackfriars, vol. LVIII.

[77] *PL* 185, 1374, *De miraculis,* c. 3, 29: "Quidam rusticanus atque pauperculus homo, a nescio quo impostore maligno audierat quia si Dominicum Corpus secum assidue circumferret, in modico tempore divitiis abundaret. Accipiens itaque die Pascha sacrosanctum Domini Corpus, integrum ore retinuit. Quod protinus assuens in margine cappae, multo secum tempore tulit, nec ei tamen aliquando paupertas et miseris defuit"; *PL* 145, 173, *Opusc.* 34; ed. Strange (1851) II, 171, *Dial.* IX, c. 6; Browe (1930) 135, 138; Trexler (1980) 56.

[78] Nussbaum (1979) 106–7, 369–70.

The fathers felt constrained to fix the frequency of communion at a minimum of once per year, at Easter or thereabouts. The council thus took account of the actual situation: people received communion very infrequently. This is significant for the extent to which the eucharistic forms were perceived as separated from what they were intended for as bread and wine: to be eaten and drunk.[79]

This attitude had been gaining greater acceptance from as early as the fourth century, in marked contrast to early Christianity when the faithful were accustomed to bring bread and wine every week as a sacrificial meal and to consume them together with the priest. The synods of Elvira in 306 and Sardika in 343 felt obliged to prescribe punishment for those who failed to fulfill this duty for more than three weeks.[80] Ambrose (+397) in the West[81] and John Chrysostom (+407) in the East[82] voiced complaints about the lack of participation in the Lord's meal. A prescription formulated by the provincial synod of Agde in 506 was repeatedly quoted until the high point of the Middle Ages, so that it almost took on the force of a general law: it uncoupled the duty to attend Mass on Sunday from the duty to receive communion, which had to be received at least at Christmas, Easter, and Pentecost.[83]

The former monk of Lérins who presided over the synod, Bishop Caesarius of Arles, spoke with contempt of all the members of the congregation who left the church at the moment of communion.[84] In order to prevent this happening, in subsequent centuries measures were taken including, as already mentioned, having communion after Mass on busy feast days. And though it was not the

[79] Mansi XXIII, 197, c. 21: "Omnis utriusque sexus fidelis, postquam ad annos discretionis pervenerit, omnia sua solus peccata confiteatur fideliter, saltem semel in anno, proprio sacerdoti et iniunctam sibi poenitentiam studeat pro viribus adimplere, suscipiens reverenter ad minus in pascha eucharistiae sacramentum, nisi forte de consilio proprii sacerdotis ob aliquam rationabilem causam ad tempus ab eius perceptione duxerit abstinendum; alioquin et vivens ab ingressu ecclesiae arceatur et moriens christiana careat sepultura. Unde hoc salutare statutum frequenter in ecclesiis publicetur, ne quisquam ignorantiae caecitate velamen excusationis assumat"; Browe (1940) 43, 44, n. 101; Nussbaum (1979) 125.

[80] Browe (1938a) 1–10; (1940) 31.

[81] PL 16, 452; Browe (1938a) 9.

[82] PG 62, 29, Eph. hom. 3, 4.

[83] Mansi VIII, 327, can. 18: "Saeculares qui natale Domini, pascha et pentecostem non communicaverint, catholici non credantur, nec inter catholicos habeantur."

[84] CCSL 103, 307, sermo 73, 2.

intention,[85] a regulation of this sort had the effect of seeming to reduce the all-important communal component, the receiving of the eucharistic gifts by the faithful, to a kind of appendage of the Mass.

Despite the prescription issued by Agde and the renewed pressure in the Carolingian era for people to receive communion regularly, something strongly emphasized by Jonas of Orleans (+844) in his *Manual for the Laity,* the reductionist tendency could not be held back. People even took little notice of the new minimum, laid down in 1215. Almost everywhere complaints could be heard about the situation in the thirteenth and fourteenth centuries.[86]

There were many causes for what happened. It is not unjustified to assume that after its recognition in 313, the Christian faith drew more and more newcomers who became Christians in name but not in deed, and the influence of the Germanic peoples, who had not gone through a maturing process in their approach to Christianity, must have contributed to the growing number of fashion-followers and indifferent believers.[87] It is also remarkable that in the early Middle Ages the rot set in at its strongest in those regions where Arianism had to be combated: in the Grecian East and in the part of the West covered by the Gallic liturgy. In the struggle against these phenomena the deity of Christ was emphasized because it was precisely that which the Arians denied. In consequence the Eucharist was characterized as the "awesome mystery" which, in the Gallic liturgy, created a gulf between the laity and the divine eucharistic gifts, a gulf that could only be bridged by piety.[88]

The purification prescriptions involving both soul and body only served to increase this pious fear. Jerome (+420) required the faithful to abstain from sexual intercourse for several days before receiving communion.[89] Caesarius of Arles (+542)[90] and the Bavarian synod of Riesback-Friesingen in 799 were no less demanding.[91] The synod of Chalons-sur Saône in 813 required of the communicant extreme dis-

[85] Browe (1931b) 760; Nussbaum (1979) 46.

[86] *PL* 106, 202–204: *De institutione laicali;* Browe (1929) 18.

[87] Browe (1932a) 5; (1938a) 133.

[88] Jungmann (1962) II, 450; Nussbaum (1969) 29–31.

[89] CSEL 54, 377, ep. 49, 15.

[90] CCSL 103, 195–200, sermo 44.

[91] *MGH Conc.* II, 52, c. 6; Mansi XIII, 1027: "Ut sanctum sacrificium sumere non tardent, sed ante aliquantos se dies ad hoc praeparare conentur, abstinentes a fornicatione nec non et licentia coniugali, ut dignos se exhibeant"; Nickl (1930) 58; Browe (1932b) 376.

cretion, citing the biblical text: "For he that eateth and drinketh unworthily, eateth and drinketh damnation to himself" (1 Cor 11:29). Purity of body and soul was a sine qua non, just as the priest Achimelech refused to give the hallowed bread to David unless his servants had not had any contact with women (1 Sam 21:4-5). The synod of Ingelheim in 826 also required three days of abstinence from sexual intercourse before communion.[92]

The awareness of impurity and its incompatibility with liturgical activities can be found in all cultures and is of pre-Christian origin. It is not unimaginable that some remnants of this were still to be found in the "culture folklorique" when the Irish monks brought the Judaic way of thinking to continental Europe. Various prescriptions contained in the book of Leviticus, whether reinforced or watered down, had been implanted in Christianity and remained in force certainly until the thirteenth century.[93] Even involuntary ejaculation and menstruation were included under the same heading of bodily impurity.[94] The same applied particularly to masturbation, following which the offender was not even allowed to touch a reliquary. Alcuin (+804) puts the question in a *speculum,* a checklist of questions drawn up for clerics and monks in preparation for confession, as to whether the penitent may not have touched the sacred vessels, books, or relics after a defilement.[95]

It is understandable that the fear of receiving communion unworthily had a grip on many.[96] In this connection it should be noted that the requirement to receive communion in a state of sobriety was strictly applied throughout the Middle Ages, so that the taverns refused to serve food or drink until after high Mass.[97]

[92] *MGH Conc.* II, 283, 552; Browe (1938a) 19.

[93] Jungmann (1962) II, 451, n. 23; Vauchez (1975) 12; the rules laid down in the penitentials from the 6th to 11th century have been quantified by Flandrin (1983) 32; Guyon (1985) 75–77.

[94] Martène (1788) III, c. 19 n. 11: "Infantibus vero et his quibus tale quid in nocte contigerit, minime dantur"; Browe (1934) 95–96; (1940) 89.

[95] *PL* 101, 499; "reliquias et s. codices et s. vasa indignus et sordide atque negligenter contrectavi?"; this *speculum* was a checklist (used by the confessor), drawn up in question form of the sins committed most frequently and designed to help the penitent in his examination of conscience.

[96] Browe (1938a) 19; Leclerq (1962) 303.

[97] Browe (1931c) 281; Jungmann (1962) II, 454–55; Nussbaum (1979) 103: "wie bereits die Juden das Paschamahl als heilige Speise nicht vollem Magen geniessen durften."

Spiritual preparation before the eighth century consisted mainly of penance, alms, and prayer. Advent and Lent in some measure guaranteed that this would be so. Confession was neither obligatory nor customary. Later the Church began to insist on confession, especially by way of preparation for Easter communion, a requirement which—all unwittingly—threw up another barrier. Regino (+915), abbot of Prüm, and Burchard (+1025), bishop of Worms, insisted on confession during Lent.[98] In the Lateran prescription of 1215, previously alluded to, the Easter confession and communion were mentioned in one breath; failure to fulfill the prescription leaving the perpetrator liable to exclusion from church and church burial.[99] In the day-to-day practice of the faith, communion and confession rather than consecration and communion came to form a unity. Both sacraments had to be received in the parish church, a monopoly that the mendical orders were, as a general rule, unable to break. The penitent was given a little instruction in the faith, accompanied by warnings, during the confession.[100]

Parishes were, however, too large and understaffed, which led to superficiality in the care of souls. This problem was made worse in the late Middle Ages by the "altarists,"[101] who were mentally insufficiently equipped, and because of their poverty, socially inadequate for the care of souls. A further material circumstance working against frequent communion was that of the offerings brought to church. When unleavened bread replaced leavened, the offerings served only to maintain the poor and the priests. To the extent that they were obligatory, they constituted an obstacle to no few of the faithful. The reverence for Christ's sufferings, the flood of relics from the East following the Crusades, the cult surrounding them and the innumerable sacramentals also took on the character or replacements for the Eucharist and clouded men's view of communion. From the eleventh–twelfth century the new forms of eucharistic devotion—to be discussed later—were just as harmful to the practice of communion since they tended rather to replace it. Moreover, individual devotion to the person of Christ required a personal encounter with the Savior, whose

[98] Browe (1932b) 375–97; (1940) 9; Devlin (1975) 144–46.

[99] See above, n. 79.

[100] Browe (1929b) 484 sqq., 503 sqq., (1932b) 394; Meyer (1965) 349; Michaud-Quantin (1971) 168–170: at the beginning of the confession the *proprius sacerdos* made sure that the penitent knew the Our Father, the Hail Mary, and the Creed.

[101] This is the name given to priests, operating mainly in the towns, whose task was to celebrate the Mass and recite the Office daily (*LW* I, 125–26).

coming demanded an ascetic preparation. Excessive communion could only be harmful.[102] In the later Middle Ages, Gerard Zerbolt of Zutphen (+1398), member of the movement of reform *Devotio Moderna*, reckoned that thousands of years of preparation and all the aid of the saints would still not be sufficient for a worthy preparation.[103]

The clericalisation of the celebration of the Eucharist constituted an obstacle to participation on the part of the people. The priest functioned in the name of the people and also received communion in the name of the people.[104] The celebration of the Mass had become a *mysterium depopulatum* and the Eucharist itself a *mysterium tremendum*.[105] The people were outwardly forced into the role of passive spectators of the awesome happening and found an answer to this new situation in the adoration of the host, really transformed into the body of Christ during the consecration of the offerings.

In the explanation of the Mass of Isidore of Seville (+636) the consecration was taken to include the whole of the Canon,[106] but from the ninth to the eleventh century it gradually came to be limited to one moment, the uttering of the words of consecration.[107] This change occurred under the influence of the theological dispute regarding Christ's presence and its resolution by the adoption of a mainly realistic approach.

The emphasis laid on Christ's actual presence caused a new "elevatio" to come into being in the twelfth century in addition to the existing

[102] Browe (1938a) 134–38, 141–44, 148, 154, 157.

[103] Ed. Woude v. d. (1951) *Over de hervorming van de krachten der ziel*, 67: "Bedenk, indien gij u gedurende duizenden jaren tot dit sacrament hadt voorbereid door reine gebeden en allerheiligste meditaties, dit nog niets zou betekenen voor een waardig ontvangen. Ook als gij alle verdiensten van de heiligen zoudt bezitten" (Reflect on this: that had you prepared yourself for thousands of years with pure prayers and the holiest of meditations for the reception of this sacrament, all of that would mean nothing for a worthy reception. Even if you had performed all the services of the saints).

[104] Brandt (1924) 233; Jungmann (1962) II, 452–53; Kidd (1958) 40; Meyer (1965) 304.

[105] Mayer (1926) 93; Nussbaum (1979) 120. This transformation, based only on observable facts, seems too absolute and too negative. See: Lukken (1990) 30: "Maintenant il est possible de discuter cette transformation non seulement d'une façon négative, à savoir que le peuple n'est plus sujet de faire, mais aussi d'une façon positive: le peuple devient destinataire ou destinateur/destinataire ou actant observateur, selon le point de vue que l'on adopte. Bien qu'il n'y ait pas d'unanimité dans ce domaine d'études, il faut dire que la sémiotique peut nuancer le parler quelque peu simpliste dans la littérature liturgique courante."

[106] PL 83, 752, *De eccles. offic.* 1, 15.

[107] Geiselmann (1933) 87–118 and passim; Jungmann (1941) 120 sqq.; (1962) II, 127 sqq.

raising up of the bread and chalice at the doxology that closes the canon. This "elevatio"—raising the host and, later, the chalice—with both hands during the consecration went back to the Jewish table ritual, where the bread and wine are taken up in a solemn gesture. In the liturgy the gesture took on a new significance, the underlining of Christ's words, "Who, the day before he suffered, took bread into his sacred hands."[108] In the East the gesture is reported as having this significance from the fourth century and in the West intermittently from the ninth century. In the twelfth century the host was raised increasingly higher and for an ever-longer period as a symbol of Christ raised on the cross.[109] Moreover, the generally increasing desire on the part of the people to see the sacred species was a further cause. The awareness of Christ's presence was intensified by the solemn upward gaze directed at the host, a precursor of the end of a Christian life: to see God himself.[110] It was also a form of protest against the doctrines of Berengarius and the Albigensian heresy. Some reports, including that of Hildebert, archbishop of Tours (+1134), show that the words that wrought the change[111] were sometimes pronounced during the "elevatio."[112]

The synodal statutes of Paris (1205–1208), drawn up by Bishop Eudes of Sully (+1208), set the time of the "elevatio" precisely in order to ensure that those present did not adore an unconsecrated host. The "elevatio" was not permitted until the words of consecration had been pronounced over the bread. In laying down this prescription the synod implicitly took sides in a new debate that had broken out after the second eucharistic dispute: was Christ only present after consecration of both bread and wine or immediately after the words "This is my body"?[113] The synod opted for the latter opinion: the "elevatio" of the host was the explicit sign that the consecration had taken place and the adoration was indeed directed towards the body of Christ. The synod further instructed the priest to raise the host sufficiently high that the faithful—to whom the priest's back was turned—could see the host clearly.[114]

[108] Browe (1933) 46–48; Jungmann (1943).
[109] Meyer (1963) 162–63; Nussbaum (1979) 127.
[110] Dumoutet (1924); Macquarrie (1972) 97.
[111] *hoc est enim corpus meum, hic est enim calix sanguinis mei.*
[112] *PL* 171, 1186, *Carmen de officio missae:* "Panis in hoc verbo, sed adhuc communis ab ara sumitur et sumptum tollit utraque manu. Nec prius in mensam demittit quam tua, Christe, verba repraesentans explicet ista super"; Browe (1933) 30, n. 22.
[113] Kennedy (1944); Quirin (1952); Nussbaum (1979) 131; Mitchell (1982) 151–63.
[114] Ed. Pontal (1971) 82: "Precipitur presbyteris ut, cum in canone misse inciperint *Qui pridie,* tenentes hostiam, ne elevent eam statim nimis alte, ita quod

The instruction fulfilled a need. Fifteen years later the "elevatio" had become the indispensable high point of the Mass, characteristic of the desire to practice eucharistic devotion, which had come to occupy a special place in the spirituality of the Cistercians and Franciscans.[115] The speed at which the devotion spread is comparable to the rate at which altars were turned around in Catholic churches following the Second Vatican Council.[116] The many forms of devotion centered on the host and which came into being around 1200 remain typical of the reverence accorded to the Eucharist until *the end of conventional Christianity* [Christendom — ed.].[117]

Whereas up to the twelfth century the obeisances made by the priest had been mainly directed towards the altar and its relics, from the turn of the thirteenth century he bowed before the consecrated bread before raising it for all to see. In the fourteenth century genuflection was added before and after the "elevatio." The faithful in the body of the church had long before been instructed to show this sign of reverence. They sank to their knees at the ringing of the bell, which was usually attached to the wall of the sanctuary.[118] When the host was only raised chest high the bell served to focus the attention of those present on the happening which, for them, was invisible.[119] From the thirteenth century it was a signal calling the people to adoration, including those in the surrounding neighborhood. In the second half of the thirteenth century the bell in the church tower was sounded for their benefit. They could then bow their heads or genuflect during their work and share in thought the sacred moment or even make their way to the church. This was the reason for the ringing of the bell at the Sanctus. In mid-fifteenth century Koblenz the sexton announced the approaching consecration at an even earlier moment—at the gospel.[120]

The Sanctus candle had the same warning effect as the bell, even though it was originally a practical measure. In the early morning

possit videri a populo, sed quasi ante pectus detineant donec dixerint *Hoc est corpus meum,* et tunc elevent eam ita quod possit ab omnibus videri"; Mansi XXII, 682; Rubin (1991) 55 n. 251; Caspers (1992) 22.

[115] Browe (1933) 28, 37; Nussbaum (1979) 122.

[116] Smits (1965) 86, n. 18.

[117] Pol v. d. (1967) *Het einde van het conventionele Christendom,* 332.

[118] Browe (1929c) 43–50; Meyer (1963) 167, 169; Jungmann (1962) II, 262, n. 51; the altar bell dates from the 15th/16th century; Nussbaum (1979) 132.

[119] Quirin (1952) 15, 22.

[120] Browe (1929c) 39; Meyer (1963) 167, 175, 264.

darkness the altar server provided light for the celebrant so that the host could at least be seen.[121]

Both the number and the duration grew: the single candle became a whole "row of wax," burning around the altar from Sanctus to Communion. In the later Middle Ages the polyphonic singing of the *Sanctus* prepared the consecration and the "elevatio," while the Benedictus closed the canon, its words thereby taking on the power of reality: "Blessed is he that cometh in the name of the Lord."[122]

The efforts made to ensure that the host was as visible as possible led to excesses. The priest was tempted to hold the host on high for a time and turn to right and to left. When genuflecting after the "elevatio," a gesture that began to become fashionable here and there at the end of the fourteenth century, he deliberately gave those present the opportunity of seeing the host three times. The "small elevatio" during the doxology of the canon sometimes literally got on top of the celebrant[123] and the Dominicans held on high the two halves of the broken host above the chalice for the faithful to adore from the Agnus Dei to the communion, an example copied by the secular clergy of the Rhineland at the end of the fourteenth century.[124]

Attempts to put a stop to such practices met with varied success. They were symptomatic of the eucharistic desire and "revival."[125] Indeed, from the thirteenth century in various dioceses "elevatio" indulgences were granted. In a fourteenth-century letter of indulgence for an unnamed Dutch convent of nuns, the ejaculation "Jesus, Son of the living God, protect me" was granted forty days indulgence.[126]

At the end of the thirteenth century, in order not to obstruct the congregation's view of the host, a start was made on pulling back the side curtains of the altar, which had been intended to ensure that the

[121] *DACL* III, 1057; Jungmann (1962) II, 261, n. 45, 176, n. 14; Meyer (1963) 167–68.

[122] Browe (1929c) 40–43; Meyer (1963) 171, 185, n. 64; Jungmann (1962) II, 164, 172, 269; Nussbaum (1979) 133.

[123] Franz (1902) 104, 176; Browe (1929c) 49; (1933) 63–64; Meyer (1963) 170, 190; Nussbaum (1979) 133.

[124] Martène (1788) I, c. 4. a. 9 n. 4: "Datum est ordini nostro, ut in missa post *Agnus Dei* ante communionem tenerent fratres hostiam elevatam super calicem, ut sic adoretur ab universo populo (. . .) et ne deponeretur usque ad communionem"; Quirin (1952) 124.

[125] Mens (1946) 157.

[126] I.e., as much from punishment for sin as if 40 days of penance had been performed; Verdam (1902) 120; Browe (1933) 170; Quirin (1952) 73–75; Nussbaum (1979) 134.

canon should proceed without being disturbed by extraneous noise. The Carthusians and the Celestines even opened the choir screens. In 1312 the Carmelites instructed the incense-bearers to ensure that the host did not disappear behind the sweet-scented clouds of smoke. At the beginning of the sixteenth century in Spain, England, and France, it became the custom to hang a black or purple curtain behind the altar so that the white host would stand out more sharply.[127]

All these provisions were inspired by the desire to see the host, to which end every opportunity was seized. During her illness Oringa of Tuscany (+1310) had herself carried to the chapel for that very purpose. After the "elevatio" the Viennese beguine Agnes Blambeckin (+1315) sought a place in the church from where she could still see the host. Geert Grote (+1384) prayed at the Friars Minor Church in Deventer before a small window through which he could see the "elevatio" in the adjacent church without being disturbed, and Dorothy of Montau (+1394) could not have satisfied her desire to see the host if she had managed to do so a hundred times a day.[128]

In the personal eye contact with the host and through the inner ejaculatory prayers, the people were expressing their deepest faith in Christ as Majesty, but also as Christ made flesh, the crucified God. Such prayers as the *Ave verum corpus Christi*, the *Ave salve caro Dei*, and *Ave sacer Christi sanguis* were very popular in the church books and missals of the later Middle Ages. Believers who did not know these prayers were recommended to say the Lord's Prayer and the Hail Mary five times each, in commemoration of the five wounds of Christ. The faithful also joined in with singing: the *Ave verum*, the *Adoro te*, or the *O salutaris Hostia* were among the hymns sung between Sanctus and Benedictus.[129] "Many prayers were heard at the sight of the body of the Lord and rich treasures of mercy were granted," wrote William of Auxerre (+1231) around 1200.

Alexander of Hales (+1245) thought along the same lines.[130] The adoration of the host was thus a personal encounter with Jesus in his sacrament and over the years ended up by almost completely replacing sacramental communion. The theological tracts, other writings,

[127] Browe (1933) 56; Quirin (1952) 87–88; Jungmann (1962) II, 260, n. 44; Meyer (1963) 176–77; Nussbaum (1979) 133–35.

[128] Meyer (1963) 190 sqq.

[129] Browe (1929c) 55; Meyer (1963) 178–87; (1965) 272.

[130] Ed. Pigouchet (1964) 261: "Multorum petitiones exaudiuntur in ipsa visione Corporis Christi: unde multis infunditur gratia"; Nussbaum (1979) 130.

and sermons emphatically encouraged the faithful of the late medieval period to practice the *manducatio spiritualis* or spiritual communion. The awe of the "Holy of Holies" already referred to, as well as the many limiting prescriptions regarding sobriety and abstention, combined with the preaching, must have created the situation in which this *manducatio* gained, in eucharistic piety, the "status" of a form of communion "equal in value." The dying no longer able to receive communion sacramentally were shown the host as a final consolation so that they could now unite themselves with Christ.[131]

Hosts, it was said, gave out light or changed into the child Jesus. These miracles were a response [of] the divine gift of the Eucharist, particularly in the circles of Cistercians and Beguines, where such visions were repeatedly witnessed in the thirteenth and fourteenth centuries.[132]

Sometimes the elevated host was seen as a real *ex opere operato* event[133] as described in the *Instruction for parish priests* written by John Mirk towards the end of the fourteenth century. The sight of the host was not only credited with spiritual benefits but also with physical good. Someone who had been present at the "elevatio" could be sure that they were guarded for the rest of the day against fire, blindness, infectious disease, or sudden death,[134] which parallels the insurance said to be offered by such objects as relics or an image of St. Christopher.[135]

In the late medieval period the tendency arose to regard the "elevatio" as a substitute for the whole of the Mass. People would slip into church when they heard the bell ringing, only to walk out again immediately after the "elevatio." It is not without reason that there were complaints about townsfolk going from church to church in order to see the "elevatio" again and again.[136] People under interdict were not above drilling a hole in the church door in order to be able to witness the "elevatio." Even the animals were not allowed to miss the event: in Gaishofen on the Danube and in the surrounding district the horses were allowed to participate in the feast of the popular St. Leonard by sticking their heads through a round hole in the outer

---

[131] Browe (1933) 58; Caspers (1992) esp. 213–30, 267.
[132] Browe (1938) 104–11; Rode (1957).
[133] Browe (1929c) 59.
[134] Ed. Kristenson (1974) 85; Nussbaum (1979) 137.
[135] Oakley (1979) 119.
[136] Browe (1929c) 65; Meyer (1963) 192; Nussbaum (1979) 137.

wall, or else the horses were ridden into the church through doors specially designed to accommodate them.[137]

The "process of independence" of the elevated host within the context of the Mass was given shape around 1300 in various new and long-lasting forms of reverence outside the Mass, forms which lasted until the 1960s: visits to the Blessed Sacrament, procession of the Blessed Sacrament, exposition of and blessing with the "Holy of Holies."

Visits to the Blessed Sacrament, kept on or close to the altar, were adopted on a wide scale from the fourteenth century by the secular clergy and the religious orders. To the extent that locked church doors made this sort of devotion impossible for the laity, they indulged in the practice only sporadically from the fifteenth century onwards until it became generalized towards the end of the Middle Ages.[138] The lamps which used to burn at the martyr's graveside and which were lit in honor of the saints and the deceased were now transformed into the sanctuary lamp, burning in a sacred silence. Its use was sparse in the eleventh century, more frequent after that, and practically general in the monastery and collegiate churches after the fourteenth century. The reverence paid to the altar, directed towards the saints and their relics, now turned into reverence paid to the tabernacle, concentrating on the sacred host, which had pushed the relics into the background.[139]

The main driving force behind this new piety originated in the desire to show reverence at the "elevatio" and to give due credence to the miracles. But a further factor which cannot be ignored is the introduction, in 1246 by Robert of Turotte, bishop of Liège, of the feast of Corpus Christi. It was brought in at the instigation of Juliana van Cornillon (+1258), representative of a group of pious women, who did not keep her reverence "under a bushel."[140] The feast was intended as a special mark of reverence towards the institution of the Eucharist, which received too little attention on Maundy Thursday. In 1264 the former cardinal-legate of Liège, Pope Urban IV, placed the feast officially in the Church's calendar.[141] It was slow in gaining popularity because of the tensions between supporters and opponents, or

---

[137] Nussbaum (1979) l.c; Rothkrug (1977) 30; (1980) 65–66.
[138] Browe (1933) 23; Delaruelle (1975) 405.
[139] Mitchell (1982) 170; Geary (1978) 29.
[140] Wegman (1986) 45.
[141] Browe (1933) 70; Stemmler (1970) 174–75; LW II, 2494.

"between the more common-sense and the more emotional approach to faith." Moreover the mainly secular opponents were perhaps suspicious of the major influence of the laity, and certainly of that of women, whose mystical tendencies were regarded as too "fanatical and too populist."[142] The feast was first introduced in the former German Empire and it was not until the second decade of the fourteenth century that it began to gain ground rapidly in England, Scandinavia, and the Romance countries.[143]

At the same time the procession of the Blessed Sacrament, originally not part of the feast day itself, began to achieve greater popularity. The lengthy hesitation in adopting the practice would seem to be related to the shockingly high costs involved. So it was that the procession did not reach full glory until some time around the sixteenth century, not only on the feast day of Corpus Christi but also on its octave and on other days of prayer, penance, and thanksgiving. In addition to the problem of money, the resistance encountered by the introduction of the feast also played a role—as did the objection to carrying the exposed host around for so long. Besides, one was afraid of blunting of veneration by the people seeing the host too frequently.[144] On the other hand, people were used to major feasts and saints' days thanks to the centuries-old practice of carrying the reliquaries in procession, housed since the thirteenth century in *ostensoria*. In line with this tradition the procession of the Blessed Sacrament was introduced on the feast day—and in addition there were several longstanding precedents: the solemn procession of the sacrament to the sick or dying, the Palm Sunday procession and its transfer to the holy sepulchre in Holy Week.

The introduction of the procession on the feast of Corpus Christi led to "exposition," a kind of static "elevatio," consisting of placing the eucharistic bread on or above the altar, either invisible in a *ciborium* covered with a *velum*, or visible in a rebuilt reliquary-ostensory (the forerunner of the monstrance), for the purposes of adoration and meditation. After the procession a Mass was celebrated during which

[142] Wegman (1986) 46.

[143] Browe (1928a) 130, 137, 143; Stemmler (1970) 172–73; Caspers (1992) 42–44, 62–66.

[144] Schannat Hartzheim, V, 408 (Council of Mainz in 1451): "Propter reverentiam Divinissimo Eucharistie exhibendam et ne populi fidelis devotio ex frequenti eius visione tepescat"; Nussbaum (1979) 158–59; Browe (1933) 91 sqq.; Martimort (1984) 267–68.

the *ciborium* or *ostensorium* was left standing on the altar. The practice was later recalled in the "Mass with exposition," celebrated on major feast days at the high altar and usually on Thursdays at a side altar with the celebration of a votive Mass.[145] Such Masses, with the exposed sacrament torn free from its liturgical context, were introduced in the north of Germany and in Hungary from the fourteenth century and in other places from the fifteenth century.[146]

Exposition of this kind could also take place completely separate from the Mass, a form which developed from the feast of Corpus Christi. In churches where the Divine Office was sung, the "bread of angels" was placed on the high altar at the beginning of the morning Office in honor of this feast and it was left there the whole day during the singing of the Office. In order to meet the demands of the people with regard to the reverencing of the host, the separate hours of the Office were extended to honorific sacramental feasts. The faithful sang hymns to the Blessed Sacrament—such as *Ecce panis angelorum*—antiphons[147] and responsories[148] that they were accustomed to sing before and after the Mass with exposition celebrated on Thursdays. It was not long before the practice was extended to cover the entire octave, a development which started in Germany in the fourteenth century and became general from the fifteenth.

Subsequently such services in honor of the Blessed Sacrament were introduced outside the octave of the feast. This happened in the fourteenth century, again at first in the Germanic lands. A century later the evening services in honor of the Blessed Sacrament were a familiar phenomenon. In other countries development was slower and did not come to full flower until during the Counter-Reformation.[149]

In 1435 the Premonstratensians demonstrated the enormous value attached to exposition of the Eucharist. From the archbishop of Trier they obtained the privilege of introducing the practice on days when the Mass was not celebrated. The "perpetual adoration" or year-long exposition was the crown on the increased "process of independence

[145] I.e., a Mass celebrated outside the context of the ecclesiastical calendar for the intentions of the donor of the *stipendium* (*LW* II, 2878).

[146] Browe (1933) 141–47; Nussbaum (1979) 162.

[147] I.e., a versicle with its own melody following a psalm; it expresses an essential idea (*LW* I, 169).

[148] I.e., part of the Divine Office that matches up with the readings and the capitula (*LW* II, 2398).

[149] Nussbaum (1979) 162–63.

of the Eucharist." And of course this gave further impetus to the practice of visits to the Blessed Sacrament.[150]

The custom known as Quarant'Ore—forty continuous hours of exposition of the Blessed Sacrament for reverence and prayer—came into being not in the Middle Ages but in the sixteenth century. It fitted well with the medieval tradition of forty hours of wake at the holy sepulchre, which had been on the increase since the tenth century as a dramatization of the events of Holy Week. In a sermon preached in the Church of the Holy Sepulchre in Milan in 1527, Gian Antonio Belotti encouraged his listeners to spend forty hours in prayer before the Blessed Sacrament at the end of Lent. He established a fraternity in order to repeat this four times annually. In 1529 the cathedral of Milan adopted the practice and in 1537 it became the custom for all the city's churches to take turns so that the adoration would be perpetual. Subsequently the "Forty Hours" devotion was spread throughout Italy by the Capuchins and throughout Germany by the Jesuits, following which it became general practice throughout Europe around 1600.[151]

A fourth type of the "process of independence of the Eucharist" outside the Mass has been mentioned: blessing with the Holy of Holies. This too grew out of the procession of the Blessed Sacrament and was first reported in the fourteenth century during a procession in Hildesheim, after which it appears more frequently in fifteenth-century sources. In all likelihood the practice was already being followed occasionally in the course of the fifteenth century during the evening services dedicated to the Virgin Mary. This latter type of service had come into being in Italy in the thirteenth century and under the name of *Hail* or *Salve*—the first word of the hymn to Mary entitled *Salve Regina*—spread throughout Europe.[152] At the beginning of the fifteenth century, in the presence of the Corpus Christi fraternity,[153] the Dominicans of Hamburg gave an undertaking that they would not practice the blessing with the Holy of Holies during the *Salve*. They agreed that every Sunday evening during the procession after Compline[154] they would place the statue of Mary, donated by

---

[150] *Ibid.*, 163.

[151] Jungmann (1952); Nussbaum (1979) 164–66; Mitchell (1982) 311–18.

[152] Mitchell (1982) 182.

[153] Dossat (1976).

[154] I.e., the Church's evening prayer (*TW* I, 443).

the fraternity, on the altar and, after singing the *Salve Regina*, would bless the faithful while the bell rang three times.[155]

However, nothing is mentioned about blessing with the Blessed Sacrament during this service dedicated to Mary, although exposition had been practiced during the *Salve* since the fourteenth century. Once the blessing had become a fixed component of the procession of the Blessed Sacrament, it eventually became an integral part of the *Salve,* later to be known as "Benediction" or blessing.

[155] Browe (1933) 158.

BIBLIOGRAPHY

Sources quoted

d'Archery, L. *Spicilegium sive collectio veterum aliquot scriptorum,* 3 vol., Paris, 1723 (repr. Farnborough, 1967–1968).

Andrieu (1931–1961), M. Andrieu, *Les Ordines Romani du Haut Moyen Age,* 5 vol., Louvain, 1931–1961.

Assemanus (1749–1766), Joseph Aloysius Assemanus, *Codex Liturgicus ecclesiae universae in quo continentur libri rituales, missales, pontificales, officia, dypticha (. . .) ecclesiarum occidentis et orientis,* ed. iterata, ad editionis principis exemplum, Ab Huberto Welter, 13 vol., Parisiis et Lipsiae, 1749–1766 (repr. 1902; 1968–1969).

Ed. Bakhuizen van den Brink (1954), J. N. Bakhuizen van den Brink, *Ratramnus, De corpore et sanguine Domini,* text établi d'après les manuscrits et notice bibliographique, Verhandelingen der Kon. Ak. v. Wetenschappen, afd. Letterkunde, Nieuwe Reeks, d. LXI, no. 1, Amsterdam, 1954.

Ed. Bartelink (1986) G.J.M. Bartelink, *Na de schriften. Twee apologeten uit het vroege Christendom, Justines en Athenagoras,* Kampen, 1986.

Ed. Beekenkamp (1941), W. H. Beekenkamp, *Berengarius Turonensis, De Sacra Coena adversus Lanfrancum,* Den Haag, 1941.

Hallinger, K. Hallinger, *Corpus Consuetudinum Monasticorum,* I–XII, Siegburg, 1964–1987.

Ed. Hanssens (1948–1950) J. M. Hanssens, *Amalarii episcopi opera liturgica omnia (Studi e Testi, 138–140),* 3 vol., Città del Vaticano, 1948–1950.

Hardouin, J. Hardouin, *Acta Conciliorum et epistolae decretales ac Constitutiones Summorum Pontificum,* 12 vol., Parisis, 1714–1715.

Ed. Kristenson (1974), G. Kristenson, *John Mirk, Instructions for parish priests,* London, 1974.

Leroquais (1927), V. Leroquais, "L'Ordo Missae du sacramentaire d'Amiens," in: *Ephemerides Liturgicae* 41 (1927) 435–55.

71

Mansi, J. D. Mansi, *Sacrorum conciliorum nova et amplissima collectio*, 31 vol., Florence-Venetië; 59 vol. Paris 1901–1923 (t. 1–48), Arnheim, 1923–1927 (t. 49–50); repr. Graz, 1960–1961.

Martène (1788), E. Martène, *De antiquis ecclesiae ritibus*, 4 vol., Venetiis, 1788.

Ed. Mingana (1927–1934), A. Mingana, *Woodbrooke Studies, Christian documents edited and translated with a critical apparatus*, 7 vol., 1927–1934.

Ed. Mohlberg (1957), L. C. Mohlberg, *Missale Francorum*, Rome, 1957.

Ed Pigouchet (1964), Ph. Pigouchet et Fr. Regnault, *Magistri Gillelmi Altissiodorentis Summa Aurea*, Paris, 1500 (repr. Minerva, G.m.b.H., Frankfurt a. Main, 1964).

Ed. Pontal (1971), O. Pontal, *Les statuts synodaux français du XIIIe siècle, précédés de l'historique de synode diocésain depuis ses origines. I. Les statuts de Paris et le synodal de l'Ouest* (XIIIe siècle), Paris, 1971.

Ed. Quasten (1936), J. Quasten, *Monumenta eucharistica et liturgica vetustissima*, Coloniae, 1936.

Schannat-Hartzheim, J. Hartzheim, *Concilia Germanie*, 8 vol., Aalen, 1970–1982 (Nachdruck der Ausgabe Köln, 1759–1790).

Ed. Strange (1851), J. Strange, Caesarius von Heisterbach, *Dialogus miraculorum*, 2 vol., Coloniae, 1851 (repr. New Jersey, 1966).

Ed. Tonneau (1966), R. Tonneau et R. Devresse, *Les homélies catéchétiques de Théodore de Mopsuesta*, Roma, 1966.

Ed. Vogel (1963), Cyrille Vogel, *Le Pontificale romano-germanique du dixième siècle*, Città del Vaticano, 1963.

Ed. Wartelle (1987), A. Wartelle, *Saint Justin Apologies,* introduction, texte critique, traduction, commentaire et index, Paris, 1987.

Ed. Woude v. d. (1951), Gerard Zerbolt van Zutphen, *Over de hervorming van de krachten der ziel*, introduced and translated by S. van der Woude, Amsterdam, 1951 (Klassieken der Kerk. tweede reeks: De Kerk in de middeleeuwen, dl. 3; original title: *De reformatione virium animae*).

Literature consulted

Andrieu (1950), M. Andrieu, "Aux origines du culte du Saint Sacrament. Reliquaires et Monstrances Eucharistiques," in : *An. Boll.* (1950) 397–418.

Angenendt (1982), A. Angenendt, "Die Liturgie und die Organisation des Kirchlichen Lebens auf dem Lande," in: *Christianizzazione ed organizazzione ecclesiastica delle campagna nell' alto medioevo: expansone e resistence* (Settimane di studio 28), Spoleto, 1982, 169–275.

Angenendt (1983), A. Angenendt, "Missa specialis," in: *Frühmittelalterlichen Studien* 17 (Berlin, 1983) 153–221.

Beekenkamp (1940), W. H. Beekenkamp, *De avondmaalsleer van Berengarius van Tours*, 's-Gravenhage, 1940.

Beck (1978), P. Beck, *Le coeur du Christ dans la mystique Rhénane*, Imprimerie Alsatia Sélestat, 1978.

Betz (1955), J. Betz, *Die Eucharistie in der Zeit der Griechischen Väter* Band I, 1: Die Aktualpräsenz der Person und des Heilwerkes Jesu im Abendmahl nach der vorephesinischen griechischen Patristik, Freiburg, 1955.

Brandt (1924), O. v. Brandt, *Bertholds von Regensburg deutsche Predigten,* Jena, 1924.

Brooks (1921), N. C. Brooks, *The Sepulchre of Christ in Art and Liturgy,* Illinois, 1921.

Browe (1927), P. Browe, "Die Hostienschändungen der Juden im Mittelalter," in: *RQS* 34 (1927) 167–98.

Browe (1928a), P. Browe,"Die Ausbreitung des Fronleichnamsfestes," in *JLW* 8 (1928) 107–43.

Browe (1929), P. Browe, "Die öftere Kommunion der Laien im Mittelalter," in: *Bonner Zeitschrift für Theologie und Seelsorge* 6 (1928) 1–28.

Browe (1929b), P. Browe, "Die Kommunion in der Pfarrkirche," in: *ZKT* 53 (1929) 477–516.

Browe (1929c), P. Browe, "Die Elevation in der Messe," in *JLW* 9 (1929) 20–66.

Browe (1929d), P. Browe, "Die scholastische Theorie der eucharistischen Verwandlungswunder," in: *TQ* 110 (1929) 305–32.

Browe (1929e), P. Browe, "Die eucharistischen Verwandlungswunder des Mittelalters," in: *RQS* 37 (1929) 137–69.

Browe (1930), P. Browe, "Die Eucharistie als Zaubermittel im Mittelalter," in: *Archiv für Kulturgeschichte* 20 (1930) 134–54.

Browe (1931b), P. Browe, "Wann fing man an die Kommunion ausserhalb der Messe auszuteilen," in: *Theologie und Glaube* 23 (Paderborn, 1931) 755–62.

Browe (1931c), P. Browe, "Die Nüchternheit vor der Messe und Kommunion im Mittelalter," in: *Ephemerides liturgicae* 45 (1931) 383–91.

Browe (1931d), P. Browe, "Die Entstehung der Sakramentsprozessionen," in *Bonner Zeitschrift für Theologie und Seelsorge* 8 (1931) 97–117.

Browe (1932a), P. Browe, "Kommunionriten früher Zeiten," in: *Theologie und Glaube* 24 (Paderborn, 1932) 592–607.

Browe (1932b), P. Browe, "Kommunionvorbereitung im Mittelalter," in: *ZKT* 56 (1932) 375–415.

Browe (1933), P. Browe, *Die Verehrung der Eucharistie im Mittelalter,* München, 1933 (Nachdr. 1967).

Browe (1934), P. Browe, *Beiträge zur Sexualethik des Mittelalters,* Breslauer Studien zur historischen Theologie (23) 1934.

Browe (1935), P. Browe, "Die Kommunionandacht im Altertum und Mittelalter," in: *JLW* 13 (1935) 45–64.

Browe (1938), P. Browe, *Die eucharistischen Wunder des Mittelalters,* Breslau, 1938.

Browe (1938a), P. Browe, *Die häufige Kommunion im Mittelalter,* Münster i. W., 1938.

Browe (1940), P. Browe, *Die Pflichtkommunion in Mittelalter,* Münster i. W., 1940.

Caspers (1992), Carles M. A., *De eucharistische vroomheid en het feest van Sacramentsdag in de Nederlanden tijdens de late middeleeuwen,* Leuven, 1992.

Corbin (1960), S. Corbin, *La déposition liturgique du Christ au Vendredi-Saint,* Paris-Lisbonne, 1960.

Delaruelle (1975), E. Delaruelle, *La piéteé populaire au moyen âge*, Turin, 1975.

Devlin (1975), D. S. Devlin, *Corpus Christi: a study in medieval eucharistic theory, devotion and practice*, University of Chicago, 1975.

Dijk, v. (1957), S. J. P. van Dijk and J. Hazelden Walker, *The Myth of the Aumbry*, London, 1957.

Dijk v. (1960), S. J. P. van Dijk and J. Hazelden Walker, *The Origins of the Modern Roman Liturgy*, Westminster, Md., 1960.

Dossat (1976), Y. Dossat, "Les confréries du Corpus Christi dans le monde rural pendant la première moitié du XIVe siècle," in *CF* 11 (1976) 357–83.

Dumoutet (1924), E. Dumoutet, *Le desir du voir l'Hostie et les origines de la dévotion au Saint-Sacrament*, Paris, 1926.

Engels (1965), P. Engels, "De eucharistieleer van Berengarius van Tours," in: *TvT* 5 (1965) 363–92.

Flandrin (1983), Jean-Louis Flandrin, *Un temps pour embrasser*. Aux origines de la morale sexuelle occidentale (VIe–IXe siècle), Paris, 1983.

Franz (1902), A. Franz, *Die Messe im deutschen Mittelalter*, Freiburg im Breisgau, 1902.

Freestone (1917), W. H. Freestone, *The Sacrament Reserved*, London, 1917 (Alcuin Club Collections, 21).

Geary (1978), P. J. Geary, *Furta Sacra, Thefts of Relics in the Central Middle Ages*, Princeton, 1978.

Geiselmann (1933), J. R. Geiselmann, *Die Abendmahlslehre an der Wende der christlichen Spätantike zum Frühmittelalter*, München, 1933.

Gerken (1973), A. Gerken, *Theologie der Eucharistie*, München, 1973.

Gschwend (1965), Kolumban Gschwend OSB, *Die depositio und elevatio crucis im Raum der alten Diözese Brixen*, Sarnen, 1965.

Guyon (1985), J. Guyon, "D'Auguste à Charlemagne, La montée des interdits," in: Marcel Bernos (1985).

Gy (1987), Pierre-Marie Gy, "La doctrine eucharistique dans la liturgie Romaine du haut moyen-âge," in *Segni e riti nella chiesa altomedievale occidentale*, 11-17 aprile 1985, vol. II, Spoleto, 1987, 533–57.

Hauser (1975), A. Hauser, *Sociale geschiedenis van de junst*, Nijmegen, 1975, (original title: *The Social History of Art*).

Häussling (1973), A. Häussling, *Mönchskonvent und Eucharistiefeier*. Eine Studie über die Messe in der abendländischen Klosterliturgie des frühen Mittelalters und zur Geschichte der Messhäufigkeit (Liturgiewissenschaftliche Quellen un Forschungen, 58), Münster, 1973.

Heitz (1963), C. Heitz, *Recherches sur les rapports entre Architecture et Liturgie à l'époque carolingienne*, Paris, 1963.

Jungmann (1941), J. A. Jungmann, *Gewordene Liturgie*, Innsbruck, 1941.

Jungmann (1943), J. A. Jungmann, "Accepit panem," in *ZKT* 67 (1943) 162–65 (also in: *Liturgisches Erbe und pastorale Gegenwart*, 1960, 366–72.

Jungmann (1952), J. A. Jungmann, "Die Andacht der vierzig Stunden und das Heilige Grab," in: *LJ* 2 (1952) 184–98.

Jungmann (1962), J. A. Jungmann, *Missarum Sollemnia*, 2 vol., Wien, Freiburg, Basel, 1962.

Jungmann (1974), J. A. Jungmann, "Rezension zu Häussling," in: *ZKT* 96 (1974) 303–6.

Kennedy (1944), L. Kennedy, "The Moment of the Consecration and the Elevation of the Host," in: *Medieval Studies* 6 (1944) 121–50.

Kidd (1958), B. J. Kidd, *The later medieval doctrine of the Eucharistic Sacrifice*, London, 1958.

Klauser (1969), T. Klauser, *A Short History of the Western Liturgy*, London, 1969.

Leclerq (1962), J. Leclerq, F. Vandenbroucke et L. Bouyer, "La spiritualité du moyen âge," II, *Histoire de la spiritualité chrétienne*, Paris, 1962.

Lukken (1990), G. Lukken, "Les transformations du rôle liturgique du peuple: la contribution de la sémiotique à l'histoire de la liturgie," in: *Omnes circum adstantes*, contributions towards a history of the role of the people in the liturgy. Presented to Herman Wegman, ed. Charles Caspers and Marc Schneiders, Kampen, 1990, 15–30.

Macquarrie (1972), J. Macquarrie, "Benediction of the Blessed Sacrament," in: *Paths in spirituality*, New York, 1972, 94–162.

Martimort (1978), A. G. Martimort, *L'Eglise en prière*, I–IV, 1983.

Mayer (1926), A. L. Mayer, "Liturgie und Geist der Gotik," in: *JLW* 6 (1926).

Mens (1946), A. Mens, "De verering van de h. eucharistie bij onze vroegste begijnen," in: *Studia Eucharistica*, 1946, Bussum, Antwerpen, 157–86.

Meyer (1963), H. B. Meyer, "Die Elevation im deutschen Mittelalter und bei Luther," in: *ZKT* 85 (1963) 162–217.

Meyer (1965), H. B. Meyer, *Luther und die Messe*, Paderborn, 1965.

Michaud-Quantin (1971), P. Michaud-Quantin, "Textes pénitentiels languedociens au XIIIe siècle," in *CF* 6 (1971) 151–72.

Mitchell (1982), N. Mitchell, *Cult and Controversy: The Worship of the Eucharist Outside Mass*, New York, 1982.

Montclos de (1971), J. de Montclos, *Lanfranc et Bérenger*, Leuven, 1971.

Neunheuser (1963), B. Neunheuser, *Eucharistie in Mittelalter und Neuzeit*. Handbuch der Dogmengeschichte, Bd. IV, 4b, Freiburg, Basel, 1963.

Nickel (1930), G. Nickel, *Der Anteil des Volkes an der Messliturgie im Frankenreich*, Innsbruck, 1930.

Nussbaum (1961), O. Nussbaum, *Kloster, Priestermönch und Privatmesse*, Bonn, 1961.

Nussbaum (1965), O. Nussbaum, *Der Standort des Liturgen am christlichen Altar vor dem Jahr 1000*, 2 vol., Bonn, 1965.

Nussbaum (1969), O. Nussbaum, *Die Handkommunion*, Köln, 1969.

Nussbaum (1979), O. Nussbaum, *Die Aufbewahrung der Eucharistie*, Bonn, 1979.

Oakley (1979), Fl. Oakley, *The Western Church in the Later Middle Ages*, London, 1979.

Pijper (1907), F. Pijper, *Middeleeuwsch Christendom. De verering der H. Hostie*, 's-Gravenhage, 1907.

Pol v. d. (1967), W. H. van de Pol, *Het einde van het conventionele Christendom*, Roermond, Maaseik, 1967.

Quirin (1952), K. L. Quirin, *Die Elevation zur hl. Wandlung in der Römischen Messe. Ihr Entstehung und Geschichte bis zum Ende des 16 Jahrhundert*, Mainz, 1952.

Rode (1957), R. Rode, *Studien zu den mittelalterlichen Kind-Jesu-Visionen*, Frankfurt am Main, 1957.

Rothkrug (1977), L. Rothkrug, "Popular Religion and Holy Shrines," in: James Obelkevich, *Religion and the People*, Chapel Hill, 1979, 20–86.

Rothkrug (1980), L. Rothkrug, *Religion Practices and Collective Perceptions: Hidden Homologies in the Renaisanze and Reformation* (Historical Reflections/Reflexions Historiques, vol. 7, no. 1), Waterloo, 1980.

Rubin (1991), M. Rubin, *Corpus Christi. The Eucharist in Late Medieval Culture*, Cambridge, New York, 1991.

Rush (1974), A. C. Rush, "The Eucharist, the Sacrament of the Dying in Christian Antiquity," in: *The Jurist* 34 (1974) 10–35.

Schillebeeckx (1967), E. Schillebeeckx, *Christus' tegenwoordigheid in de Eucharistie*, Bilthoven, 1967.

Semmler (1980), J. Semmler, "Mönche un Kanoniker im Franken reiche Pippins III und Karls des Grossen," in: *Untersuchungen zu Kloster und Stift Veröffentlichungen des Max Plank-Instituts für Geschichte, 68, Studien zur Germania Sacra, 14* (Göttingen, 1980).

Smits (1965), L. Smits, *Actuele vragen rondom de transsubstantiatie en de tegenwoordigheid des Heren in de eucharistie*, Roermond-Maaseik, 1965.

Southern (1975), R. W. Southern, *The Making of the Middle Ages*, Esse, 1975 (original ed. 1953).

Stemmler (1970), T. Stemmler, *Liturgische Feiern und Geistliche Spiele*, Studien zu Erscheinungsformen des Dramatischen im Mittelalter, Tübingen, 1970.

Trexler (1980), R. C. Trexler, *Public Life in Renaissance Florence*, New York, 1980.

Vauchez (1975), A. Vauchez, *La spiritualité du moyen âge occidental*, Paris, 1975.

Verheul (1974), A. Verheul, *Grondstructuren van de eucharistie*, Brugge, Boxtel, 1974.

Vogel (1980), C. Vogel, "Une mutation cultuelle inexpliquée: Le passage de l'eucharistie communautaire à la messe privée," in *Revue des sciences religieuses* 54 (1980) 231–50.

Wegman (1986), H. A. J. Wegman, "Theologie en Piëteit," in: *De Gelovige Thomas*. Beschouwingen over de hymne 'Sacris sollemniis' van Thomas van Aquino, Annalen van het Thymgenootschap, v. 74, n. 2, red. A. G. Weiler and G. A. M. Berkelaar, Baarn, 1986, 36–49.

Wegman (1991), H. A. J. Wegman, *Riten en Mythen*, Liturgie in de geschiedenis van het Christendom, Kampen, 1991.

Edward Schillebeeckx, O.P.

5. The Dogma of the Council of Trent on Transubstantiation: Its Development and the Categories in Which It Is Expressed*

GENERAL BACKGROUND: THE RELATIONSHIP BETWEEN A DOGMA AND THE FORM IN WHICH IT IS EXPRESSED

We know from the whole history of theology that it is always dangerous simply to repeat a formulation of faith which was made in a different climate of thought in the past and that if we do so it is hardly possible to speak of a *living* affirmation of faith. According to the Constitution on Revelation, it is impossible to grasp the real biblical meaning of Scripture without a knowledge of the various literary genres and the distinctive forms of thought of the writers of the Old and New Testaments. What theologians openly apply to Scripture, which is inspired, they must just as openly venture to apply to conciliar statements. What is remarkable, however, is that some Christians show more reverence for these statements than they do for the Bible. Nevertheless we must persevere in putting this method into practice if we are to be faithful to God's revealing word. We should be failing in reverence for the word of God if we were simply to put forward our own limited interpretations and representations as the norm for the authentic faith of our fellow-Christians.

On the other hand, however, we can never find the word of God anywhere in its pure state. Phrases like "the wording of the dogma," as opposed to its essence, although they may be quite correctly applied in a *retrospective* situation, are fundamentally misleading. They give the impression that we can dress a dogma up in words and strip it of its words with the ease of a child playing at dressing and undressing a doll. In the thought of a past age concerning the faith, which may be for us *now* an outmoded way of thinking, it is possible for us to make a distinction between what was "really affirmed" (and this, in any event, was already an interpretation) and the way in

* E. Schillebeeckx, *The Eucharist* (New York: Sheed and Ward, 1968) trans. by N. D. Smith, Part I: The Tridentine Approach to Faith, 23–86.

which this affirmation was expressed—its "wording." But in those past times this *manner of presentation* was vital to the question of whether the statement concerning the faith was or was not true. Those Christians of the past could present the faith only in the way they did present it—*for them* the dogma stood or fell with the form in which *they* expressed it. Hence it is clear that in its historical situation the teaching authority of the Church could not but press for a specific *idea* or wording of the dogma, because in the intellectual climate of the time a denial of the manner of presentation of the dogma inevitably suggested a denial of the real article of faith it expressed. Indeed such a challenge to the manner of presentation very often did more than *suggest* a denial of doctrine: an inflexible disregard for the form of expression frequently meant a genuine denial of the real content of the dogma itself!

It is only after the passage of time has produced a different climate of thought that meaningful questions can be raised concerning the "wording" of the dogmatic definitions of the past; in other words, that the process of finding new interpretations faithful to these definitions can begin. As long as man's perspective and climate of thought have not changed, he will take over the dogma as a whole—that is, together with the framework within which he must necessarily think in order to experience the dogma meaningfully. No one can ever anticipate history, although all kinds of implicit tendencies betray— afterwards—that the future has been prepared in the past. When history has moved forward, texts from the past acquire a new fulfillment. Thus, every generation is able to study Plato or Augustine, for example, anew—the past lives again and again in a new way, and indeed in such a way that the distinctively Platonic and distinctively Augustinian sense and meaning of their works is inwardly really fulfilled and not by way of "inegesis" [eisegesis — ed.], but by faithful exegesis! In the same way there can be no end to the interpretative rereading of the Bible. In every generation the Church rereads Holy Scripture, and she has been doing this for two thousand years, during which time the Bible has gradually been revealing its *own* meaning thanks to the light in which the past comes to stand in the present. The same applies to conciliar texts. The fact that the biblical and conciliar statements convey a mystery does not eliminate the historical character of human thought and faith.

Therefore in examining, in faith, statements made in the past by the Church, we must take present problems into account. Otherwise we hardly need to examine these earlier statements at all—we shall know in advance what we shall find. It will be the dogma together with its historical framework of thought and wording, as this is reconstructed for us by the historian, and, as believers, we shall be precisely where we started! Bonaventure and Thomas "demythologised" the "profession of faith." Berengarius was obliged to sign in the light of their new Aristotelian way of thinking: in other words, they took it out of the "sensualistic" framework within which a Roman synod in the eleventh century had formulated the real presence of Christ in the Eucharist. Some epigons are clearly unable to show moderation, but this does not mean that by an appeal to the Council of Trent we should call a halt to the genuine effort being made at the moment throughout the whole world (and especially in Western Europe) to understand the real content of "transubstantiation." If we were to do this, we should perhaps (the possibility is *a priori* there) be invoking the authority not of a dogma but of an earlier way of thinking! The authority of the Church's pronouncements would be maintained against modernists, but the fact that we were only appealing to the earlier framework of thought would be lost to sight, whereas the so-called modernists are really deeply concerned with the problem of making the inviolable *dogma* itself once again relevant to the faithful of today by separating it from a framework of ideas within which faith can no longer thrive in the present age.

But this "separation" must be done with great care, because we are concerned here with a mystery we cannot lay hold of and grasp in our hands, as we can the earth, for example. What we have here is one of the most delicate of all the living mysteries of the Catholic faith which cannot be stripped of its splendor without causing great harm to the faithful.

THE TEXT OF THE DOGMA: ITS ORIGIN, GROWTH, AND FINAL DRAFTING

Before the Council of Trent, certain *theologi minores* (conciliar experts who were not bishops), with a view to making the discussions in the council about the Eucharist easier, had studied Protestant publications and compiled a list of statements which, in their opinion, could not be accepted by a Catholic.[1] These statements were first

---

[1] *Concilii Tridentini Acta,* ed. Goerres Gesellschaft, pt. 5, 869–961; pt. 6, 123; pt. 7, 111–43 (see pt. 1, 608–9).

examined by the assembled theologians.[2] The result of their work was then handed to the fathers of the council, who used the text as a basis for their discussions and as a basis on which the council (in the present case at least) would build up its dogmatic definition. The discussions in plenary congregations which began in Trent were interrupted by the threat of plague, and the council was transferred for a time to Bologna. Later, they were resumed in Trent and brought to a conclusion.

All that concerns us here, at least directly, is the genesis of canon 1 and canon 2.[3] The very first basic text of the statements which were condemned by canons 1 and 2, in the form in which it was distributed for discussion in the plenary congregation of February 1547, was as follows.

1. "In the Eucharist, the body and blood of our Lord Jesus Christ is not truly (present), but as in a sign, just as it is said that there is wine in a signboard outside a tavern (a cup or some other symbol on a signboard at the entrance to a drinking house). That is the error of Zwingli, Oecolampadius and the Sacramentarians."[4]

2. (in fact 3 here) "In the Eucharist, the body and blood of our Lord Jesus Christ is truly (present), but at the same time with the substance of bread and wine, so that there is no transubstantiation, by a hypostatic union of (Christ's) humanity with the substance of bread and wine. For Luther says. . . ."[5]

I shall, for the time being, not consider the question as to how far these theologians accurately reproduced the Reformers' views in these texts.

The first draft (first schema) of the two canons was made on the basis of these two theses and distributed to the council fathers before the plenary discussions which began on May 9, 1547:

1. "If anyone should maintain that the sacrament of the Eucharist does not truly *(re vera)* contain *(contineri in sacramento)* the body and blood of our Lord Jesus Christ, but (that these) are only there *(ibi esse)* as in a sign or a symbolic form *(in figura)*, let him be excommunicated."[6]

[2] *Ibid.*, pt. 1, 615; pt. 5, 869–79, 960 ff., 1008; pt. 6, 123 ff.

[3] Denzinger, 883–84 (1651–52).

[4] *Concilii Tridentini Acta*, pt. 5 869; to be condemned, see pt. 7, 142; see pt. 7, 111–12 (Sept. 2, 1551, with a slightly changed text).

[5] *Ibid.*; also pt. 7, 112 (slightly changed). Also an affirmation to be condemned: pt. 7, 142.

[6] *Ibid.*, pt. 6, 124.

2. "Should anyone maintain that the sacrament of the Eucharist contains the body and blood of our Lord Jesus Christ in a manner which is different from that which the holy Catholic Church has hitherto preached and taught, that is, by a unique and wonderful changing of the whole substance of bread into the body and of the whole substance of wine into the blood, so that, under the two species and, in breaking or separation, in each particle (or part), the whole Christ is contained, which change was very suitably called *(nuncupata est)* transubstantiation by our fathers,[7] let him be excommunicated."[8]

These texts were submitted to the fathers of the council for discussion. In the congregation of May 17–23, 1547, various *censurae,* or amendments, were suggested by the fathers. Those which concern us here are the following. In canon 1, some of the fathers objected to *re vera,* "truly," and preferred terms which were rather more emphatic—*vere et realiter, realiter et veraciter, substantialiter et realiter,* or *vere et substantialiter.*[9] In canon 2, the interpolation of the clause "while the species *(species)* of bread and wine nonetheless remain"[10] was demanded, because no mention had been made of this in the official schema which had been discussed (in contrast to various personal schemas, which had not been debated). These amendments were examined on May 17 by a commission of *theologi maiores* (theologians who were at the same time bishops).[11] The formula *vere et realiter* was accepted.[12] In addition, the word "contained in" *(contineri)* in the same canon 2 was replaced by "is present" *(esse).* What is remarkable is that some of the bishops (although they proved to be in a minority) objected to the word *praesentia* and preferred the more objectivistic words *esse* or *contineri in.*[13]

An extremely interesting suggestion, put forward by Bishop Th. Casellus in the conciliar debate and defended by him in the commission (of which he was a member), was rejected with one vote in favor

[7] It is clear from other texts that the phrase "our fathers" here referred to the Fathers of the Church and to the fathers of, among others, the Fourth Lateran Council: *Concilii Tridentini Acta, op. cit.,* pt. 6, 156.

[8] *Ibid.,* pt. 6, 124.

[9] In the summary of the discussions: pt. 6, 142.

[10] Pt. 6, 136.

[11] Pt. 6, 145–57.

[12] Pt. 6, 146.

[13] Pt. 6, 134, 135, and 140, as against 135, 136, 137, 138, and 140, where the word *praesentia* was agreed to.

(his own): "because of the scholastics," as he said, he preferred to speak more precisely of a "sacramental change" *(conversio sacramentalis),* instead of the exuberant but rather meaningless adjectives "unique and wonderful" in connection with the *conversio.*[14] From the sacramental theological point of view, I personally think that this was one of the best suggestions that was made during these sessions. It was, unfortunately, not taken up, and the acts of the council do not tell us why. The bishop was clearly reacting against a "sensualistic" and crudely realistic view of the Eucharist, whereas the fathers of the council never stressed those points on which Catholic and Protestant Christians were in agreement (in our case, the *sacramentality* of the *whole* eucharistic event), but only reacted against the Reformers in their canons.

The canons were consequently revised, and the second, amended schema was submitted to the plenary congregation for discussion on May 25, 1547:

1. "If anyone should maintain that the *most holy* sacrament of the Eucharist does not *truly and really (vere et realiter)* contain the body and blood of our Lord Jesus Christ, but only as in a sign or a symbolic form *(in figura),* let him be excommunicated."[15]

2. "Should anyone maintain that, in the sacrament of the Eucharist, the body and blood of our Lord Jesus Christ is *(present)* in a manner which is different from that which the holy Catholic Church has hitherto *held,* that is, by a unique and wonderful changing of the whole substance of bread into the body and of the whole substance of wine into the blood, *while the species (species) of bread and wine nonetheless remain,* so that, under each part, the whole Christ is present (is contained), which change was very suitably called transubstantiation by our fathers, let him be excommunicated."[16]

The amended schema was examined by the plenary congregation on May 25, 1547, and all kinds of new amendments were suggested.[17] One remarkable suggestion was that the word "species" should be

[14] Pt. 6, 139.

[15] Pt. 6, 155.

[16] Here and in the later amendments I have italicized additions that were new in comparison with the preceding schema. Omissions will be revealed by a comparison of the texts.

[17] Pt. 6, 156–69, with the summary, 159–60.

changed to "accidents."[18] The commission of *theologi maiores* discussed the new suggestions on May 27. As the commission could not decide whether to allow the word "species" to stand or whether to replace it by "accidents," the matter was put to a vote. The result was an equal number of votes for each word, and the text (which was "in possession") remained unchanged.[19] The new text went back to the council and the two basic canons at least (those with which we are concerned here) were accepted without new corrections. They were, however, not published.

For many different reasons, these texts on the Eucharist were left untouched for about four years. It was not until September 1551 that the question was taken up again (this time, once more in Trent itself).[20] Although the canons which were formulated at Bologna were taken as a point of departure,[21] everything would seem to point to the fact that the whole question was fundamentally reexamined. On the basis of the previous theses, the theologians drew up a number of theses taken from the works of Protestant writers. The two which had been the basis of the two dogmatic "canons" remained in fundamentally the same form (as mentioned above).[22] These theses were, at least as far as their content was concerned, again taken as a basis for the two later canons (which express in the form of an anathema what the Protestant affirmations assert positively), after having first been discussed both by the theologians[23] and by the bishops.[24] As far as our two canons are concerned, only a few new elements appeared. Bishop Martin Ayala (of Guadix in Spain) asked that "and not only by its saving efficacy" *(in virtute)*[25] should be interpolated in canon 1 after "not only as in a sign." This was not, as has often been said, aimed at Calvin (who was never named in connection with transubstantiation),

[18] Pt. 6, 157 and 159. (See also pt. 7, 185: "quae per se subsistere possit.")

[19] Pt. 6, 160-61.

[20] Pt. 7, 110–204.

[21] Pt. 7, 177.

[22] Pt. 7, 111–12. Only the first "thesis" *(articulus)* was made more concise and matter-of-fact and was given a new interpolation: "In the Eucharist, neither the body and blood *nor the divinity* of our Lord Jesus Christ is truly (present), but only as in sign. This is the error of Zwingli, Oecolampadius and the Sacramentarians" *(ibid.,* 111). This should be compared with the previous text (see above, n. 4 of the present chapter).

[23] Pt. 7, 111–43.

[24] Pt. 7, 143–76.

[25] Pt. 7, 162.

but was inserted simply "in order more clearly to condemn the position of the heretics." In the case of the Eucharist, it was clearly not even sufficient to say that it was a *signum efficax,* an effective sign of salvation. The amended canons, which were distributed on October 3, 1551, were as follows:

1. "If anyone should maintain that the most holy sacrament of the Eucharist does not truly, really and *substantially* contain the body and blood *together with the soul and divinity* of our Lord Jesus Christ and *thus the whole Christ,* but (that these) are only there (present) as in a sign or figure *or (only) by efficacity,* let him be excommunicated."

2. (in fact 3 in this text) "Should anyone maintain that, in the *most holy* sacrament of the Eucharist, *the substance of bread and wine remains (in existence) together with the body and blood of our Lord Jesus Christ* or that, *according to detestable and profane modernist words (vocum novitates), Christ is "impanated"* (united with the remaining substance of bread) *and should deny this* wonderful and unique changing of the whole substance of bread into the body and of the whole substance of wine into the blood, while the species of bread and wine nonetheless remain, which change our fathers *and the universal Catholic Church* have very suitably called transubstantiation, let him be excommunicated."[26]

The list of adverbs, "truly, really and substantially"—*vere, realiter* and *substantialiter* (see the earlier texts)—only gave greater emphasis to the original *re vera,* "authentically real," the aim being to eliminate any possibility that the meaning might be reduced. The word "substantially," however, has a special shade of meaning that I shall explain later.

A discussion of these new canons reveals a number of interesting facts (some of which are only considered in *The Eucharist,* Part II). For example, a bishop suggested that, in the expression "truly present," the distinctively sacramental character of the eucharistic presence should be stressed by inserting the words "really and sacramentally"[27] and by leaving out "by efficacy," because Christ is also present *in virtute* in the Eucharist.[28] The text about the "impanated Christ" was also criticized by the fathers of the council, who

[26] Pt. 7, 178.
[27] Pt. 7, 183: "realiter et sacramentaliter."
[28] Pt. 7, 183, 184, and (three interventions) 185.

said that no Protestant had ever made such an assertion.[29] It was only at this stage too (a few days before the declaration of the dogma) that the idea of preceding the negative, condemnatory canons by a concise, positive exposition of Catholic teaching was brought up.[30] The text that was amended by the commission (the schema of October 9, 1551, which was, in fact, as far as canons 1 and 2 are concerned, exactly the same as the definitive text of the dogma; see later) was as follows:

1. "If anyone should *deny* that the most holy sacrament of the Eucharist truly, really and substantially contains the body and blood together with the soul and divinity of our Lord Jesus Christ and thus the whole Christ, but should say that they (body, blood, etc.) are only (present) as in a sign or figure or (only) by (their) efficacy, let him be excommunicated."

2. "Should anyone maintain that, in the most holy sacrament of the Eucharist, the substance of bread and wine remains (in existence) together with the body and blood of our Lord Jesus Christ and should deny this wonderful and unique changing of the whole substance of bread into the body and of the whole substance of wine into the blood, while the species of bread and wine nonetheless remain, which change *the Catholic Church* very suitably *calls* transubstantiation, let him be excommunicated."[31]

The changes were therefore very slight. What is striking is that the historical relativity of the Church's use of the word "transubstantiation" was acknowledged. Whereas there had previously been an inclination to regard the use of the term, despite some protests, at least materially as scriptural, patristic, and conciliar custom and even to attribute it to the *universal* Church (as the previous schemas had done—"our fathers and the universal Catholic Church") there was a sudden change in this schema, which did not refer to the past and simply stated "the Catholic Church" (leaving out the word "universal") very suitably calls (that is, *now* in any case) "transubstantiation." The bishops—more were present at the council in 1551 than in 1547 and more too from outside Italy—had strongly criticized this generalized and, from

---

[29] Pt. 7, 182 (twice), 183, and 184.

[30] The so-called *capita:* pt. 7, 177 and 185. Mgr. A Foscararius (Modena) and Mgr. A. Ayala (Guadix, Spain) were given the task of formulating these *capita* (pt. 7, 188), which were revised by the working commission. See the definitive text: Denzinger, 873a–882 (1635–1650).

[31] Pt. 7, 187.

the historical point of view, basically incorrect assertion.[32] The theory of an "impanation," regarded as a kind of extension of the "hypostatic union," was also omitted completely because, as one bishop maintained, no Protestant had ever expressed such an opinion.[33]

The new canons were once again submitted to the council for discussion and the amendments were dealt with by a commission. Apart from the transposition of two small words for the sake of style, there were no changes in the two canons which concern us here. This schema was therefore at the same time the definitive and dogmatic text, which was solemnly approved on October 11, 1551.[34]

SOME HERMENEUTIC AFTERTHOUGHTS

The basic intention of the fathers of the council was made clear in *cap.* 4 of the "Decree on the most holy sacrament of the Eucharist," a commentary on canon 2—it was *precisely because* Christ understood the handing over of his body under the form of bread in a very real sense that the Church's conviction (which this synod wishes to proclaim explicitly now) has *therefore* always been that the entire substance of the bread is changed into the body of Christ our Lord and the entire substance of the wine is changed into the substance of his blood by the consecration of bread and wine. This change was, in a suitable and appropriate manner, called transubstantiation by the holy Catholic Church.[35] As a result of this, canon 2 goes on to say, the substance of bread and wine is no longer present after the consecration—the really present reality is the body and blood of Christ, the entire concrete Christ (in his divinity and in his humanity), "while the species of bread and wine nonetheless remain." This happens by virtue of a change which the Church very suitably calls transubstantiation.

It is clear from the acts of the council that there was no discussion at all about the concept "change" *(conversio)*—this was accepted by everyone without further ado. There was some doubt, however, about whether the term "transubstantiation" should be insisted upon also.

[32] See esp. pt. 7, 183 and (three interventions) 184, also 125.

[33] "Non est error temporis praesentis" (pt. 7, 163; see also pt. 7, 183 and 184).

[34] Pt. 7, the *capita,* 200–3 and the canons 203–4. See also Denzinger, 883 and 884 (1651–1652).

[35] Denzinger, 877 (1642). The past tense, "was called," is preserved in the *caput.* These *capita* were, however, not discussed in detail by the council itself and, unlike the canons, they have no precise dogmatic value. They form, as it were, an explanatory *nota praevia,* although of a rather more official kind.

The expression had, after all, only a short tradition behind it, and one father of the council, apparently counting centuries as years, even went so far as to claim: "Say rather that the Church has been making use of this word for a few years."[36] It was therefore not primarily a question of the word or the expression "transubstantiation." Certain bishops even asked for this word to be suppressed, believing that a council ought not to take over such a (recently introduced) current term.[37]

On the other hand, many of the council fathers pointed to the new word *homoousios*, "consubstantial" ("homoousian," of the same nature or substance), which also did not occur in Scripture, but which the earlier Fathers of the Church seemed to have found necessary in order to expose christological heresies.[38] Divergent views about faith, in other words, made it necessary to use new words. The term was consequently accepted, especially since it had been explicitly and firmly rejected by Luther.[39] In other words, like the word "homoouisian" previously, the term "transubstantiation" was, for the Council of Trent, a political banner of the orthodox faith, very suitably proclaiming, in the sixteenth-century situation, the difference between the Reformers' and the Catholic view of the Eucharist. As such, the word itself explained nothing. It was simply intended as a kind of distinguishing mark by which the Christian could make his own position in the doctrine of the Eucharist immediately clear. It has lost this significance in our own times—even Protestant theologians have discovered and accepted the suggestive force of the word "transubstantiation." It has lost its function as a banner because it can now be used to fly over ships with different cargoes.

The fathers of the Council of Trent set out with much more important questions in mind than simply this terminology, the relative value of which is clearly displayed in the final statement, "it is a very suitable term." No more was claimed for it than this. What is more, the bishop of Vienna even asked, fully three days before the dogma was solemnly published, for the term "transubstantiation" to be omitted![40] What, then, was basically at stake? The council wanted to safeguard the significance of the "real presence" of the Eucharist

[36] *Concilii Tridentini Acta, op. cit.,* pt. 7, 184.

[37] Pt. 7, 188 (see also 182 and 125).

[38] For example, pt. 5, 944. In the debate of 1551, this argument was constantly occurring: pt. 7, 114–86; especially in the case of Melchior Cano: pt. 7, 125.

[39] Pt. 5, 188; pt. 7, 112.

[40] Pt. 7, 188.

within the Church. Zwingli, Oecolampadius, and the Sacramentarians had exclusively emphasized the symbolic significance. The Catholic Church had always proclaimed the sacramental species of the Eucharist to be "signs," and the Council of Trent had nothing to say against this. Canon 1 therefore only condemned the thesis according to which the eucharistic presence was interpreted "exclusively and only" *(tantummodo)* as a sacramental symbolism, as is, for example, the case with baptism and the other sacraments.

Furthermore, the council said, it was not sufficient to regard this eucharistic presence as being of the same order as Christ's presence in the other sacraments, because he was really present "by efficacy" in those sacraments; that is, Christ's personal act of giving himself acquired, in the sign of the sacramental symbolic action of, for example, baptism, a visible form for anyone who received the sacrament. In baptism there was therefore a real giving of himself on the part of Christ in a symbolic act. But in this interpretation, the distinctive quality of Christ's presence in the Eucharist was not guaranteed. Something more profound was accomplished in it. The council did not say, therefore, that there was a real presence of Christ only in the Eucharist. It was not until the time of Scotus that the real presence of Christ was identified for the first time with his specific presence in the Eucharist—and this was unfortunate, for is not Christ also really present (non-eucharistically) in the service of the word and in the assembled community of believers (as explicitly professed in the Second Vatican Council's Constitution on the Liturgy, c. I, n. 7)? But Christ's real presence in the Eucharist is something else.

Each of these different forms of Christ's single real presence has its own distinctive mode of reality. But the Council of Trent had the task of defending and professing the distinctive mode of Christ's real presence *in the Eucharist*. That was the council's basic intention, and it is in the light of this that the canons must be read and interpreted. (To constitute a real synthesis, any review of this presence—that is, Christ's real presence in the Eucharist—should involve, at the same time, a consideration of this eucharistic presence against the background of Christ's real presence in the entire liturgy. This real presence in the whole liturgy includes not only Christ's presence in the liturgical proclamation of the word, but also his real presence in the community of believers gathered for the celebration of the Eucharist. But unfortunately, as I have already said, this background must be assumed here without further exposition. I take this course reluctantly, with the aim of concentrating attention on the one point—Christ's real presence in the Eucharist.)

We are at once aware of three different levels in the Tridentine dogma:

1. At the very center of the dogma is the Tridentine affirmation of a specific and distinctive *eucharistic* presence—namely, the real presence of Christ's body and blood under the sacramental species of bread and wine—a presence which is understood in so deep and real a sense that Jesus was able to say: This here, this is my body; I hand it over to you for you to eat, so that you may have communion with me. For this reason, Christ is "truly, really and substantially" present, and not *only* present "as in a sign" or "by efficacity" (canon 1) or simply at communion, but also before (after the liturgy of the consecration) and afterwards. The insistence of the Tridentine dogma on the *lasting* character of Christ's real presence in the Eucharist points to the special and distinctive reality of this particular presence.[41]

2. The Council of Trent was unable to express this eucharistic real presence in any other way than on the basis of a change of the substance of bread and wine into the substance of Christ's body and blood (canon 2).

3. This change of bread and wine was very suitably called transubstantiation (the concluding sentence of canon 2).

I have already discussed this third and fairly relative level; in other words, the question of terminology. The question which immediately presents itself now is, What is the relationship between the first and the second levels, between the first and the second canons? Are they two different dogmas? The introductory *cap.* 4 clearly establishes the connection: *because* there is a specifically eucharistic real presence, there must *therefore* be a "change of the one substance into the other." This emerges even more clearly from the previous stage(s) of canon 2: "Should anyone maintain that in the sacrament of the Eucharist, the body and blood of our Lord Jesus Christ is (present) *in a manner which is different* from that which the holy Catholic Church has hitherto held, that is, by a changing . . . etc."[42] The council was clearly

---

[41] Denzinger, 886 (1654), although *cap.* 5 says explicitly that this presence ultimately continues to be directed towards sacramental communion: "ut sumatur institutum" (Denzinger, 878 [1643]).

[42] See above, n. 8 (pt. 6, 124), also n. 15 (pt. 6, 155), referring to the second schema of the canon. The same is clear from Seripando's personal draft. (The first

concerned with the distinctive character of the presence of Christ in the Eucharist—with no more than this, but also with no less than this. This was very suggestively illustrated by the interventions on the part of various bishops, some of whom expressed the opinion that what the council wanted to express positively as a change of substance by the term transubstantiation had already been said in as many words in the first statement, namely, that Christ was "truly, really and substantially" present in the Eucharist.

This view was expressed particularly in the session of 1551. No separate justification was provided for the error of canon 2, for many bishops maintained that the opposite was apparent from the falsehood of the first thesis (canon 1).[43] The second canon was only a different formulation of what had already been said in the first canon. In other words, the canon dealing with transubstantiation added nothing new, as far as its *content* was concerned, to the canon dealing with the specifically and distinctively real presence in the Eucharist. Eucharistic "real presence" and "transubstantiation" were, in the minds of the fathers of the council, identical as affirmations. But, despite this identity, Melchior Cano especially pointed out at the council that the new formulation did not therefore belong to faith in quite the same way as the first statement did. This theologian—who had, in his time, been particularly concerned with the method of theology—

---

official draft was based on Seripando's preliminary study.) Seripando's words were: "If anyone should maintain that the body and blood of Christ are present in the Eucharist *in any other manner* than in the manner which the Church . . . etc." (pt. 6, 131). The statement of Mgr. Musso, the bishop of Bitonto and the official defender of the text in its final stage, was especially strongly worded, namely, canon 1 says how transubstantiation is ("quomodo sit transsubstantiatio") and canon 2 says how transubstantiation comes about ("quomodo fiat sit transsubstantiatio"), pt. 7, 188. The eucharistic *praesentia realis* therefore *is* transubstantiation.

[43] Again and again we find the phrase repeated: "(art. 2, here still art. 3) continetur in primo" or (art. 2) "haereticus est ex primo," as, for example, in pt. 7, 149, 158, 161, 165, and (twice) 170. As far as I know, there was only one father who did not clearly see the relationship and asked for the second canon to come first (pt. 7, 183), apparently reasoning that transubstantiation was there "first" and the eucharistic presence then came about because of it. The council itself, on the other hand, reasoned the other way about—starting from the biblical affirmation of the eucharistic real presence. It would similarly be wrong to claim that some of the fathers of the council wanted to delete the second canon (as implied in the first). (Some authors have obviously been caught by the fact that, in some stages of the discussions, our "canon 2" became "canon 3," because an entirely different canon was inserted as "canon 2" between our two canons.)

appeared, in other words, to *sense* that it was possible to give orthodox affirmation to the content of the first canon while at the same time remaining skeptical about the *formulation* of the second.[44]

If we look at this historical result with the modern problem in mind, we at once see the red light—the fathers of the Council of Trent could not establish or express the real presence of Christ in the Eucharist unless they insisted on the acceptance of a transubstantiation of bread and wine. But, in that case, the theologian is immediately confronted with the question: Is this necessary connection between the "real presence" in the Eucharist and "transubstantiation" an *inner* necessity of the dogma itself or is it something that was necessary, in the spiritual and intellectual climate of the age; to thought—the only way in which the dogma of the eucharistic real presence could, *at that time*, readily be established? If the latter is the case, then the affirmation of a "change of substances" was no more than a formal repetition of the eucharistic "real presence"—in other words, different logical terms were being used in the second canon to say the same, as far as the content was concerned, as had been said in the first. The solution to this problem is vital to the question as to whether the Tridentine dogma of the real presence of Christ in the Eucharist displays an aspect of "wording," to which the Church, then, is not bound for all time, or whether it does not in fact display this aspect. To judge from the various drafts of the definitive canon 2, from the purport of *cap.* 4 and from the interventions on the part of several fathers of the council, it is in any case quite clear that the fathers were really concerned with the unique and distinctive (Catholic) quality of the real presence of Christ in the Eucharist. But it is also clear that these fathers were firmly convinced that they could not safeguard this distinctively eucharistic presence of Christ unless they also insisted on the acceptance of a "change of substances." What has obviously emerged, then, is that the final statement was without doubt secondary and that it was there purely to explicate the first statement in a polemical context.

On the other hand, however, despite the fact that many bishops claimed that canons 1 and 2 were, as far as their contents were concerned, identical, the council ultimately devoted a separate canon to the second affirmation—that is, to transubstantiation. From one point of view at least, it is even possible to say that the Council of Trent placed the emphasis on the second affirmation—*because* there is a

---

[44] Pt. 7, 125.

specifically eucharistic real presence, the council *therefore* insists on transubstantiation (*cap.* 4). We can therefore, and indeed must, say that the council was pointing directly towards transubstantiation, *because* the *real* intention was to safeguard the eucharistic real presence—as *cap.* 4 says, "quoniam . . . ideo. . . ." This means, in other words, that the Council of Trent was unable to express this unique presence in any other way but on the basis of a transubstantiation. Anyone denying this transubstantiation would at the same time be denying this particular presence, and this was what was at stake in the Catholic faith.

Both Bonaventure and Thomas, for example, presented it in the same way. They took as their point of departure the distinctive quality of the sacramental presence of Christ's body and blood—that was the biblical datum, the dogma, and therefore the norm for their speculation about this aspect of faith. From this point of departure, they came to a "theological conclusion"—*because* a presence *of this kind* cannot come about unless it does so by means of a change of the reality of the bread into the reality of Christ's body, we must *therefore* accept transubstantiation.[45] Both Bonaventure and Thomas began with the indisputable fact of faith—here is a distinctive real presence.[46] Because of what this inevitably implied for them, they spoke, in the *second* place—that is, on the basis of theological reasoning—of a change of the substance of the bread. In comparison with the first dogmatic statement of *faith*, their affirmation of this change of substance is a *theologoumenon*, despite the fact that, even before the time of Bonaventure and Thomas, certain Roman synods had already spoken about *substantialiter converti*.[47]

[45] Thomas, *ST*, III q. 75, a. 4 (transubstantiation) *after* a. 1 (eucharistic real presence). Bonaventure, *In IV Sent.*, d. 11, pars. 1, art. unicus, q. 1-q. 6: 241–53 *(de transsubstantiatione) after* d. 10: 216–38 (on the real presence).

[46] A presence that is difficult to define: "quodam speciali modo, qui est proprius huic sacramento" (Thomas, *ST*, III, q. 75, a. 1, ad. 3). As a non-local presence, it is a *spiritual* presence of Christ's true body, born of the Virgin Mary and risen from the dead. The term *praesentia realis* (as applied to and characteristic of the Eucharist) was not known in the thirteenth century. Thomas himself used many different expressions—a "praesentia corporis Christi" (*ST*, III, q. 75, a. 1, ad. 4), "spiritualiter" *(ibid.)*, "esse in hoc sacramento" (*ST*, III, q. 75, a. 1), "hoc sacramentum ipsum Christum realiter continet . . . secundum rei veritatem" *(ibid.)*, "veritas corporis et sanguinis Christi" *(ibid.)*, "invisibiliter" *(ibid.)*, "non in propria specie, sed sub speciebus huius sacramenti" *(ibid.,* ad. 2), "esse sub sacramento" (*ST*, III, q. 76, a. 6), etc.

[47] See n. 8 of the introduction.

Innocent III had referred to *transsubstantiari* in 1202[48] and the Fourth Lateran Council had used the term *transsubstantiatio*.[49] In this context at least, Thomas did not even refer to these texts. For him, it was first and foremost something that was necessary to thought— this distinctively eucharistic real presence could not be established in any other way but by proposing a change in the substance of the bread.[50] It was also precisely the same for Bonaventure, but, *in addition* to regarding this as necessary to thought (the opposite being *contrarium rationi*), he was *also* to appeal to the universal tradition of the Church.[51] For Thomas especially, the "change of the substance" of the bread and wine was a theological conclusion drawn *from* the datum of faith of the unique eucharistic presence. It was only then—in the *third* place, as it were—that Thomas appealed to the Aristotelian doctrine of the substance and its accidents.[52]

The whole affair, then, was full of subtle distinctions in the entire tradition that preceded the Council of Trent. A clear distinction was above all made between the real datum of *faith*, which was, in the last resort, biblical,[53] and the way in which this datum was expressed and

[48] Denzinger, 416 (784).

[49] Denzinger, 430 (802).

[50] " . . . et propter hoc relinquitur quod *non possit aliter corpus* Christi incipere esse de novo in hoc sacramento *nisi per* conversionem substantiae panis in ipsum" (Thomas, *ST*, III, q. 75, a. 2).

[51] "*Communiter* tenet ecclesia quod est ibi conversio" (Bonaventure, *In IV Sent.*, d. 11, pars. 1, art. unicus, q. 1: pt. 4, 242 B, 243 B; and q. 3:246 B). Thomas certainly referred to the condemnation of Berengarius in connection with the latter's *praesentia corporalis* (*ST* III, q. 75, a. 1) and in connection with his affirmation that the *substantia panis*, in his opinion, remained after the consecration (*ST*, III, q. 75, a. 2). But, whereas, in the first case, he referred to the fact that the Church obliged Berengarius to retract his statement, he did not, in the second case (a. 2) make use of argument based on the authority of the Church, but only of purely rational argument. He recognized more clearly than Bonaventure the difference "in level" between the affirmation of the eucharistic presence (which was, for him, a datum of faith) and the "change of the substance" (which was, for him, a cogent theological conclusion).

[52] In *ST*, III, q. 77, after having spoken, in q. 75–76, about the eucharistic presence and then, after this, about the "change of the substance" of the bread.

[53] See, in addition to the well-known technical and exegetical studies, the excellent synthesis provided by J. Betz in *Die Eucharistie in der Zeit der griechischen Väter*, Pt. II-1, *Die Realpräsens des Leibes und Blutes Jesu im Abendmahl nach dem Neuen Testament*, Freiburg i. Br., second enlarged edition (1965). A concise but careful study of the *praesentia realis* in Paul and John has been provided by B. van Iersel, "De 'praesentia realis' in het Nieuwe Testament," *Praesentia realis*, Nijmegen (1963) 7–18 (*Sanct. Euch.* 55 [1963], July and August).

interpreted. As we have already seen, some of those who were present at the council sensed this difference in level. There was, however, this important distinction—the Council of Trent was an "ecumenical council" testifying here, on the basis of its supreme authority, to the fact that it could not uphold the biblical affirmation of faith in its purity without at the same time affirming the change of the substance of the bread and the wine. In such circumstances, too, it is important to take into account the difference between a "*theological* development" of the doctrine and a "development of *dogma*." In other words, something that has once been recognized in theology simply as a theological conclusion may, at a later stage, be affirmed by the mind of the whole Church and ultimately even by the official charism of the Church's teaching authority as a true datum of *faith*. We have therefore not yet finished with the simple assertion that there were at the Council of Trent statements at two different levels of not quite equal value.

In the light of the report on the Protestant assertions made by the conciliar theologians and submitted to the fathers of the council, the first canon (the one dealing with Christ's real presence in the Eucharist) was clearly directed against Zwingli, Oecolampadius, and the Sacramentarians, who appeared to misrepresent the unique and distinctive character of the eucharistic presence. Neither Luther nor Calvin was mentioned in this connection. The Tridentine theologians had a distinct feeling for what was Catholic in Luther's view of the eucharistic presence. On the other hand, they were also aware of a fundamental difference between Luther's total view and the Catholic view—Luther accepted this unique presence only during the liturgy and therefore at communion (only *in usu*) and was sharply opposed to the Roman practice of "reserving" the sacrament. This could at least possibly have indicated a different view of the real presence in the Eucharist, a view which seemed to be expressed in Luther's opinion that the bread remained simply bread after the consecration. It was this that made his theory of "companation" (his theory that Christ and the bread coexisted) suspect, and it was for this reason that the second canon about the "change in the substance" of the bread was added, as a polemical move against Luther, who had, moreover, violently attacked the term "transubstantiation."

This shows once more that the fathers of the Council of Trent were really concerned with no more and no less than the pure question of *faith* in the real presence of Christ in the Eucharist. We can hardly, of course, ask how the council would have reacted to a possible argument on the part of one of its theologians reasoning from a completely different frame of thinking and maintaining that there might well be other possible ways of thinking about and interpreting meaningfully this "true, real and substantial" presence of Christ's body and blood in the Eucharist. No such different point of view or way of thinking existed among Catholics in the sixteenth century, and none of the Tridentine theologians could have thought and reasoned in advance of his own time. All that we can do now, reflecting about the Tridentine doctrine, is to repeat that the *only* aim of the Council of Trent was to proclaim the unique and distinctive character of the eucharistic presence as an inviolable datum of faith.

THE CONCEPT OF "SUBSTANCE," THE TRADITION OF THE CHURCH, AND THE ARISTOTELIAN DOCTRINE OF SUBSTANCE AND ACCIDENTS

It is, however, quite possible that the second statement made by the Council of Trent (canon 2, on "transubstantiation") also contained two different levels. These may be formulated as follows. In the first place, the council wished to affirm a *conversio* in the radical sense of the word and expressed this by the statement of a "change of substance." The second level is that of the Aristotelian doctrine of substance and accidents. So far, we have not yet established whether these two levels are in fact present or not in canon 2, and this is clearly what we must do now.

Generally speaking, most modern historians of the Council of Trent maintain that this council completely dissociated itself from the Aristotelian philosophy of nature, claiming that this is especially evident from the deliberate avoidance of the word "accidents" and the use of the word *species* (or "forms"). Although I do agree that the fact, also put forward by these writers, that the council stated in at least five different places that it only wished to make a stand against the Reformation and had no intention of settling scholastic disputes between Catholic theologians is undoubtedly correct,[54] I believe that the view that the council deliberately avoided using the word "accidents" is historically incorrect and lacking in discernment. It is true, of course, that the word "accidents" was never used in any of the *official*

[54] See *Concilii Tridentini Acta, op. cit.*, pt. 7, 189. Mgr. Cornelio Musso, the Bishop of Bitonto, who was appointed to defend the editing of the canons, said this explicitly. It was also a general attitude on the part of the whole council, by order of Cardinal Crescentius, the first president of the council and a papal legate.

Tridentine schemas. But it was used in unofficial texts which formed the basis for the official schemas. An example of this is Seripando's schema, in which it was explicitly stated: "(change in the substance of bread and wine), while the accidents continue to exist without subject."[55] In the final sessions on the Eucharist a bishop suggested that the word "species" should be changed to "accidents" (see above). The commission which had to study the amendments submitted under Cardinal Cervini decided not to change the text because, as we have seen, there was an equal number of votes for each word.[56] The word *species* ("forms") consequently remained, and the justification for this decision is significant—the term *species* had a firm tradition behind it, and it had already been used by the Fourth Lateran Council, by the Council of Florence, and many theologians.[57] The other four votes said "utraque lectio placet" (*ibid.*)—in other words that both terms were equally good. The practical result was that the word "species" was retained because the text was juridically already "in possession." There is no mention in the whole of this discussion of any criticism of the word "accidents" as an Aristotelian term. The fathers of the Council of Trent were not trying to dissociate themselves from the word "accidents" for the very good reason that, whether they were strict Thomists or Scotists or whatever they were, they were all in their own way Aristotelian scholastics in their manner of thinking, and for all of them the words "species" (*species*) and "accidents" (*accidentia*) meant exactly the same in their *thinking* about faith and within the framework of faith.

This is precisely where so many of the historians of the Council of Trent go wrong—they are obstinate in their belief that the fathers wanted in one way or another to dissociate themselves from the Aristotelian manner of thinking. In this they are producing an anachronism and committing a hermeneutical blunder, which incidentally makes the modern reinterpretation of the dogma all the more difficult. As we have said, no single man, situated at a definite point in the history of the evolution of human thought, can be expected to dissociate himself from his own way of thinking (for him, an integral part of himself) and anticipate this history—in this case, to think

[55] *Ibid.*, pt. 6, 131.

[56] See above, under footnotes 18 and 19 of this chapter.

[57] *Concilii Tridentini Acta, op. cit.,* pt. 6, 160–1. The Fourth Lateran Council: Denzinger, 424 (793); see 414 (782); *Decretum pro Armenis* (Council of Florence): Denzinger, 698 (1321) (see the Second Council of Lyons: Denzinger, 465 [860]).

some four centuries ahead! Although there were individual differences, the Aristotelian doctrine of substance and accidents formed the framework within which all the fathers of the Council of Trent thought. In reflecting about the datum of faith (of the unique real presence of Christ in the Eucharist), in considering it, not as a puzzle or a magic formula, but as a mystery of faith, they were bound to do so within their Aristotelian frame of reference. How could they have thought in any other way? Putting a distance between themselves and this way of thinking would, for them, have been the equivalent to a refusal to think at all meaningfully about this mystery of faith! It is moreover historically unfair to see a "break" in the fathers' thinking about faith in the earlier conciliar texts in order to make it easier for us to think about these texts now in a new way. These modern authors believe that their theory facilitates reinterpretation of the Tridentine dogma, but in fact it only makes it more difficult! For, only if it becomes clear historically that the Tridentine dogma, without in fact sanctioning a particular philosophy, certainly expressed the datum of faith in Aristotelian terms will it be evident to the theologian (reasoning from the present stage of philosophical thought) that the dogma is bound to contain an aspect of "wording" which is historically determined and therefore unmistakably relative.

Some scholars have attempted to find out (in isolation from the modern problem and from their own manner of thinking about faith) precisely what the fathers of the Council of Trent believed and taught in connection with the Eucharist. To do this, they have tried to make a "reconstruction" excluding the older, then essential, ways of thinking. But a true interpretation of Trent is only possible—*objectively*—if both our own contemporary way of thinking and that of the fathers of the council are brought to bear on the problem. This will be made clearer later on.

There is a great deal of evidence to show that there was not one of the fathers of the council who did not think of the dogma in Aristotelian terms. There was certainly a feeling—ultimately biblical—that what was at stake was the distinctively *Catholic* character of the eucharistic presence; but, in order to insist on this distinctively Catholic quality, the fathers could not but express everything in contemporary terms (that is, in Aristotelian scholastic terms) *insofar* as it was necessary to do so in order to safeguard the dogma. They were certainly aware of the difference between philosophy and faith, but they inevitably thought about faith in the concepts and categories, and within the whole framework, of their own thought. This does not imply any sanctioning by the Church of an Aristotelian philosophy; nonetheless, the whole Aristotelian doctrine of substance and accidents was the *framework of thought* within which the fathers of the council reflected about faith. If it was ever to emerge, from the philosophical point of view, that the Aristotelian doctrine of substance and accidents was no longer tenable, there would be no reason for the dogma itself to suffer in any way. The Aristotelianism applied by Catholic theologians to the Eucharist was, after all, a radical "transubstantiation" of the authentic, historical Aristotelianism, which would never have tolerated any such division between substance and accidents! This insight certainly brings us one step closer to a solution of the problem.

Long before the Council of Trent, John Wycliffe (1320–1384) wrote the book, *De eucharistia tractatus maior*[58] in which, with reference to the real presence in the Eucharist, he quoted "three views" current in the Middle Ages—those of Thomas, Scotus, and Berengarius.[59] He himself favored the symbolic interpretation of Berengarius, and his justification of this is interesting. Wycliffe was an Aristotelian at Oxford University. Faithful to the authentic, historical Aristotelianism which could not admit any division between substance and accidents, he denied transubstantiation and consequently, at that time, he also denied the specifically Catholic view of the real presence in the Eucharist. Any division between substance and accidents, Wycliffe maintained, was metaphysically impossible. His refusal to think of the eucharistic presence in these Aristotelian categories meant, within the *same* framework of thought, that Wycliffe could see no other way out of the difficulty than to understand this presence purely symbolically, and this further implied that he was bound to formulate the eucharistic presence thus conceived in Aristotelian terms as follows: (1) the substance of bread and wine remains; (2) the accidents of bread and wine do not continue to exist without subject; (3) there is consequently no "corporeal presence" *(praesentia corporalis)* of Christ.[60]

This Aristotelian expression of a real presence not conceived in accordance with Catholic ideas forms the exact obverse of the Tridentine formulation, which expressed the Catholic view of the eucharistic presence in broadened Aristotelian terms. This clearly

[58] Ed., J. Loserth, London (1892).

[59] *Ibid.*, 29–30.

[60] See Wycliffe's condemnation by the Council of Constance (Denzinger, n. 581–83 [1151–53]).

confirms what I have already said about Trent—within the Aristotelian framework of thought that prevailed in the Middle Ages, it was impossible to safeguard the distinctively Catholic character of Christ's real presence in the Eucharist without affirming transubstantiation. The fact that Wycliffe regarded himself as obliged, on the basis of authentic Aristotelianism, to deny transubstantiation led him inevitably to deny the dogma of faith in the real presence in the Eucharist. Once again, then, we may say that the concept "transubstantiation" points to nothing more, but also to nothing less, than the Catholic feeling for the biblical and distinctively eucharistic real presence of Christ within the medieval framework of thought.

At the Council of Constance, the Church condemned Wycliffe because of his purely symbolic interpretation of the eucharistic presence (Berengarius). But this condemnation was also inevitably expressed in the Aristotelian terms in which both Wycliffe and the Church thought at the time. The council therefore condemned Wycliffe's thesis that the accidents of bread and wine did not continue to exist without subject after the consecration. This shows even more clearly than in Trent the correlation between the eucharistic presence and the Aristotelian view of substance and accidents. In the Middle Ages, this correlation was decisive to any view—either Catholic or non-Catholic—of the eucharistic presence.

The matter does not, however, end there. Although Trent was in fact much more sober in its Aristotelianism than the Council of Constance, it is true to say that all the fathers of the Council of Trent had the more pronounced Aristotelian formulae of Constance in mind when they condemned the Reformers' view of the eucharistic presence. The influence of the Council of Constance on that of Trent has been analyzed by E. Gutwenger, who has, however, quite incorrectly inferred from this that Trent indirectly sanctioned the Aristotelian doctrine of substance and accidents as an inevitable ontological implication of the Catholic view of the eucharistic presence.[61] It is certainly true that, in connection with the change of the substance of bread and wine, the fathers and the theologians of the Council of

---

[61] "Substanz und Akzidenz in der Eucharistielehre," *Zts. f. Kath. Theologie*. 83 (1961) 257–306. G. Ghysens, on the other hand, is also incorrect in dissociating the way the fathers of the Council of Trent thought about faith from their Aristotelian views, in which they expressed at least the "remaining of the *species*" in a way as meaningful to themselves. See "Présence réelle et transsubstantiation dans les définitions de l'Eglise catholique," *Irén*. 32 (1959) 420–35.

Trent made constant reference to the Council of Constance.[62] Seripando's own preliminary study, which was an important source for the final text, was virtually composed of formulae from Constance.[63]

Finally, Trent also took up the condemnation of Wycliffe's three points again, but did it, as far as the Aristotelian mode of expression was concerned, rather more soberly—although the fathers of the Council of Trent still continued to think about faith within the framework of Aristotelian thought, they were at least more existentially sensitive to the difference between philosophy and faith. That is why the doctrine of substance and accidents was, both for Constance and for Trent, more than simply a question of "wording." The fathers of the Council of Trent were not explicitly aware of this aspect of wording. Indeed, they could not be, nor had they any need to be, aware of it. For them, thinking and experiencing as they did, it was not simply a question of "wording," but the only possible way of thinking meaningfully as Catholics about the presence of Christ in the Eucharist, at least in connection with the "remaining of the species." That is why it is impossible for us to comprehend the content of faith of the declarations of the Council of Trent if we try to grasp the way in which the fathers thought about faith precisely insofar as they dissociated themselves from their "Aristotelianism." That would be an attempt to trace what Trent believed in isolation from its concrete faith—an attempt to catch *in flagrante delicto* a way of thinking about faith after having previously eliminated all the factors which might lead us to this capture. Only a generation of believers living at a later period in the development of human consciousness and therefore further removed from the Aristotelian metaphysical philosophy of nature in its medieval form—and capable at least of seeing this philosophy more clearly if they have not rejected it altogether—can be aware that this medieval mode of thought was historically conditioned and hence, in the concrete sense, a form of "wording" for what the Council of Trent was really trying to express. But, in that case, this later generation will not be able to grasp the genuine *content of faith* of the Council of Trent if they methodically set aside their own (and later) way of thinking. If we, living in the twentieth century, are to discover the genuine content of the Tridentine faith in connection

---

[62] *Concilii Tridentini Acta, op. cit.*, pt. 5, 873–74, 876–77, 883–92, 906, 914, 916, 923, 926, 929, 950, 1010, 1013.

[63] Especially "remanentibus accidentibus sine subiecto" (*ibid.*, pt. 6, 131).

with Christ's presence in the Eucharist, we must also enter intimately into this content of faith, reassessing it and making it actual and present, because we can never really grasp it in its "pure state."

But we have not yet established apodeictically whether or not there is an important factor of "wording" in the Tridentine doctrine. We have seen that there were three "levels" in Thomas, for example, which were ultimately fused. First, there was Thomas' affirmation of the unique presence of Christ that was "peculiar to this sacrament." Second, he affirmed a radical change or a change of the substance of bread and wine, which he personally (that is, when he was not engaged in translating his own most deeply held conviction into traditional terms) called a "change of being" *(conversio totius entis)*. By this, he meant that the *reality* of bread was something quite different after the consecration—it became the body of Christ.[64] Third, he made use of the Aristotelian theory of substance and accidents. Thomas distinguished these three levels in the concrete structure of his treatise and discussed them separately, passing from the first to the second and then on to the third. We can sum them up as the level of *faith* (the special eucharistic presence), the *ontological* level (the change of being or *trans-entatio*), and the level of *natural philosophy* (the *trans-substantiatio*). Ultimately, of course, these three levels formed one single vision—as a believer, he thought about the dogma in ontological terms and in terms of natural philosophy. "Here I stand, I can do no otherwise!" He could not separate one from the other because if he did so the dogma of faith itself would be in danger for him. But then *we* are at once confronted with the question as to whether the ontological can and must not be preserved even if the level of natural philosophy is no longer serviceable for us. We are also faced with a second question—Does the level of faith also in fact imply the *ontological* level? Did not one theologian, Bishop Casellus, suggest in Trent itself (or rather, in Bologna) that it was right to speak of a "change," but that this should be thought of at the level of sacramentality or symbolic activity and thus be called a "sacramental change" *(conversio sacramentalis)*?[65]

[64] "Conversio *totius entis*," "se extendens ad *totam naturam* entis"—"change of the *whole being*," "extending to the *whole nature* of the being" (*ST*, III, q. 75. a. 4). "Id quod *entitatis* est in una, potest Auctor entis convertere ad id quod est entitatis in altera"—"The Author of being can change what is *of the reality* in one into what is of the reality in the other" (*ST*, III, q. 75, a. 4, ad. 3).

[65] See above, n. 14 of this chapter.

It is *a priori* quite conceivable that anyone who has to reject the specifically Aristotelian character of the doctrine of substance and accidents (we are, after all, not bound by faith to an Aristotelian philosophy) may still be able to keep to an ontological "change," on the basis of which the answer to the question "What *is* that?" after the consecration can no longer simply be "It is bread." In such a case, it is perfectly clear that a demythologization of this kind of the Aristotelian element in the Tridentine dogma is still completely faithful to the Catholic belief in the real presence of Christ in the Eucharist. But, in the light of the modern problem, we are obliged to ask the further question, leaving aside the consideration of the Aristotelian philosophy of nature (which, *as believers,* we might in any case just as well drop): Did Trent really mean to insist on an *ontological* aspect or does this too come within the scope of what at the present time may be called the aspect of *"wording"* of the Tridentine dogma? In my opinion, this question brings us to the very heart of the modern problem.

It is historically clear that theologians and the Church had already spoken of a "change of the substance" of bread and wine even before the Aristotelian doctrine of substance and accidents had penetrated into the West.[66] What is more, the Greek Fathers, Ambrose, and the theologians of the Carlovingian period had, in their thinking, clearly followed a direction which led to the conviction that the Catholic view of the eucharistic presence could not be maintained without a *real* change of the bread (without any allusion to an Aristotelian philosophy of nature). The fathers of the Council of Trent were certainly informed about the way in which the Fathers of the Church conceived the eucharistic presence, at least in broad outline and without critical identification of individual authors. Centuries before the Latin Church had begun, in the late Middle Ages, to use the word *transsubstantiatio,* the Greek Fathers had been speaking of a *trans-elementatio* or *meta-stoicheiōsis* (the elements, *stoicheia,* of bread and wine, changing into Christ's body and blood). Why, then, should the Latin Church not speak of *trans-substantiatio*? a doctor of Paris, John Consilii, exclaimed in a very sound argument.[67] Reference was made in the

---

[66] See above, Denzinger, 355, 416, and 430 (700, 784, and 802). See also above, the bibliography under footnote 1 of the introduction, and below under n. 70 of this chapter.

[67] *Concilii Tridentini Acta, op. cit.,* pt. 5, 945. He referred to Theophylactus (*PG,* 123, 1307), but this brings us to as late as the eleventh century. In fact, the term can be found as early as in Gregory of Nyssa, *Oratio catechetica,* 37, 4, ed. Strawley,

Council to Tertullian, Ambrose, Jerome, Cyprian, Gregory of Nyssa, Gregory Nazianzen, Basil, Augustine, Irenaeus, and others.[68] The fathers of the council were therefore able to conclude, "Although the word (transubstantiation) is of more recent date, the real faith (*fides et res*) is nonetheless very old."[69]

Of course, the fathers of the Council of Trent were not aware of the distinctive character of the patristic view of the eucharistic change. Although the Greek Fathers remained outside the Aristotelian influence in the first three centuries of Christianity especially, they had always spoken about a *radical change* of bread and wine; that is, into Christ's body and blood. In the ancient Western liturgies, the terms used in this context were *transformare, transfigurare, transfundere,* and *transmutare.* The ancient Eastern liturgies used the terms *metapoieisthai, metaballesthai, metarrythmizesthai,* and *metastoicheuousthai,* and these technical terms were derived from the Greek Fathers.[70] Let me give just one example, from Theodore of Mopsuestia: "Christ did not say, 'This is the *symbolum* of my blood,' but 'This is my blood,' a *change* of the wine takes place."[71] The ancient Church was as firmly convinced of a real change of the bread and the wine as was the medieval Church.

But the categories in which the ancient Church thought about this datum were rather different from those in which the Church thought about it later, because the former was more orientated in her thinking towards the ancient world.[72] The early Christian vision was much

---

151,8–152,8 (*PL* 45, 97). Theophylactus was quoted again and again in Trent: *Concilii Tridentini Acta, op. cit.,* pt. 5, 884; pt. 5, 874 and 915.

[68] *Ibid.,* pt. 5, 874, 884, 915, and 944; pt. 7, 163.

[69] *Ibid.,* pt. 5, 945.

[70] As early as 1855, a study was written dealing with the terms used by the Greek Fathers for this change: E. Pusey, *The Doctrine of the Real Presence, as Contained in the Fathers from the Death of S. John the Evangelist to the Fourth General Council,* Oxford and London (1855) 162–66. The same study was taken up again, more critically, by J. Betz, *Die Eucharistie in der Zeit der Griechischen Väter,* Pt. I-1, Freiburg i. Br. (1955) 300–18.

[71] *Fragmenta in Matt. 26, 26* (*PG* 66, 713). See also Cyril of Jerusalem, *Catech. Mystag.,* 5, 7 (*PG*, 33, 1113, and 1116)—Cyril cited the miracle of Cana as a guarantee of this miraculous eucharistic *conversio, ibid.,* 4. 2 (*PG*, 33, 1097, and 1099); Gregory of Nyssa, *Oratio catechetica,* 37, 2, 3, and 4 (*PG*, 45, 93–97)—"by the power of the blessing, the nature of what we see is *transelementalised*"; Cyril of Alexandria, *Comm. in Matth,* 26, 26 (*PG*, 72, 452–53); John Damascene, *De Fide orthodoxa,* 4, 13 (*PG*, 94, 1144); John Chrysostom, *Homilia de proditione Judae,* 1, 6 (*PG*, 49, 380) *In Matth. homilia,* 82, 5 (*PG*, 58, 744).

[72] See J. Betz, *op. cit.,* 301.

more dynamic—corporeal things were, for the earliest Fathers of the Church, what they were because they were controlled by Powers, and a change of a thing meant that other Powers seized it and took possession of it. They said therefore that a Christian was a person whose flesh had been seized by the Pneuma, by God.[73] Moreover, these Greek Fathers regarded material things as being "without qualities; they can invest themselves with all qualities as the Creator desires."[74] "To be changed" in the context of the Eucharist therefore meant that Christ, the Logos, took possession of the bread and the wine and made it his body and blood, that he appropriated them, making them his own body and blood. The terms *metaballein* and *metapoiein* used by the Greek Fathers for this eucharistic change meant precisely "to change by appropriating to oneself, by taking possession of." In this way, the Greek patristic view of the eucharistic change was in a sense an extension of the "hypostatic union," the Incarnation. What was a problem of secondary importance for the scholastic theologians of a later period—that is, that the divinity of Christ, the Logos, was present "concomitantly" in the Eucharist— was the most important question for the Greek Fathers precisely because they regarded man's justification as a deification. The Logos took possession of the sacrificial gifts by the Holy Spirit's descent on them, just as he had taken possession of his body from the Blessed Virgin. The way the change took place was thus the same as that in which the Logos appropriated his body at the Incarnation.

It was, so to speak, a cultic and sacramental incarnation of Christ— the Holy Spirit descended on the offering, "penetrated" the elements and made them the body and blood of Christ, and this could only take place within the mystery of liturgical worship. The Logos thus took possession of these sacrificial gifts of bread and wine, which then acquired a "pneumatic power" through being in the possession of the life-giving Logos. The Incarnation in this way continued to be living and effective in a cultic and sacramental manner in the Eucharist. In other words, the bread and wine were, by virtue of the descent of the Holy Spirit, changed into the "body-and-blood," in the body that was hypostatically of the Logos. Instead of natural powers, the saving power of Christ was now effective in the sacrificial gifts. In this way, the bread and wine were, after the consecration, to be sacra-

[73] Irenaeus, *Adv. Haereses*, V, 9, 3, ed. Harvey, pt. 2, 343.
[74] Origen, *Contra Celsum*, 3, 41 (GCS, pt. 1, 237).

mental *forms* in which the body of the Logos *appeared*. They had, in other words, lost their natural independence as things of nature—they had been dispossessed of themselves *(de-substantiatio)* and possessed by the Logos, received into the body of the Logos *(trans-substantiatio)*.

The basic patristic intuition was the same as that of the Tridentine dogma, but it was expressed within a different framework of thought. The Greek Fathers did not in any sense think of a substance situated "behind" the accidents. In their view of the change of the substance of the bread and wine, they did not see the substance as opposed to the accidents, but in its independent being. The bread and wine lost *this* substance and acquired a radically new independent being or reality, that of the body of Christ, the saving organ of the Logos. It cannot be denied that what we have here is a real transubstantiation which was not conceived in Aristotelian terms and which in a dynamic way possesses great ontological density. Just as Trent sanctioned the word *transsubstantiatio* in the sixteenth century, so did the Greek Church also eventually sanction, in the seventeenth-century synod, the word *metaousiōsis* (a non-patristic term, but a translation of the Latin *transsubstantiatio* and thus dependent on the Latin Church).

This all goes to make it quite clear that, although the fathers of the Council of Trent thought of the "change" *(conversio)* in Aristotelian terms, this Tridentine "change" does suggest a *reality* of which the early Church was also deeply convinced, but which she did not express in an Aristotelian context. This should be sufficient confirmation of the idea that canon 2 of the Council of Trent does suggest a reality *of our faith* which need not of itself be interpreted in the Aristotelian sense.

We must now take another datum into account. The *word* "transubstantiation" was without doubt partly formed with a biblical echo in mind. Medieval theology developed within the study of *Sacra Pagina* (Holy Scripture), the first branch to emerge being grammatical theology, the next dialectical, and finally speculative theology. The terminology of theology was therefore interspersed with biblical words (from the Vulgate and other early Latin translations) even when the division between *lectura* (biblical exegesis) and *quaestio* (speculative theology) had gradually become established. Biblical words, about which a *quaestio* had previously been asked in the *lectura,* continued to be used in speculative discourses even if they no longer had any direct connection with the content of the original biblical text. The use of biblical words (often no longer directly associated with their biblical context) in independent speculation was a characteristic of medieval theologians who, in this sense—that is, terminologically— thought "biblically." Now the Latin translation of the words "daily bread" in the Matthaean version of the Our Father ("give us this day our daily bread," Matt 6:11) was *panis supersubstantialis*,[75] and it has struck me in the Acts of the Council of Trent that theologians especially made a connection between the idea of transubstantiation and this "biblical" *panis supersubstantialis*.

One of the bishops, John Fonseca, in fact said explicitly that it was heretical to deny transubstantiation, because it was contrary to the Our Father, "da nobis panem supersubstantialem."[76] Whenever early scholastic theologians who, especially since the time of Boethius, had become familiar with speculations about "substance" read these words in the Latin translations of the Bible, their minds at once began to work like electronic brains, and they made connections. I have not made a special study of this question, as there is still too much material that is in manuscript and has not yet been published—it remains a "feeling" that is based on a few indications, which are nonetheless very suggestive. But I do feel convinced that the Latin Bible in the early scholastic period was partly responsible for the new word-formation "transubstantiation" and not the typically Aristotelian theory of substance and accidents.[77]

What, then, did "substance" mean in the tradition of the Church? Even in the patristic and the early medieval periods, this word had already a long history that was independent of the precise relationship between substance and accidents. It was used in two ways. The prescientific meaning of the word was *reality*, as opposed to *appearance* or something abstract (an *ens rationis*). It was used to mean everything that suggested the idea of "firmness," "steadfastness," or "stability," just as we still refer to "something substantial" both in

[75] A rendering of the Greek *epi-ousion* which was translated in the Latin version of Luke 11:3 as *panis quotidianus*.

[76] *Concilii Tridentini Acta, op. cit.*, among other places, pt. 7, 150. See also the statements of other bishops and theologians: pt. 7, 129 and 140.

[77] The first time, as far as we know, that the word *transsubstantiatio* was used was in the *Sententiae* of Roland Bandinelli, who later became Pope Alexander III, thus between 1140 and 1153 (see ed. Gietl, 231). Bandinelli did not, however, put it forward as a neologism. It would seem that the word was formed in the school of Laon between 1100 and 1130. In the second half of the twelfth century it was in current use.

connection with, for example, a meal or a conference and in connection with the foundation of our faith, that the Epistle to the Hebrews called the *substantia* or *hypostasis* of "things hoped for," that is, the firm foundation (Heb 11:1). In the Christian literature of the first centuries, substance therefore always indicated *reality*. In addition, the word substance also came to be used scientifically in connection with Trinitarian and christological polemics. *Substantia* was here linked with the Greek word *ousia*, which originally also pointed to the "firmness of being" of the *reality*. An Aristotelian influence already made itself felt in the patristic period, with the result that a twofold (scientific) concept of substance became current in a theological context—the *substantia prima* or the concrete reality, the reality that is firm in its being, the existing reality, and the *substantia secunda* or an abstract formalization of this concrete reality (the so-called *essentia* or *quidditas abstracta*).

This twofold meaning caused a great deal of theological confusion (which we can ignore here). The result of these theological fluctuations was that the word "substance" was used in theology (especially in contrast to "person") both for a non-spiritual, concrete reality (*substantia prima* or *ousia prōtē*) and in the sense of "abstract essence."[78] Thus, someone (presumably Faustus of Riez) already referred in the fifth century to a change of visible things (bread and wine) into the substance of the body and blood of Christ.[79] In the theology of the Carlovingian and early scholastic periods, then, *substantia panis* simply meant the *reality* bread, not in itself in relation to the Aristotelian connection between substance and accidents. Quite apart from the Aristotelian philosophy of nature, the Church had for a long time been speaking about a *real* change or a change of the *substance* of the bread and wine in connection with the Eucharist. It is quite clear from the very first polemics about the eucharistic presence between

[78] See, among others, J. de Ghellinck, "L'entrée d'essentia, substantia et autres mots apparentés dans le latin médiéval," *Arch. Lit. Med. Aevi* (Bull. du Cange) 16 (1942) 77–112; *id.*, "Essentia et substantia. Note complémentaire," *ibid.* 17 (1942), 29ff. and 133 ff.; F. Erdin, *Das Wort Hypostasis*, Freiburg i. Br. (1939); F. Sassen, *De vraag naar het zijn in de eerste eeuwen der scholastiek* (Meded. Kon. Ned. Akad, van Wetensch.) Amsterdam (1937). See also H. de Lubac, *Corpus mysticum*, Paris (1944) 171–76 and 243–48.

[79] See *PL*, 30, 272 (known to the theologians of the Middle Ages via the *Decretum Gratiani*). See also *PL*, 67, 1052–56 and *PL*, 100, 203. It was only from the time of the polemics against Berengarius in the eleventh century that *substantia* became a key-word in the doctrine of the Eucharist.

Ratramnus[80] and Radbert[81] in the ninth century (long before the polemics around Berengarius in the eleventh century) that the sacramental sign of the "bread"—in the sense in which the Church understood the *signum* of this particular sacrament in contrast to the *signa* of the other sacraments—of necessity implied a *real* and, in this sense, substantial or radical change of the bread. Even Ratramnus, branded as a heretic by Radbert, whose thought was rather strongly "sensualist," accepted a fundamental change of the bread, but emphasized the sacramentally veiled character of this event *(in figura)*. Indeed, so much stress was laid on the "sign" that not only was Christ's body and blood *referred to,* but this body and blood was concretely and really present for me here and now, "in," "under," "via," or "through the medium of" (the best formula was sought) the sacramental form of bread and wine.

It was essential and fundamental to the dogma of faith that there should be no *reality* bread after the consecration, since, if the ultimate *reality* present in the Eucharist were to be called bread, there would be simply bread (a reality cannot at the same time be two realities!) and the eucharistic presence could only be conceived symbolically. The whole of the Catholic life of faith was opposed to this. The fundamental reality that the Catholic faith affirms is, after all, "This here, this is my body," given to you as *spiritual* nourishment not only for your "soul" but also for your body. The affirmation of Trent in canon 2, that there is a fundamental, radical, and, in this sense, substantial change of the bread, is a purely dogmatic datum of faith, confirmed by the whole tradition of the Church. It was only in an attempt to explain the "remaining of the species" that the theory of substance and accidents arose in the minds of the fathers of the council, with the result that, speaking *traditionally* of the "substance" of bread, they inevitably produced a contrast between substance and accidents. Dogmatically, however, the "change of substance" as an affirmation of reality was contrasted exclusively with "only as in a sign of figure" and "only by efficacity" (canon 1). That was the immediate meaning of substance in the whole of the earlier dogmatic tradition.

Independent of the Aristotelian framework, then, the ultimate question is whether the Catholic view of the eucharistic presence can be

<hr/>

[80] See the critical edition by J. N. Bakhuizen van den Brink, *Rathramnus. De corpore et sanguine Domini,* Amsterdam (1954).

[81] Paschasius Radbertus, *De corpore et sanguine Domini (PL,* 120, 1267–1350); see J. Ernst, *Die Lehre des hl. Paschasius Radbertus von der Eucharistie,* Freiburg i. Br. (1896).

thought of without a *real* and, in this sense, ontological change of bread and wine. Is this implication something that was necessary to thought in the Middle Ages, or is it clear from the affirmation of the whole of patristic thought which was orientated in the same direction and (despite "spiritualizing tendencies" that were constantly arising) the whole of pre-Tridentine theology that it is primarily an inner ontological implication of the dogma of the eucharistic presence and *for this reason* a universally valid necessity—in other words, a dogmatic requisite of faith? The affirmation of the eucharistic presence is so closely bound up with the affirmation of a real change of bread and wine that the affirmation of this change is the concrete content of the dogmatic statement—the real Tridentine dogma as an affirmation of reality.

THE PROBLEM: WHAT IS REALITY?

We have, however, still not settled the hermeneutic problem. It is only now that we are faced with the central question, What is reality? In this problem we should be careful to distinguish reality in a naively realist view of human knowledge from reality in an idealist theory of knowledge and to bear in mind that both these views are different from Merleau-Ponty's extension of idealism to include corporeality, from Sartre's or from De Petter's view of the *en-soi*. Let me give one example to make this clear.

The Calvinist theologian F. J. Leenhardt reacted against Zwingli's purely symbolic view of the presence of Christ in the Eucharist which had a considerable influence on later Reformed thought. Leenhardt wanted to retain the word transubstantiation, but to use it in the light of the Protestant view of reality. Reality, according to Leenhardt, is determined by the creative word of God ("the true reality of things is to be found in what God wants these things to be for the creature"[82]) and consists of a twofold relationship—its relationship to God and its relationship to the creature, man. The true reality of something is thus situated in what God gives to man through these things. The truth or reality of things is therefore not to be found *in* these things themselves, in what we, as men, see and experience of these things: "the substance of a reality is in the divine intention which is realized in it" (*ibid.*). Only faith, then, is able to grasp this substantial reality: "Only faith is capable of knowing what things are in God's will, what their destination is, their raison d'être, and that it is here that the

---

[82] F. J. Leenhardt, *Ceci est mon corps,* Neuchâtel and Paris (1955) 31.

essence of their being, their ultimate substance, is to be found" *(Ibid.).* If Christ himself said in the sovereign freedom of his power, "This is my body," this means that the "substance," the reality with which I am concerned in the Eucharist, is not bread for me—I who understand this reality as a believer—but the true body of the Lord with which I can nourish myself: "faith will acknowledge that this bread . . . no longer has the same substance."[83] From the human point of view, the bread remains inwardly unchanged—it is still ordinary bread. But for the eyes of faith, it is *really* no longer bread, but the body of Christ, given to me to eat. According to this ontology of faith, the bread is no longer ontologically bread, but the truly present body of the Lord. The "bread" is therefore more than simply the "sign of Christ's presence"—"the sign . . . *realizes* this presence."[84] Christ, then, does not give us believers bread to eat, but really himself.

This view of reality is clearly very different from the Catholic view. It is, of course, true that we would not disagree with Leenhardt's primary affirmation, that God himself is the ultimate ground on which all reality is founded, that reality is what it is by divine constitution. But the Catholic view of reality cannot admit the "extrinsicism" of the creative word of God. He claims in addition that through this creative word things are what they are, in an absolute and inward manner.[85]

But does Leenhardt's modern Calvinist view[86] of the real presence imply a difference *in faith* from the Catholic religious view (and experience of the Eucharist) or merely a difference *in ontology,* which is of no further interest to the life of faith? I am of the opinion that, however different philosophy and faith may be, our view of reality cannot possibly be separated completely from our conviction of faith. To make a division of this kind seems to me to be unjustified, because the judgment of faith is by definition a judgment about reality,

[83] *Ibid.,* 33.

[84] *Ibid.,* 36: "Le signe . . . réalise cette présence."

[85] Thomas's affirmation in this connection is still very meaningful: "unumquodque dicitur bonum *divina bonitate*"—"each thing is said to be good with the *divine goodness*" (that is Leenhardt's view), "nihilominus unumquodque dicitur bonum similitudine divinae bonitatis *sibi inhaerente,* quae est formaliter sua bonitas denominans ipsam"—"nonetheless each thing is said to be good in the likeness of the divine goodness *inhering in it,* which is formally its goodness by which it is thus named" (*ST,* I, q. 6, a. 4).

[86] For a historical study of Calvin, see G. P. Hartveldt, *Verum Corpus. Een studie over een central hoofdstuk uit de Avondmaalsleer van Calvijn,* Delft (1960).

and a difference of opinion about what constitutes reality naturally involves a difference in faith—or at least it has an influence on the density of the concrete sense of faith. Some accretions of the Catholic "devotion to the tabernacle" are certainly accretions, but they have nonetheless a specific orientation. They were able to develop in the first place only on the basis of the specifically Catholic view of reality, just as the specifically Zwinglian development of an evacuation from the Eucharist of the real presence of Christ had its origin in the Protestant view of reality. Basically, the Reformation wants to hold onto the reality of a specific presence of Christ in the Eucharist, but it is still hesitant about accepting the realism of Leenhardt or that of the Taizé community.[87] It is, then, possible to some extent to distinguish, in both the Catholic and the Protestant "accretions," the *orientation* of the fundamental views of both and therefore to sense the real danger to which each view is exposed through its basic tenets. In the meantime, both Catholics and Protestants are nowadays reacting against the accretions to their own basic tenets.

There is, then, a decided difference between the Catholic and the Protestant views of reality, and this difference has made itself felt in Christology, in ecclesiology, in Mariology, in the doctrines of grace and the sacraments, and in eschatology, to mention only the most fundamental themes. A. Hulsbosch put his finger on an essential point when he said that Rudolf Bultmann saw reality one-sidedly as a *pure relationship,* that is, as a relationship which took on no form *in* the reality which is man and the creature.[88] For the Catholic, however, this relationship is *filled*—precisely in what the creature is inwardly (I may even say, as a "secular" being), it is a transcendental relationship to God. Thus God's saving activity with regard to man is also primarily and totally a sovereign and free act of conferring grace, but this act is so real that "created grace" in man is, as it were, its other side. The creature does not need to give way to God when he approaches, as water has to give way to a piece of wood that is plunged into it. On the contrary, the creature is completely permeated by God without any withdrawal whatever. God is not a fellow creature who occupies his own space beside me and to whom I have to yield if he wants to occupy my space as well. He is, even when he confers grace, transcendent through interiority.

[87] M. Thurian, *L'Eucharistie,* Neuchâtel and Paris (1959).
[88] "Het verstaan van de Schrift," *Ts. v. Theol.* 5 (1965) 1–27.

It is undeniably true that since the Counter-Reformation Catholic theologians have tended to fix their attention on this naturally *creative* aspect (gratuitously *ex nihilo* and therefore transcendent through interiority) that is present in all conferring of grace, and consequently they have often neglected to consider the most distinctive aspect of grace, the intersubjectivity between God and man (God's address to man and man's response in faith). In the case of the Eucharist too, the fundamental event—Christ's *de facto* giving of himself here and now, his real *presentation* of himself in the Eucharist—has all too frequently been lost sight of and the real *presence* as an "objective datum" has been given one-sided attention in isolation from this event. Once again, then, I should like to emphasize that this one-sided treatment is an accretion; nevertheless in itself it follows from what constitutes the basic, authentically Catholic meaning of the Eucharist—that is, the creative aspect that is present in every act in which God approaches man to confer grace on him. Have modern authors, who rightly emphasize that the Eucharist in Christ's hands is a symbolic act on the part of the man Jesus (the Son of God), given sufficient thought in this connection to the vital conviction of the Fathers of the Church (a conviction that has, unfortunately, lost much of its vitality for us) that the Eucharist was the work of the divine Holy Spirit, the *Spiritus Creator?*

The "ontological aspect" of the Eucharist, God's gift of salvation in Christ and thus his saving activity here and now in a sovereign free act of self-giving, is precisely this "creative aspect." This aspect may be regarded as "created grace," which is implicit in all God's communication of himself in grace, but which has an unexpectedly profound ontological density in this particular gift of himself in the Eucharist, since it takes hold of the secular reality of the bread creatively and is not simply a transcendent "naming from outside" which leaves the *secular* reality as it was before (those who accept this do not, after all, accept any transcendence *in* the interiority itself). And it is precisely *that* aspect which the Council of Trent indicated with the word *conversio* (the change of the bread), thus continuing the whole Christian tradition in a pure form. In the second canon, the council made the datum of faith of this change, which was only implicit in the first canon, explicit. In other words, the presence of an *ontological aspect* in the *sacramental* giving of the bread is without doubt a datum of faith and not simply an aspect of "wording." The *reality* of Christ's gift of himself in the sacramental bread is involved here.

According to the Catholic view of revelation and thus of the whole order of salvation, grace itself comes to us in a historical, visible form, on the horizontal level of human history (and, included in this, on the level of the cosmos or the corporeal world), and not simply vertically, like rain falling from heaven. What comes to us from heaven—grace—in fact comes to us *from the world*, from human history with its secular environment. Our personal relationship with God in grace is at the same time a relationship of fellow-humanity and thus of orientation towards the secular world. In a cosmic piece of bread, grace is conferred on me by Christ in the Eucharist. But Christ's act of giving himself and of conferring grace precisely in and through the consecrated bread has a creative aspect, first and foremost not with regard to me, but *in* the gift of this bread as Christ's *sacramental* giving of himself—in its ultimate reality, this bread is therefore simply no longer bread—and then, through my communion in faith, also in me. The bodily activity of eating is therefore (for the believer, that is) a saving activity. The cosmic reality does not remain outside this process of grace, nor is it involved in it simply by an extrinsic word of God—the consecrated bread itself *is* the grace that is conferred here; that is, Christ himself in a sacrament to be eaten as a sacrificial meal, nourishment for the whole man. The secular world itself is intrinsically involved in Christ's gift of himself in the Eucharist and therefore—and this, in my opinion, brings us to the deepest meaning of the Tridentine dogma of transubstantiation (an analysis of the "meaning for me now" of this dogma will follow in a later chapter)—the secular world already *shares* in the eschatological situation of the glorified corporeality which will be deified entitatively. But we are still in the "already now" and "not yet" that characterizes the period of salvation between the resurrection and the *parousia,* and the consecrated bread and wine therefore still belong, in their new meaning as "new creation" of the order of salvation, to "this old world" also. For this reason, transubstantiation contains two dimensions—a *change of being* of the bread and wine (in which Christ's glorified body is really offered through the Holy Spirit), but *within the terrestrial, but now* (through this change of being) *sacramental form* of bread and wine, which remain subject, in this secular world, to the terrestrial laws of corporeality (in this case, of the vegetable product of cultivation that we eat as bread and drink as wine in our daily lives). Transubstantiation thus has two dimensions of one and the same undivided reality. This is the essential meaning of the dogma.

In asserting, on the witness of the entire Christian tradition (in accordance with "Pneuma-christology"), that an ontological aspect is present in the Eucharist, a change of *being*, we should not forget that we are at the same time dealing here with an ontological aspect of a *sacramental symbolic activity* on the part of Christ and therefore with a profound objective reality of precisely this symbolic activity which is, of its nature, orientated towards the sacramental response of the believer. *A priori*, we ought not to look for realities in the Eucharist outside the sphere itself of sacramentality—to do so would be to leave the standpoint of faith and the Eucharist. This is, after all, our aim—the *sacramental parousia!* In this perspective, the "ontological dimension" or intrinsic reality of the consecrated bread, as Christ's sacramental giving of himself, may indeed be open to an interpretation which is different from that of scholasticism. Scholasticism had, after all, a tendency to look for the ontological aspect "in depth," so to speak, *behind* the phenomena themselves, with the consequence that, in connection with anthropology, for example, the "substance of the soul" was given a greater ontological density than man's psychical activity as a person—as though a meaningful human action did not have a greater ontological depth than a *substantia animae* which had, as it were, sunk to the zero of its freedom and personal activity! It is impossible for a "substantialist" metaphysical view such as this, which had, in later scholasticism, assumed rather more daring proportions than in the earlier scholasticism of the High Middle Ages, to provide an intelligible interpretation of the unsuspected ontological depth in a human meaning given by the man Jesus, the Son of God, glorified in the Holy Spirit. But this is anticipating the following chapter.

The Eucharist is, of its very nature, an event of the period between the resurrection and the parousia, a period during which earthly realities become historical manifestations of the gift of grace here and now and—in the sacramental liturgy, within the mystery of the Church's community of grace led by its office; that is, especially in the Eucharist—are withdrawn from their secular independence, their "being themselves," to the extent of becoming the sacramental form in which the heavenly bodiliness of Christ himself—that is, of his real presence for me—appears. There is in the Eucharist, as distinct from the other sacraments, a specific earthly real presence of the Christ who is nonetheless heavenly and remains heavenly in the sacrament. It is, of course, a *sacramental* earthly presence, due to Christ's real act of making himself present *in* the gift of the holy bread placed at the disposal of all who wish to approach this sacrament in faith. For this reason, the true reality in the Eucharist is no longer bread, but simply the body and blood of Christ in a sacramental form—that is the content of the Tridentine dogma which will be examined theologically in the following chapter in the light of our modern attitude. This modern approach has already been embodied, implicitly and existentially perhaps, in the foregoing analysis of the Tridentine doctrine. Otherwise the dogma would simply have been re-presented mechanically, and the eucharistic presence would have been seen only within its medieval intellectual framework and not in its openness to a modern Catholic interpretation which at the same time remains faithful to the Catholic tradition. Apart from this modern approach we, as believers, should never be able to seize the full implications for us of our Catholic faith. After all, we simply cannot formulate our belief as Christians did in the Middle Ages, or even as the apostles did; yet it is the same faith which we possess and experience—exactly the same faith, but with the dynamic identity of a living faith which is caught up in the movement of history.

This dogma of transubstantiation as Christ's saving action of making himself present to us and of transforming from within the sacrificial gifts of earthly food (gifts which were already universally sacrificial symbols in the natural religions and raised by Israel to the level of symbols of the saving event of the Pasch), thus making of them a new creation, a saving sacrificial gift in time for eternity, must be so formulated now, in a modern theological way, that the new formulation does not contradict the original, inviolable datum of faith or minimize it.

Louis Bouyer

6. Cranmer and the Anglican Eucharist[*]

A very different example of a Protestant liturgy susceptible of a Catholic interpretation was offered in the middle of the sixteenth century by the first Anglican eucharistic liturgy. But in this instance, the intention was not to reintroduce a Catholic sense into Lutheran formulas, but rather the possible introduction of a Zwinglian sense into the Catholic formulas (something which, as we have seen, Zwingli had already tried in his first and completely provisional liturgy). We mean naturally the text composed by Cranmer and published in 1549 in his first *Prayer Book.*

This book itself proceeds from a still-born liturgy: the one that had been patronized by the archbishop of Cologne, Hermann von Wied, and which was composed by Bucer in collaboration with Melanchthon. It reflected something from most of the Lutheran *ordines* that were already published, especially the two divergent *ordines* of Brandenburg, while making an effort, like the Swedish liturgies, to come closer also to the ancient liturgies. The energetic opposition of the chapter, upheld by the university, prevented this composition, published in 1543, from ever having any local use. Charles V forbade its use and Hermann, excommunicated by Paul III in 1546, died deprived of his see in 1552. Although it was never used at Cologne, the book to which he gave his name did have some success among the Lutherans of Hesse and the Saar and a few places in Alsace.[1]

For his liturgy of the English Mass, Cranmer took from it only the formula of general confession of sins at the beginning and the biblical verses (the "comfortable words") which accompanied the absolution that followed. But he took no inspiration from its eucharistic preface

[*] L. Bouyer, *Eucharist*, trans. Charles Underhill Quinn (Notre Dame, Indiana: University of Notre Dame Press, 1968) 407–419.

[1] Cf. Luther D. Reed, *The Lutheran Liturgy*, 2nd ed. (Philadelphia, 1960) 102 ff.; Y. Brilioth, *Eucharistic Faith and Practice, Evangelical and Catholic* (London, 1930) 202. It will be noted that an English translation of the Cologne *Ordo* appeared in 1548. See the introduction of *The First and Second Prayer Books of Edward VI*, in the *Everyman's Library* edition (new ed., London, 1952) with a bibliographical and historical note by E. C. Ratcliff, viii.

in which there seemed to have been a combination of Gallican and Eastern influences and which was followed by the institution narrative immediately after the Sanctus. Actually, if Cranmer's personal literary taste caused him to retain as many as possible of the traditional formulas to which Henry VIII remained strongly attached (just as he was to the Catholic doctrines on the sacraments), he was not and never had been more Lutheran than his master. Nonetheless, he had abandoned the medieval doctrines on the Eucharist, although he took great care not to let Henry see this, and immediately adopted a radical Zwinglianism. He was to try, with the same prudence shown by Zwingli in Zurich, first to insinuate it beneath a phraseology which was still Catholic in appearance at the end of Henry's reign, and then with the Protestantism of the government of Edward VI to express it plainly.

Dom Gregory Dix has established irrefutably that the interpretation long given by catholicizing Anglicans of the difference between his Eucharist of 1549 and the one he produced in 1552 is untenable. Far from being still Catholic or, at the most, "Lutheranized," the first Eucharist is only Catholic in appearance and simply disguises under a veil of ambiguities the same doctrine which is so frankly stated in the second, a doctrine which is not only "reformed" but properly Zwinglian. But, like Zwingli's first liturgy and still more skillfully, Cranmer's first liturgy retains all that could be kept of the ancient formulas in making them susceptible of a completely different understanding. The same prudence guided him, not only for the sake of the king, but because of the sentiments of the mass of the people and a great part of the English clergy, which had remained basically Catholic. We must just add that his refined humanism caused him to bring to his task the taste of an antiquarian and an artist, without which the astounding and lasting success of this ambiguous composition would be incomprehensible.[2]

Here is this text, which is basic for the whole history of the Anglican liturgy:

"It is very mete, righte, and our bounden dutie that wee shoulde at all tymes and in all places, geue thanks to thee, O Lorde, holy father, almightie euerlastyng God . . .

---

[2] See Gregory Dix, *The Shape of the Liturgy,* 648 ff. and Stella Broom, *The Languages of the Book of Common Prayer* (London, 1965).

"Therefore with Angels and Archangels, and with all the holy companye of heauen: we laude and magnify thy glorious name, euermore praisyng thee, and saying: Holy, holy, holy, Lorde God of Hostes; heauen & earth are full of thy glory: Osanna in the highest. Blessed is he that commeth in the name of the Lorde: Glory to thee O lorde in the highest.

"Almightie and euerliuying God, whiche by thy holy Apostle haste taught us to make prayers and supplicacions, and to geue thankes for al menne: We humbly beseche thee moste mercifully to receiue these our praiers, which we offre unto thy diuine Maiestie, beseeching thee to inspire continually the uniuersal churche, with the spirite of trueth, unitie and concorde: And graunt that al they that do confesse thy holy name, maye agree in the trueth of thy holye worde, and liue in unitie and godly loue. Speciallye we beseche thee to saue and defende thy seruaunt, Edwarde our Kyng, that under hym we maye be Godly and quietly gouerend. And graunt unto his whole consaile, and to all that be put in aucthoritie under hym, that they maye truely and indifferently minister iustice, to the punishemente of wickednesse and vice, and to the maintenaunce of Goddes true religion and vertue. Geue grace (O heauenly father) to all Bishoppes, Pastors, and Curates, that thei maie bothe by their life and doctrine, set furthe thy true and liuely worde, and rightely and duely administer thy holy Sacramentes. And to al thy people geue thy heauenly grace, that with meke heart and due reuerence, they may heare and receiue thy holy worde, truly seruying thee in holiness and righteousnes, all the dayes of their life: And we most humbly beseche thee of thy goodness (O Lorde) to coumfort and succour all them, whyche in thys transystory life be in trouble, sorowe, nede, syckenes, or any other aduersitie. And especially we commend unto thy mercifull goodnes, this congregacion which is here assembled in thy name, to celebrate the commemoracion of the most glorious death of thy sonne; And here we do geue unto thee moste high praise, and hartie thankes for the wonderfull grace and vertue declared in all thy sainctes, from the beginning of the worlde: And chiefly in the glorious and most blessed virgin Mary, mother of thy sonne Jesu Christe our Lorde and God, and in the holy Patriarches, Prophetes, Apostles and Martyrs, whose examples (O Lorde) and stedfastnes in thy fayth, and kepying thy holy commaundementes: graunt us to folowe. We commend unto thy mercye (O Lorde) all other thy seruauntes, which are departed hence from us, with the signe of faith, and nowe do reste in the slepe of peace: Grant unto them, we beseche thee, thy mercy, and euerlasting peace, and that at the day of the generall resurreccion, we and all they which bee of the misticall body of thy sonne, may altogether be set on his right hand, and heare that his most ioyfull voice: Come unto me, O ye that be blessed of my father, and possesse the kingdom, whiche is prepared for you, from the begynning of the worlde: Graunt this, O father, for Jesus Christes sake, our onely mediatour and aduocate.

"O God heauenly father, which of thy tender mercie, diddest geue thine only sonne Jesu Christ, to suffre death upon the crosse for our redempcion, who made there (by his one oblacion once offered) a full, perfect, and sufficient sacrifyce, oblacion, and satysfacyon, for the sinnes of the whole worlde, and did institute, and in his holy Gospell commaund us, to celebrate a perpetuall memory, of that his precious death, untyll his comming again: Heare us (o merciful father) we besech thee: and with thy holy spirite & worde, vouchsafe to blesse and sanctifie these thy gyftes, and creatures of bread and wyne, that they maie be unto us the bodye and bloude of thy moste derely beloued sonne Jesus Christe. Who in the same nyght that he was betrayed: tooke breade, and when he had blessed, and geuen thanks: he brake it, and gaue it to his disciples, saiying: "Take, eate, this is my bodye, which is geuen for you, do this in remembraunce of me. Likewyse, after supper toke the cuppe, and when he had geuen thankes, he gaue it to them, saying: drynk ye all of this, for this is my bloude of the newe Testament, whyche is shed for you and for many, for remission of synnes: do this as oft as you shall drinke it in remembraunce of me."

At this point, a rubric prescribes that the priest, as he takes the bread and then the cup into his hands, remain turned towards the altar, without any elevation or showing of the sacrament to the people. The prayer continues:

"Wherefore, O Lorde and heauenly father, accordyng to the Instytucyon of thy derely beloued sonne, our sauiour Jesus Christ, we thy humble seruauntes do celebrate, and make here before thy diuine Maiestie, with these thy holy giftes, the memoryall whyche thy sonne hath wylled us to make, hauing in remembraunce his blessed passion, mightie resurreceyon, and gloryous ascension, renderying unto

120

thee most hartie thankes, for the innumerable benefites procured unto us by thesame, entierely desiryng thy fatherly goodnes, mercifully to accepte this our Sacrifice of praise and thankes geuing: most humbly beseeching thee to graunt, that by the merites an death of thy sonne Jesus Christ, and through faith in his bloud, we and al thy whole church, may obteigne remission of our sinnes, and all other benefites of hys passyon. And here wee offre and present unto the (O Lorde) oure selfe, oure soules, and bodies, to be a reasonable, holy, and liuely sacrifice unto thee: humbly besechyng thee, that whosoeuer shalbee partakers of thys holy Communion, maye worthely receiue the moste precious body and bloude of thy sonne Jesu Christe; and bee fulfilled with thy grace and heauenly benediccion, and made one bodye with thy sonne Jesu Christe, that he maye dwell in them, and they in hym. And although we be unworthy (through our manyfolde synnes) to offer unto thee any Sacrifice: Yet we beseche thee to accepte thys our bounden duetie and seruice, and commaunde those our prayers and supplicacions, by the Ministery of thy holy Angels, to be brought up into thy holy Tabernacle before the syght of thy dyuine maiestie: not waiyng our merites, but pardonyng our offences, through Christe our Lorde, by whome, and with whome, in the unitie of the holy Ghost: all honour and glory, be unto thee, O father almightie, world without ende. Amen."[3]

This English Eucharist seems to have been very badly received by the laity, who as a whole were in no way anxious to abandon the Latin liturgy with which they had always been familiar. But it is incontestable that the mass of the clergy which had come in contact with humanism, even though it was still so attached to Catholic doctrines, saw no objection to using these Anglicized formulas rather than the canon of the Roman Mass. Somewhat later Bishop Gardiner relied on two passages from this text to uphold against Cranmer himself the permanent legitimacy within the Anglican Church of the teaching which had always been that of the Catholic Church. In the first place, he cited these words from Cranmer's canon, immediately before the institution narrative: "Hear us, O merciful Father, we

[3] Bard Thompson, *Liturgies of the Western Church* (Cleveland and New York, 1961) 255 ff. From the *Everyman's Library* edition mentioned above (221 ff.), it will be noted that Cranmer retained the proper prefaces of Christmas, Easter, Ascension Day, Whitsunday, and Trinity, but in a paraphrased text (which is at times reduced as in the case of Trinity, and at times expanded as for Whitsunday).

beseech thee: and with thy Holy Spirit and word, vouchsafe to bless and *sanctify* these thy gifts, and creatures of bread and wine, that *they may be unto us the body and blood* of thy most dearly beloved Son Jesus Christ." With these he connected the words that followed in the same narrative: "most humbly beseeching thee, that *whosoever shall be partakers of this holy Communion, may worthily receive the most precious body and blood of thy Son. . . ."* To which he again added this formula from the preparatory prayer for communion: "Grant us therefore . . . so to eat the flesh of thy dear Son Jesus Christ, and to drink his blood *in these holy mysteries,* that we may evermore dwell in him. . . ." But Cranmer replied drily that to interpret these texts as the Bishop of Winchester did was "a plain untruth."

Indeed, we must pay close attention to the sense that Cranmer, in Zwingli's wake, gives constantly to the evangelical formulas concerning the eating of Christ's body (or flesh) and his blood becoming our drink. His *Defence* repeats tirelessly that the only possible sense of these expressions is "to believe in our hearts, that His Flesh was rent and torn for us upon the cross and His Blood shed for our redemption." As he says again, this eating is in no way specific to the Eucharist; we eat and drink Christ and feed on him as long as we are members of his body (obviously the mystical body), with the result that he may be eaten and drunk in the Old Testament just as well as today. Under these conditions the Supper was instituted "that every man eating and drinking thereof should remember that Christ died for him, and so should exercize his faith, and comfort himself by the remembrance of Christ's benefits." Not only does he expressly reject every idea of a sanctification of the elements other than the material fact of their being set aside for the celebration, but even Calvin's idea of a spiritual but real eating of the body and blood of Christ present in heaven is quite foreign to him. For him, "to eat the flesh and drink the blood" is only a metaphor for believing (in the presence of the bread and wine, but without this presence as well) in the benefits of the cross which the word of the Gospel alone allows us to know. One could not be clearer than he on this point.

The same is true, for stronger reasons, in regard to the sacrificial expressions that he may use in his eucharistic prayer. The "sacrifice of praise and thanksgiving" (still according to this *Defence*) is set off against the propitiatory sacrifice whereby Christ has reconciled us with God. It is "another kind of sacrifice . . . which doth not reconcile us to God, but is made of them that be reconciled by Christ, to testify our duties unto God, and to shew ourselves thankful unto Him; and therefore they be called sacrifices of laud, praise and thanksgiving. The first kind of sacrifice Christ offered to God for us; the second kind we ourselves offer to God by Christ. And by the first kind of sacrifice Christ offered us also unto His Father; and by the second we offer ourselves and all that we have, unto Him and His Father. *And this sacrifice generally is our whole obedience unto God, in keeping His laws and commandments."*

Not only, then, is the propitiatory sacrifice offered by Christ alone and our sacrifice of pure gratitude and obedience completely distinct, but we cannot say that Cranmer even left the way open for some sort of presence of the Savior's sacrifice in the Eucharist, so that it might become the source of our obedient act of thanksgiving. For him, there is no presence in the Eucharist of any sacrifice other than this latter. "In this eating, drinking and using of the Lord's supper, we make not of Christ a new sacrifice propitiatory for remission of sin. But, the humble confession of all penitent hearts, their 'knowledging' of Christ's benefits, their thanksgiving for the same, their faith and consolation in Christ, their humble submission and obedience to God's will and commandments, is a sacrifice of laud and praise, accepted and allowed of God no less than the sacrifice of the priest." In other words, according to him, there is no other sacrifice (and his liturgy does not speak differently) than the faithful's feelings of gratitude and their disposition to obey God in all things.[4]

Evidently, the fact that no other alternative than either a recommencement of the cross or a purely subjective "sacrifice" occurred to him and to so many other Protestants, shows the extent that the notion of sacrificial and sacramental memorial had decomposed in the religious mentality of the end of the Middle Ages. But in these circumstances what happens to this "sacrifice" whose sole presence they are still willing to acknowledge in the Eucharist? Cut off in this way from any actual relationship to Christ's sacrifice, on the basis of a sacramental presence, this sacrifice of our praise, our gratitude, and our obedience becomes, as Eric Mascall points out, a completely

---

[4] On all of this, see Gregory Dix, *op. cit.,* 648–58, which we have merely summarized. The more recent work of A. Kavanagh, *The Concept of Eucharistic Memorial in the Canon revised by Thomas Cranmer, Archbishop of Canterbury* (St. Meinrad, Ind., 1949) shows the purely subjective character of the "Memorial" in Cranmer's understanding.

Pelagian sacrifice: man does offer it after Christ and as a response to his sacrifice, but it is no longer solely by virtue of his own.

Once we have understood this transposition of all the traditional notions, we can admire the skill (which is much more refined than that of Zwingli himself in his first Eucharist) with which Cranmer in his liturgy succeeded in retaining even in its details the schema of the ancient Roman Eucharist. In adapting it not only to his ideas but to the language and rhetoric of his age, he produced a work which, literarily, is not without analogy with the remodeling of the ancient Eucharists that we have seen come about in fourth-century Syria. In this reworking, however, he was not as daring as men were then. He limited himself to regrouping into one series the different intercessions and commemorations which seemed to be scattered throughout the Roman canon. Instead of bringing them together as a conclusion, he assembled them as a block in the first section, arranging them around the *Te igitur,* the *Memento of the living,* and then the *Communicantes* and the *Hanc igitur.* But he allowed to remain in their original places what we have called the pre-epiclesis of the *Te igitur,* the consecratory epiclesis of the *Quam oblationem,* immediately preceding the institution narrative, and the second epiclesis, arising from the anamnesis in the *Supra quae* and the *Supplices,* and beseeching that the Eucharist have its full effect in those who celebrate it.

If we pay close attention to the interpretations given by Cranmer himself to the formulas he uses, all of these prayers and the anamnesis itself seem to be deprived of their original content. But, since they retain practically all of the ancient expressions, with the minimum of retouching that was necessary in order to be able to bend them to the devitalized sense in which he understood them, a person who is without the key to his perpetually metaphorical language can be easily taken in. One might think that one were simply rereading the old canon in a more obviously coherent order and in a casing of devout humanist rhetoric. It is true that those terms that were hardest to allegorize in this way, like oblation and sacrifice, surreptitiously disappeared from those places where they could only have one meaning which he no longer was willing to give them. But they are found elsewhere, where they are used either of the cross of Christ alone or of the Christians' offering of themselves, and one must be very alert to observe that the eucharistic celebration is never expressly envisioned as an objective connection between the two. If one were vaguely suspicious about the sleight-of-hand that had taken place, the fact that all the secondary details of the old prayers have remained in their original places, from the initial call to God's fatherly clemency to the references to the heavenly altar and the angel of the sacrifice, concluding with the opposition between the inadequacy of our own merits and the limitless generosity of divine grace, would be enough to reassure us of the author's good intentions. If a formula that is too unequivocal happens to be paraphrased, this is always done under the cover of a biblical allusion chosen with such infallible dexterity, and the whole is expressed in such a melodious and consistently unctuous literary setting that even after the very pointed declarations of the *Defence,* it is hard to be persuaded that so much skill and so much devotion is in the long run merely the skill of speaking piously in order to say nothing.

It is more easily and readily forgotten that Cranmer, when he is not concerned with emptying the properly sacrificial or sacramental formulas of their content, shows himself to be a liturgist of equal stature with the greatest of antiquity. The most felicitous characteristic of his skill is the delicacy with which from the beginning to the end of the prayer he was able to keep the basic act of thanksgiving constantly uppermost with a word or an expression. He does this so well that it is everywhere present and runs through this lengthy prayer like a golden thread binding it together. The same must be said for the theme of the Church and her unity: from one end of the Eucharist to the other, beginning with the first part of the intercessions as their connecting link, it is constantly recalled through a succession of impeccable strokes of the bow before it finally emerges in a magnificent crescendo. The recall of the "grace and heavenly benediction" of the Roman canon is specified here in the unforgettable final invocation, that we become one body with Christ and that he abide in us and we in him.

Particularly successful also is the "retractatio" of the *Quam oblationem* through which Cranmer introduces the combined mention of the Spirit and the Word to "bless and sanctify" the eucharistic elements. Was his wish, through this addition, to reconcile the tenor of this prayer which remains typically Roman not only with the Syrian epiclesis but with the old Alexandrian epicleses like Serapion's? It seems that he was not sufficiently familiar with the Eastern liturgies to have such a synthesis in mind, and therefore that it was merely the result of his instinctive good taste.

Dom Gregory Dix is probably right in supposing that at this point he was only inserting an explanation of the eucharistic consecration that had come from Paschasius Radbertus,[5] but which the whole of the Middle Ages had reproduced attributing it to St. Augustine. This eucharistic liturgy of Cranmer's is an incontestable masterpiece. The rhythmical perfection of his language and style succeeded in making it so attractive that those who made use of it in good faith as a fully Catholic liturgy always found their disillusionment with it most painful. But, once one has become advised of the perpetual ambiguities that allow it to clothe the most rigid denial of their whole content in the most traditional expressions, we have to admit that it is an equivocal masterpiece. It is only right to acknowledge that Cranmer had too uneasy a conscience about his work to want it to be perpetuated. Hardly three years had gone by before the progress of Protestant ideas in England permitted him to speak openly, at least in the upper classes.

Instead of his Eucharist of 1552, that of the second *Prayer Book*, being merely an unhappy decomposition of a first and still Catholic liturgy, succumbing to the pressure of the continental reformers (as conservative Anglicans have long tried to persuade themselves), it is a fully thought-out work in which he was finally able to say openly what he had been merely able to insinuate in the preceding book. If he did take many elements from his first text, this proves but one thing: the extent to which that text had already been impregnated with ideas that had long been his. It sufficed to get rid of the artificially imposed framework of the Roman canon for the paraphrase that he had made of it to be reorganized in accordance with his own logic and to allow its real meaning to become finally uncovered.

In the 1552 liturgy all the intercessions and also the mentions of sacrifice that were still connected with the anamnesis were removed from the eucharistic prayer, which was quite natural since any propitiatory or impetratory character was denied it. The intercessions simply took the place of the old *oratio fidelium* after the sermon. Meanwhile, the mentions of the "sacrifice," returned to their proper place, reveal its true nature: they figure now only in the prayer of "thanksgiving" (in the non-liturgical sense of the term), that follows the communion. Cranmer himself was so aware that his "sacrifice of thanksgiving," in the sense that he understood the term, had no necessary connection with the communion, that he retained these formulas only in an *ad libitum* prayer. The postcommunion of 1549 (which

[5] *De corpore et sanguine Domini*, 12; PL, 120, col. 1310 C.

made no mention of sacrifice) could be substituted for it at will. He further modified it also so that it no longer read: "we give thee thanks . . . that thou has nourished us in these holy mysteries with the body and the blood of our Saviour . . ." but only: "we give thee thanks that thou consentest to nourish us, who have received these holy mysteries, with the body and blood of our Saviour. . . ." In other words, it is no longer in the communion that we are nourished with Christ's body and blood (in the very special sense in which he understands this expression), but only in the remembrance of his passion, reawakened at the very most through the celebration of the Supper.

On the other hand, in this reworking, not only was everything that remained of the ancient epicleses removed, but also the anamnesis as in the Lutheran liturgies. Consequently, with the exception of an apology inserted after the eucharistic preface and the Sanctus, all we have is the institution narrative. Merely a few connective words were kept to introduce it. But, detached as they are from their former context, it is now clear that the purpose of these words is not only to exclude any notion of the sacramental presence of the sacrifice which the Lutherans were the first to reject, but to exclude as well the idea of the real presence of the body and blood of Christ that they still retained:

"Almighty God oure heauenly father, whiche of thy tender mercye dyddest geue thine onely sonne Jesus Christ, to suffre death upon the crosse for our redempcion, who made there (by hys one oblacion *of hymselfe* once offered) a full, perfecte and sufficiente sacrifice, oblacion, and satysfaccioin for the synnes of the whole world: and dyd institute, and in hys holye Gospell commaunde us, to continue a perpetuall memorye of that his precious death, untyll hys comynge again. Heare us O mercyfull father wee beeseche thee: *and graunte that wee receyuing these they creatures of bread and wyne, accordynge to thy sonne our Sauioure Jesu Christes holy institucion, in remembraunce of his death and passion,* may be partakers of his most blessed body & bloud: who in the same night that he was betrayed, etc. . . ."[6]

It is enough to compare this text with the preceding one, and particularly the italicized passages which were modified, in order to convince ourselves about the intention which governed both these changes and the keeping of the introductory formula in its polished state: its purpose was to exclude the very idea of any sort of a real

[6] Bard Thompson, *op. cit.,* 280.

presence of the body and blood of Christ in the sacrament along with any idea of a sacramental presence of the sacrifice.[7]

After the various re-establishments of Anglicanism, first after the Catholic interlude of Mary Tudor under Elizabeth and then after Cromwell, no one dared to return to the 1549 text. It was only the expurgated prayer of 1552 that was retained, but in 1662 it was given the name "Prayer of Consecration." For his part, Cranmer was careful not to give it this title, since he knew better than anyone that it was unsuitable if one understood it in its obvious sense. Did not he himself say that there could be no other consecration of the bread and wine in the Eucharist than the separation that sets them aside at the offertory for liturgical use, and that this involved no other change?

[7] Cf. Gregory Dix, *op. cit.*, 650.

Dominic E. Serra

7. The Roman Canon: The Theological Significance of Its Structure and Syntax[*]

Eucharistic prayers are commonly divided into five distinct families. The determining characteristics of each family include the order of appearance of the various constitutive elements and their relationships one to another. Thus the prayers of each family bear a distinctive structure and syntax. It is now well accepted practice to note the placement of the dominical words within the thanksgiving for redemption or alternatively within the supplication as one of the distinguishing features on which the classification of anaphoras is based. The concern of this study will be not the *fact* of the placement of the words within one or other of these elements but the *consequences* of such placement for the understanding of how the words function within the anaphora known as the Roman Canon. How they function within the prayer is determined in large measure by the syntactical relationship of the narrative to the rest of the prayer. Our purpose is to determine what the grammar and syntax of the Roman Canon can tell us about the theological function of the supper narrative within this ancient text.

The manuscript of the *Gelasian Sacramentary* provides us with a text of the Roman Canon which is virtually identical to the prayer currently used by Christians of the Roman Rite, among whom it is generally known as "Eucharistic Prayer I."[1] The Gelasian manuscript of

[*] Originally published in *Ecclesia Orans* [Rome] 20 (2003) 99–128.
[1] *Liber sacramentorum romanae aeclesiae ordinis anni circuli (Sacramentarium gelasianum)*, ed., Leo C. Mohlberg, Rerum ecclesiasticarum documenta, Series Maior, Fontes 4 (Rome: Herder, 1981) 183–86, nos. 1242–55. Cf. *Missale Romanum ex decreto sacrosancti oecuminici concilii Vaticani II instauratum auctoritate Pauli PP. VI promulgatum* (Vatican City: Typis Polyglottis Vaticanis, 1975) 447–55. In addition to some very minor variations, the Gelasian text does not include the prayer for the dead found in many other ancient sources and in the text used today. In fact, the *Memento etiam* is not to be found in several of the Gelasians of the eighth century and in some of the best manuscripts of the *Gregorian Sacramentary*, including the *Cambrai 164*, the *Vaticanus Reginensis 337*, and the *Trento: Castel del Buonconsiglio*,

the mid-eighth century reflects the authentic Roman practice of the early seventh century.[2] However, it is not our earliest evidence of the canon's existence. Ambrose of Milan, in one of his mystagogical sermons, quotes the Eucharistic Prayer of his church, which bears a great similarity to the central portion of our text.[3] Some twenty years earlier, between 370 and 374, the anonymous author commonly called Ambrosiaster comments on a portion of a text which scholars believe to be the Roman Canon.[4] Gordon Jeanes has recently suggested that Zeno of Verona, whose sermons he assigns to the 360s, also gives evidence of knowing the Roman Canon as the prayer of his church.[5] Thus, it is quite probable that at least the main portion of the Roman Canon was composed during the pontificate of Damasus (366–384) just as the city of Rome was adopting Latin as its liturgical language.[6]

1590. See Leo Eizenhöfer, *Canon missae romanae, I: Traditio textus* (Rome: Orbis Catholicus, 1954) 38–39; Jean Deshusses, ed., *Le sacramentaire Grégorien,* vol. 1, Spicilegium Friburgense 16 (Louvain: Éditions Universitaires Fribourg Suisse, 1979) 90. Since the commemoration of the dead seems originally to have been included in the canon only on weekdays when particular deceased persons were prayed for, its absence from some documents need not suggest its being a late addition. On this matter see Michel Andrieu, "L'Ordo VII et le canon de la messe romaine: la question du *memento* des morts," *Les Ordines Romani du haut moyen-âge,* vol. 2 (Louvain, 1948) 269–81; Antoine Chavasse, *Le Sacramentaire Gélasien* (Tournai: Desclée, 1958) 496–97; and G. Di Napoli, "Il lento processo di formazione del Canone Romano," *Ecclesia Orans* 17 (2000) 229–68.

[2] Cyrille Vogel, *Medieval Liturgy: An Introduction to the Sources,* revised and trans. by William G. Storey and Neils Krogh Rasmussen (Washington, D.C.: Pastoral Press, 1986) 67–69.

[3] *De sacramentis,* 4, 21–27. See B. Botte, ed., *Ambrose de Milan. Des sacrements. Des mystères. Explication du symbole,* Sources Chrétiennes 25bis (Paris: Cerf, 1961) 114–16; Leo Eizenhöfer, *Canon missae romanae, II: Textus propinqui.* Rerum ecclesiasticarum documenta, Subsidia studiorum 7 (Rome: Herder, 1966) 12–13. A comparison of Ambrose's text to that of the Roman Canon may be found in Enrico Mazza, *The Origins of the Eucharistic Prayer,* trans. Ronald E. Lane (Collegeville: The Liturgical Press, 1995) 246–52.

[4] Mario Righetti, *Manuale di storia liturgica,* vol. 3, *La messa, commento storico-liturgico alla luce del Concilio Vaticano II* (Milan: Editrice Ancora, 1966) 459 and Enrico Mazza, *The Eucharistic Prayers of the Roman Rite,* trans. Matthew J. O'Connell (Collegeville: The Liturgical Press, 1986) 57–58.

[5] Gordon P. Jeanes, *The Day Has Come!: Easter and Baptism in Zeno of Verona,* Alcuin Club Collection (Collegeville: The Liturgical Press, 1995) 7–17 and 191–96.

[6] Mazza, *Eucharistic Prayers,* 57; Allan Bouley, *From Freedom to Formula: The Evolution of the Eucharistic Prayer from Oral Improvisation to Written Texts* (Washington, D.C.: Catholic University Press, 1981) 206–13; Righetti, *Manuale,* 3:459–60.

With the addition of the Sanctus early in the fifth century,[7] of the *Communicantes* and *Hanc igitur* later in the same century,[8] and with the inclusion of some phrases attributed to Popes Leo and Gregory,[9] the Canon achieved its present form by the dawn of the seventh century. Having its origin in the mid-fourth century, its full development complete by the start of the seventh, and its solid and constant manuscript tradition in place by the eighth century, the Roman Canon is indeed a venerable text. The extant manuscripts of the Celtic and Gallican liturgical books, the *Stowe Missal,* the *Bobbio Missal,* and the *Missale Francorum* reveal that by the time of their composition in the seventh and eighth centuries, the Canon was well on its way to replacing all other Eucharistic Prayers previously used by those Western non-Roman churches.[10]

The Canon is ancient, existing in one form or another since the time of Damasus, and its use is exclusive; no Eucharistic Prayer but the canon would be used in the Roman Rite until the composition of three new prayers in 1968.[11] Some sixteen centuries of uninterrupted and exclusive use by Roman Rite Christians make the Canon one of the most time-honored of current liturgical texts.[12]

[7] Pierre-Marie Gy, "Le sanctus romain et les anaphores orientales," *Mélanges liturgiques offerts au R. P. Dom Bernard Botte, O.S.B.* (Louvain: Abbaye du Mont César, 1972) 167–74; Bryan D. Spinks, *The Sanctus in the Eucharistic Prayer* (Cambridge: Cambridge University Press, 1991) 93–98.

[8] B. Capelle, "Problèmes du *Communicantes* de la messe," *Rivista Liturgica* 40 (1953) 187–95; L. Eizenhöfer, "*Te igitur* und *Communicantes* im römischen Messkanon," *Sacris Erudiri* 8 (1956) 14–75; Righetti, *Manuale,* 3:375–85; Mazza, *Eucharistic Prayers,* 65–68.

[9] Leo the Great is credited with adding the words, "*sanctum sacrificium, immaculatam hostiam*" to the *Supra quae,* and Gregory the Great expanded the *Hanc igitur* to include the phrase, "*diesque nostros in tua pace disponas . . .*" thus allowing it to stand on its own as a permanent part of the canon even in the absence of a special intention. See Mazza, *Eucharistic Prayers,* 58, 66–68, and 80.

[10] Jordi Pinell, "Libri liturgici gallicani," *Anàmnesis,* vol. 2 *La liturgia panorama storico generale,* eds. Salvatore Marsili and others (Casale Monferrato: Marietti, 1978) 185–87.

[11] Concerning the singularity of the Roman Canon see Bouley, *From Freedom,* 213–15. On the promulgation of three new Eucharistic Prayers see Sacred Congregation of Rites, *Prece eucharistica,* 23 May 1968, *Notitiae* 4 (1968) 156–60.

[12] Some of the important studies of the Roman Canon consulted are the following: Joseph A. Jungmann, *The Mass of the Roman Rite: Its Origins and Development (Missarum Sollemnia),* trans. Francis A. Brunner (New York: Benziger Brothers, 1951–1955) 1:49–60, 2:101–274; Righetti, *Manuale,* 3:342–475; Cipriano Vagaggini,

THE CLASSIFICATION OF EUCHARISTIC PRAYERS: STRUCTURE AND THEOLOGY

Eucharistic Prayers are divided by scholars into five families. The prayers of each family bear a distinctive structure and syntax determined by the order of appearance and interrelationship of such elements as the thanksgiving, the epiclesis, the anamnesis, the offering, the supper narrative, and the intercessions.[13] Two families will concern us in this study, the West Syrian and the Roman.

The West Syrian Family, also known as the Antiochene Family to which belong the Byzantine anaphoras of St. John Chrysostom and St. Basil, begins with an introductory dialogue, continues with an expression of praise and thanksgiving in which God's acts of creation and redemption are rehearsed, the Sanctus is sung, and the thanksgiving is continued emphasizing the saving deeds in Christ. This final christological thanksgiving culminates in a recital of the Lord's words at the Last Supper and the remembrance of the paschal mystery commanded by those words. Only then is the prayer of offering taken up and an invocation made for the descent of the Holy Spirit for the transformation of the elements into the body and blood of Christ for the sake of those who will receive them as the fruits of the sacrifice. This movement toward supplication in the pneumatic epiclesis generates a series of petitions for the needs of the Church, the hierarchy, the living, and for the dead. The prayer ends with a doxology and the people's Amen.[14]

The supper narrative appears within the anamnetic thanksgiving of all anaphoras belonging to the Antiochene Family. The Lord's promise concerning the bread and cup declared in the dominical words makes it possible for the Church to seek the descent of the Holy Spirit for the transformation and fruitfulness of the gifts. The movement from anamnetic thanksgiving to epicletic supplication is negotiated by the action of sacrificial offering. The Holy Spirit's presence is invoked upon the gifts or offerings thus rendering them truly pleasing to God and capable of bringing salvation to all who receive them

---

The Canon of the Mass and Liturgical Reform, trans. Peter Coughlan (Staten Island, N.Y.: Alba House, 1967); Ralph A. Keifer, "The Unity of the Roman Canon: An Examination of its Unique Structure," *Studia Liturgica* 11 (1976) 39–58; Mazza, *Eucharistic Prayers*, 49–87; Mazza, *The Origins*, 240–86.

[13] Anton Hänggi and Irmgard Pahl, eds. *Prex eucharistica* (Fribourg Suisse, 1968) 101, 204, 375, 423, 461.

[14] *Ibid.*, 204–5.

properly. This structure is evident in the following quotation from the Eucharistic Prayer of St. John Chrysostom. Immediately following the supper narrative, which concludes the christological thanksgiving, the text turns to supplication by way of the anamnesis/offering:

"We, therefore, remembering this saving commandment and all the things that were done for us: the cross, the tomb, the resurrection on the third day, the ascension into heaven, the session at the right hand, the second and glorious coming again; (aloud) offering you your own from your own, in all and for all . . . . We offer you also this reasonable and bloodless service, and we pray and beseech and entreat you, send down your Holy Spirit on us and on these gifts set forth; and make this bread the precious body of your Christ, [changing it by your Holy Spirit,] Amen; and that which is in this cup the precious blood of your Christ, changing it by your Holy Spirit, Amen; so that they may become to those who partake for vigilance of soul, for fellowship with the Holy Spirit, for the fullness of the kingdom of heaven, for boldness toward you, not for judgement or condemnation."[15]

When we turn our attention to the Roman Canon, the sole example of a Eucharistic Prayer of the Roman Family, [16] a very different structure presents itself. Here the narrative appears within the supplicatory section of the prayer. It is not part of the anamnetic thanksgiving for the deeds of redemption in Christ but instead follows the thanksgiving. The prayer as we know it today has a very brief thanksgiving, all of which precedes the Sanctus. The Roman Canon moves abruptly from the song of the angels to supplication. Most of its supplication focuses on the repeated petition that God recognize the offering to be acceptable for the good of those who will partake of it and those for whom it is offered. This is a matter to which we shall return. For now it suffices to note, that while the Antiochene anaphoras place the supper narrative at the culmination of the anamnetic thanksgiving, the dominical words in the Roman Canon are found in the context of the supplication that follows the thanksgiving. Anyone

---

[15] *Ibid.*, 226. The English translation is from R. C. D. Jasper and G. J. Cuming, trans. and eds., *Prayers of the Eucharist: Early and Reformed* (New York: Pueblo, 1987) 133. The omission represented by the ellipsis is the congregation's acclamation and a rubric.

[16] The post-Vatican II additions to the Eucharistic Prayer repertoire of the Roman Rite represent hybrid texts and are not purely Roman in structure.

who is familiar with the literature will find nothing surprising in this brief review. The most recent observations concerning the placement of the account of the Last Supper may be found in works by Giraudo,[17] Mazza,[18] Power,[19] and Kilmartin.[20]

This inquiry into euchological structures will offer some fresh insight about several important theological issues. The first of these is ecumenical in that the relationship of the narrative to the rest of the anaphora may suggest its relationship to the epiclesis and give us another way of looking at the long-standing disagreement between East and West on the question of the consecratory significance of each of these two elements.[21] The second is related to the ecumenical concerns of the first. It is the issue of the action of the presiding bishop or presbyter as an action done *in persona Christi* and/or *in persona ecclesiae*.[22] I believe that the syntactical structure of the Roman Canon may shed some light on this topic, which has implications for the theology of the role of the ordained presider vis-à-vis that of the assembly. A third issue that will arise as a result of this study will be the relationship of the eucharistic sacrifice to the narrative as it eluci-

---

[17] Cesare Giraudo, *La struttura letteraria della preghiera eucaristica*, Analecta Biblica 92 (Rome: Biblical Institute Press, 1981).

[18] Enrico Mazza, *The Origins*.

[19] David N. Power, *The Eucharistic Mystery: Revitalizing the Tradition* (New York: Crossroads, 1992).

[20] Edward J. Kilmartin, *The Eucharist in the West: History and Theology* (Collegeville: The Liturgical Press, 1998).

[21] For a summary and discussion of this issue see John H. McKenna, *Eucharist and Holy Spirit: The Eucharistic Epiclesis in Twentieth-Century Theology (1900–1966)*, Alcuin Club Collections 57 (Great Wakering: Mayhew-McCrimmon, 1975) esp. 173–207, and his more recent analysis in "Eucharistic Prayer: Epiclesis," *Gratias agamus: Studien zum eucharistischen Hochgebet für Balthasar Fischer*, eds. A. Heitz and H. Rennings (Freiburg: Herder, 1992) 283–91. See also Robert F. Taft, "The Epiclesis Question in the Light of the Orthodox and Catholic *Lex Orandi* Traditions," *New Perspectives on Historical Theology: Essays in Memory of John Meyendorff*, eds. Bradley Nassif and Tony Nassif (Grand Rapids, Mich.: Eerdmans, 1995) 210–37; Edward J. Kilmartin, "The Active Role of Christ and the Holy Spirit in the Sanctification of the Eucharistic Elements," *Theological Studies* 45 (1984) 225–53.

[22] Important contributions to the understanding of this issue are found in Bernard D. Marliangeas, *Clés pour une théologie du ministère: In persona Christi, in persona ecclesiae*, Théologie historique 51 (Paris: Beauchesne, 1978); Dennis M. Ferrara, "Representation of Self-effacement? The Axiom *In Persona Christi* in St. Thomas and the Magisterium," *Theological Studies* 55 (1994) 195–224; Id., "*In Persona Christi*: Towards a Second Naïveté," *Theological Studies* 57 (1996) 65–88.

dates the relationship of that sacrifice to the eucharistic presence of Christ under the forms of the offered gifts.[23]

THE TEXT OF THE ROMAN CANON

The Roman Canon was the only prayer used in the eucharistic liturgy of the Roman Rite during the sixteen hundred years preceding the Second Vatican Council. It was prayed daily by many of those who were responsible for the development of the eucharistic theology as it came to be formulated and clarified during the scholastic period and further defined at the Council of Trent. It is the prayer Roman-rite Christians have considered canonical in their discussions with the East on the relative importance of the epiclesis and of the [supper — ed.] narrative. Thus, the text of the Roman Canon suggests itself as a primary source of eucharistic theology, a font of the *lex orandi* concerning the meaning of the Eucharist.

Since the issue before us requires attention to the details of the text of the Canon as it comes to us from our earliest sources, I have relied upon the critical edition established by Bernard Botte.[24] The edition of the Roman Mass Ordinary by Botte and Christine Mohrmann[25] as well as the textual study and critical edition of the *textus receptus* by Leo Eizenhöfer[26] also have been consulted. The more recent edition and notes by Eizenhöfer and Irmgard Pahl also have proved useful.[27] In addition, the results of my own examination of five of the earliest manuscripts in which the Roman Canon appears have contributed some evidence one cannot expect a printed edition to supply.[28] This

[23] Robert F. Taft, "Understanding the Byzantine Anaphoral Oblation," *Rule of Prayer, Rule of Faith: Essays in Honor of Aidan Kavanagh, O.S.B.*, eds. Nathan Mitchell and John F. Baldovin (Collegeville: The Liturgical Press, 1996) 32–55; Kenneth W. Stevenson, *Eucharist and Offering* (New York: Pueblo, 1986).

[24] Bernard Botte, *Le canon de la messe romaine: Édition critique, introduction et notes* (Louvain: Abbaye du Mont César, 1935).

[25] Bernard Botte and Christine Mohrmann, *L'ordinaire de la messe: Texte critique, traduction et études* (Paris: Cerf and Louvain: Abbaye du Mont César, 1953).

[26] Eizenhöfer, *Canon missae Romanae, I: Traditio Textus.*

[27] Eizenhöfer and Irmgard Pahl, "Liturgia Romana," *Prex eucharistica*, eds. Hänggi and Pahl, 423–47.

[28] The documents examined include facsimiles of two non-Roman, Western manuscripts: *The Bobbio Missal* and *The Stowe Missal*; the microfilm copies of two early documents of Roman provenance within the family of Gregorian Sacramentaries: *Cambrai 164*, and the early eighth-century sacramentary from the city of Trent, *Buonconsiglio 1590*; and the facsimile of the *Gelasianum Vetus (Vat. Reg. lat. 316)*. These

textual study will reveal some facts about the Canon's structure and syntax, which I believe have theological implications. The way in which the Canon's structure and syntax influenced the composition of the postconciliar Eucharistic Prayers introduced in 1968 will be noted.[29] The resultant information will be compared with the structure of the Antiochene Anaphoral Family in order to afford us the possibility of exploring the ecumenical implications.

It is currently believed that the Roman Canon in its earliest form (of which there is no extant text) lacked the Sanctus, *Communicantes, Hanc igitur, Nobis quoque peccatoribus,* and the *Memento etiam* petition for the dead, and that its only Amen came at the conclusion of the final doxology. Even the *Memento domine* is probably not original, and the *Per quem* may have been used only when the blessing of oil and other produce concluded the Canon. If the evidence from Ambrose of Milan is taken into account, the *Quam oblationem* may have had a different intent and the *Supra quae propitio* was preceded by only the first portion of the *Supplices te rogamus.*

Enrico Mazza has proposed that the Roman Canon may be one of those prayers of such great age that it lacked even the account of the Last Supper. This account, with its recital of the dominical words, may have been added some time after the prayer was composed and used in the eucharistic celebrations of the ancient Roman Church. If Mazza is correct, the decision to place the dominical words in the canon at the precise point at which they now appear, and the grammatical devices used to join the words to the existing text, can be expected to be suggestive of the theological relationship of the supper account to the canon as understood by those responsible for the placement. Even if Mazza's opinion fails to be probative, the placement and relationship remain suggestive of the theological meaning of the dominical words in the Roman Canon. Due to the absence of any textual evidence for Mazza's theory, this study will rely upon the text of the Canon in the form it achieved in the time of Gregory the Great and in which form it appears in the earliest sacramentaries. Notice will be taken of the earlier forms where it clarifies the discussion. Using the text of the

were studied at the Hill Monastic Manuscript Library at Saint John's University in Collegeville, Minnesota, with the kind assistance of the library staff, recognized here with gratitude.

[29] These are the prayers usually referred to as "Eucharistic Prayer II, III, and IV." Other prayers approved for particular occasions and for specific regions will not be considered here.

manuscript tradition given in the critical edition by Botte,[30] our prayer exhibits the following structure. The Latin incipits of each section will be used throughout and square brackets mark those sections most scholars believe to be later additions included in the Canon before the extant manuscripts were composed:

Dialogue
Vere dignum (Preface)
[Sanctus]
Te igitur (We therefore pray)
[*Memento domine*] (Remember Lord)
[*Communicantes*] (In fellowship with)
[*Hanc igitur*] (Therefore Lord)
Quam oblationem (Which oblation)
Qui pridie (Who the day before)
Unde et memores (Therefore also Lord)
Supra quae propitio (Vouchsafe to look upon)
Supplices te rogamus (We humbly beseech you)
   . . . [*ut quotquot*] (that all who)
   . . . [*per Christum dominum nostrum*] (through Christ our Lord)
[*Memento etiam*] (Remember also)
[*Nobis quoque*] (To us sinners)
[*Per quem*] (Through whom)
Per ipsum . . . Amen.

When laid out in this way, the canon looks like a collection of independent prayers rather than a unified Anaphora. This impression is exacerbated by the use of the phrase *per christum dominum nostrum* at the end of several sections. A closer look will reveal that many of these prayers are joined to a preceding text by the use of some grammatical device such as a conjunction, a transitional adverb, or a relative pronoun introducing a relative clause. We shall now examine some of these.

Immediately after the preface of thanksgiving and its concluding Sanctus, the prayer turns to supplication for the acceptance of the offering for the sake of the Church with its hierarchy and for others (*Te igitur* and *Memento*). Thus our first connecting construction is the conjunction *igitur*. In Jungmann's monumental work on the Roman

---

30 Botte, *Le canon*, 30–47.

Mass, it is noted that *igitur* could not have been intended to join this portion of the prayer to the preceding Sanctus, but must be a vestige of a grammatical structure that linked it to the preface before the Sanctus was added.[31] Jungmann cites several ancient prefaces which include some allusion to the offering.[32] Although it is impossible to be sure just how common such prefaces were prior to the developments we see in the early medieval sacramentaries, such references to the sacrifice occurring within the preface could certainly make sense of the *igitur* which introduces a petition for the acceptance of the offering. This view has been taken also by Cipriano Vagaggini[33] and Pietro Borella[34] and more recently by Enrico Mazza.[35]

Of the next three sections, the *Communicantes* and the *Hanc igitur* are believed to have been added to the earliest form of the canon just prior to the pontificates of Leo the Great and Gregory the Great, respectively.[36] These texts were probably used only on certain occasions such as a great feast, in the case of the former, and when particular persons were the object of special supplication, in the case of the latter. Both end with *per Christum dominum nostrum*, which heightens their independence from the rest of the prayer. Since some of the manuscripts represent the *Communicantes* as a part of the final sentence of the preceding text, and for other reasons, the *Memento domine* is thought by some to be later than the earliest elements in the canon.[37]

The second grammatical link for us to consider is a relative pronoun, introducing what appears to be a relative clause beginning with the words, *quam oblationem*, literally, "which oblation." What precedes this clause in the received text of the canon is a petition, just discussed, for the acceptance of the oblation of the Church and for peace and salvation, the *Hanc igitur*. A petition beginning with the words "which oblation" can logically follow such a prayer for the ac-

[31] Jungmann, 2:148–49.

[32] *Ibid.*, 149–51.

[33] Vagaggini, 29–32, 39–41.

[34] Pietro Borella, "Evoluzione storica e struttura letteraria del canone della messa romana: Le intercessioni, loro antichità," *Il Canone: studio biblico, teologico, storico-liturgico*, eds. Louis Ligier and others (Padua: Centro Azione Liturgica, 1968) 118–19, 141–42.

[35] Mazza, *Origins*, 251–61.

[36] Righetti, 3, 376–385; Botte, *Le canon*, 55–59.

[37] Mazza, *The Eucharistic Prayers*, 64–65; Jungmann, 159–71.

ceptance of an oblation and function grammatically as a relative clause, but between these two petitions is the concluding phrase, *"per christum dominum nostrum."* This division suggests that the relative pronoun *quam* may function here as a connective relative, normally used at the start of an entirely new sentence with the effect of joining the ideas of the two sentences.[38] In either case, the word suggests a relationship between the two concepts. Since the section from the *Quam oblationem* through the *Supplices te rogamus* is thought to belong to an older stratum of the Canon than does the *Hanc igitur,* and for that matter, the *Communicantes,* our prayer may originally have been joined to the end of the *Memento domine.*[39] At a yet earlier stage, it may have followed the *Te igitur.* In both cases, the preceding prayer does not conclude with the phrase "through Christ our Lord" and would then allow for the *quam* to function as a relative pronoun introducing a relative clause making a further petition for the acceptance of the offering spoken of in either or both the *Te igitur* and the *Memento domine.*

The *Quam oblationem,* as we have it in the manuscripts of the Roman sacramentaries, asks that God hold the offerings (spoken of throughout the earlier petitions) acceptable so that they will become the body and blood of Jesus Christ.[40] It clearly states that the offerings become the body and blood of Christ as a result of their being recognized by God as the acceptable sacrifice. The supper narrative also finds a place in this sentence as a relative clause within this relative clause which seeks the acceptance of the sacrifice. Thus, the second relative pronoun, *qui,* initiates the recital of the dominical words in the *Qui pridie.* The construction is the following:

---

[38] This use of the relative pronoun is discussed in John F. Collins, *A Primer of Ecclesiastical Latin* (Washington, D.C.: The Catholic University of America Press, 1985) 84. See also Charlton T. Lewis and Charles Short, *A Latin Dictionary* (New York: Oxford University Press, 1993) 1510.

[39] This appears to be the arrangement to which Ambrose bears witness in *De sacramentis* 4, 14: "Nam reliqua omnia quae dicuntur in superioribus a sacerdote dicuntur: laus deo, defertur oratio, petitur pro populo, pro regibus, pro caeteris . . . ," Botte, ed. (SC 25bis) 108.

[40] It is well-known that Ambrose's form of this petition asks God to accept the offerings because they are the sacramental reality of Christ's body and blood. *De sacramentis* 5, 21: "Fac nobis, inquit, hanc oblationem scriptam rationabilem, acceptabilem, quod est figura corporis et sanguinis domini nostri Iesu Christi," Botte, ed. (SC 25bis) 114.

Quam oblationem tu deus in omnibus quaesumus benedictam adscriptam ratam rationabilem acceptabilemque facere digneris ut nobis corpus et sanguis fiat dilectissimi filii tui domini dei nostri iesu christi.

Qui pridie quam pateretur accepit panem in sanctas ac venerabiles manus suas elevatis oculis in caelum ad te deum patrem suum omni-potentem tibi gratias agens benedixit fregit dedit discipulis suis dicens accipite et manducate ex hoc omnes hoc est enim corpus meum. Simili modo posteaquam caenatum est . . ."[41]

(Which oblation, O God, we beseech you to make) wholly blessed, approved, ratified, reasonable and acceptable; that it may become for us the body and blood of your dearly beloved Son Jesus Christ our Lord;

who on the day before he suffered, took bread in his holy and reverend hands, lifted up his eyes to heaven to you, O God, his almighty father, gave thanks to you, blessed, broke, and gave it to his disciples, saying, "Take and eat from this, all of you; for this is my body." Likewise after supper . . .[42]

Next, we have the transitional adverb *unde,* which indicates that the subsequent offering of the sacrifice in commemoration of the paschal mystery will result from the earlier petition for the accept-ability of the offerings that made them identifiable with the body and blood of the Lord. God is asked to look upon these gifts with a propi-tious and serene countenance in order that they be accepted just as were the offerings of Abel, Abraham, and Melchisedech. Likewise, these offerings are to be transferred to the heavenly altar for the good of all who receive them. Here is the text:

Unde et memores sumus domine nos tui serui sed et plebs tua sancta christi filii tui domini dei nostri tam beatae passionis necnon et ab inferis resurrectionis sed et in caelos gloriosae ascensionis offerimus praeclarae maiestati tuae de tuis donis ac datis hostiam puram hostiam sanctam hostiam immaculatam panem sanctum uitae aeternae et calicem salutis perpetuae.

Therefore also, Lord, we your servants, and also your holy people, having in remembrance the blessed Passion of your Son Christ our Lord, likewise his resurrection from the dead, and also his glorious ascension into heaven, do offer to your excellent majesty from your gifts and bounty a pure victim, a holy victim, an unspotted victim, the holy bread of eternal life and the cup of everlasting salvation.

[41] Botte, *Le canon,* 36–38.

[42] English translation from Jasper and Cuming, 164–65. The portions set within parentheses are my revisions of that translation.

Supra quae propitio ac sereno uultu respicere digneris et accepta habere sicuti accepta habere dignatus es munera pueri tui iusti abel et sacrificum patriarchae nostri abrahae et quod tibi obtulit summus sacerdos tuus melchisedech sanctum sacrificium immaculatam hostiam.

Vouchsafe to look upon them with a favorable and kindly countenance, and accept them as you vouchsafed to accept the gifts of your righteous servant Abel, and the sacrifice of our patriarch Abraham, and that which your high priest Melchizedek offered to you, a holy sacrifice, and unblemished victim.

Supplices te rogamus omnipotens deus iube haec perferri per manus angeli tui in sublime altare tuum in conspectu diuinae maiestatis tuae ut quotquot ex hac altaris participatione sacrosanctum filii tui corpus et sanguinem sumpserimus omni benedictione caelesti et gratia repleamur per christum dominum nostrum.[43]

We humbly beseech you, almighty God, bid these things be borne by the hands of your angel to your altar on high, in the sight of your divine majesty, that all of us who have received the most holy body and blood of your Son by partaking at this altar may be filled with all heavenly blessing and grace; through Christ our Lord.[44]

Next we find the commemoration of the dead *(Memento etiam),* a prayer that ministers and people may participate with the saints, *(Nobis quoque),* and the *Per quem,* used as a transition from the blessing of oil when this is added during Holy Week. The Trinitarian doxology follows, and the prayer is sealed with the people's Amen.

From this outline of the central and most ancient portions of the Roman Canon, once the prayer moves from anamnetic thanksgiving to supplication, one can see that the divine acceptance of the offering becomes the primary concern. The acceptability of the offerings causes them to be identified with the Body and Blood of the Lord and that identification, in turn, is the source of the Church's confidence which inspires its petition for the benefits of the sacrifice for all who receive them. The narrative of the Last Supper functions in the schema as a warrant for this confident supplication. The offerings will become the Body and Blood of the Lord, who promised that it would be so when he spoke about the bread and the wine at the Last Supper. It is no wonder, then, that the narrative is introduced as a subordinate clause *(Qui pridie)* of the previous subordinate clause *(Quam oblationem)* which asks for the acceptance of the offering.

[43] Botte, *Le canon,* 40–42.
[44] Jasper and Cuming, 165.

141

These petitions for acceptance reach their culmination after the supper narrative *(Qui pridie)* and anamnesis *(Unde et memores)*; they rehearse the scriptural exemplars of worthy offerers *(Supra quae propitio)* and seek the identification of the eucharistic offering with the heavenly liturgy for the good of all who will receive the holy gifts *(Supplices te rogamus)*.

Analysis

The meaning of every subordinate clause depends upon the meaning of the sentence in which it functions. The *Quam oblationem* must be understood as part of the sentence which seeks God's acceptance of the offering for the good of the Church with its ministerial hierarchy *(Te igitur)* or possibly of the next sentence for the intentions of various offerers *(Memento domine)*. Likewise, the *Qui pridie* must be interpreted within the context set by both these earlier petitions for the acceptance of the offering. Thus the dominical words within the second relative clause *(Qui pridie)* function as a warrant for making the petition for the transformation of the gifts found in the first subordinate clause *(Quam oblationem)*, and the petitions of both these clauses serve the intention of the main clause of this sentence, that God hold the offering acceptable for the sake of the Church and others for whom it is offered. This second subordinate clause presents the reason that such a petition could have any chance of meeting with a positive action by God. Thus it is clear that the dominical words function as part of the supplication for the acceptance of the offerings; the narrative serves as the justification for confidence on the part of the petitioning Church.

It has long been noticed that the narrative finds its place within the supplicatory portion of the Roman Canon, but no attention has been given to the grammatical and syntactical transformation resulting from its placement in a relative clause subordinate to a petition. It ceases to function grammatically as an independent statement and takes on the nature of the sentence to which it has been subordinated. It functions as part of the petition it justifies. This reality has been ignored or gone unnoticed in discussions of the function of the narrative. Usually it is treated as an isolated element, a narrative, or a declarative statement placed in the midst of supplications and simply producing a hiatus in the petitioning. It is commonly interpreted by its narrative structure alone. No attention is paid to its grammatical subordination to the supplication. In fact, the relative pronouns *quam* and *qui,* are usually preceded by periods rather than by commas and are capitalized in most modern texts of the Roman Canon.

We find precisely this arrangement in Botte's critical edition of the canon, cited above, and in the critical edition of the Mass Ordinary by Botte and Mohrmann. While Eizenhöfer's study of the canon does the same, he notes otherwise in his description of the manuscripts. There he notes the incipits of each section of the canon and indicates capitalizations, letter size, and color.[45]

THE MANUSCRIPTS

Facsimiles and microfilms of five of the oldest and most reliable manuscripts are available at the Hill Monastic Manuscript Library at Saint John's University in Collegeville, Minnesota. An examination of these documents supports my observations. These manuscripts offer no reason to introduce a period just before the *Quam oblationem* and *Qui pridie.* Nor should it be taken that the manuscripts suggest that these clauses be treated as independent sentences requiring the capitalization of their first words.

The first microfilm copy of a manuscript I examined was that of the *Cambrai 164,* considered to be the most ancient and reliable manuscript of the *Gregorian Sacramentary.* It is believed to be a copy of the document sent by Pope Hadrian to Charlemagne, a fact that earned it the name *Hadrianum ex authentico.* This manuscript locates the *Quam oblationem* immediately after the *Hanc igitur.*[46] The *Hanc igitur* is concluded with a punctuation that resembles a period placed above the line. This punctuation is found in many other places in the text separating clauses beginning with such words as *sed* and *et* and *ut* from the preceding clauses where it obviously functions as a comma. The word *quam* begins with a small letter, identified by Eizenhöfer as *paulo maior,*[47] and the final line of the *Hanc igitur* occupies only two thirds of that line.[48] This appears to be a device by which the scribe draws attention to this clause without separating it definitively from the preceding text. The same device is used to highlight the dominical words, *accipite et manducate* and *accipite et bibite,* while avoiding to set them up as sentences independent of their grammatical context.[49]

---

[45] Eizenhöfer, 1:5–14.
[46] *Cambrai 164,* fol. 39 recto.
[47] Eizenhöfer, 1:11.
[48] *Cambrai 164,* fol. 39 recto.
[49] *Ibid.,* fol. 39 verso.

The manuscript provides no punctuation and no capitalization to set off the *qui pridie* from the rest of the sentence, allowing it to be rendered . . . *dilectissimi filii tui domini dei nostri iesu christi qui pridie quam pateretur. . . .*[50]

Another important manuscript of the *Gregorian Sacramentary* consulted in its microfilm copy is the *Trento, Castello del Buonconsiglio, Cod. 1590.* Here we find the only example in the manuscripts I consulted of a clear capitalization of *quam,* but as is typically the case in such manuscripts, the capitalization does not guarantee a grammatical independence since it is used liberally in the middle of sentences throughout this manuscript. No punctuation precedes this clause and a raised period, the equivalent of a comma, concludes it. The *Qui pridie* immediately follows without capitalization.[51]

Two Gallican documents, *The Bobbio Missal* and *The Stowe Missal,* were consulted in their facsimile editions. Neither of these capitalizes the first words of the clauses we are studying nor do they set them off by means of punctuation.[52] The very same can be said for the arrangement of these sections of the canon found in the manuscript facsimile of the *Sacramentarium Gelasianum Vetus (Vat. Reg. lat. 316).*[53]

It is clear from my study of the manuscripts that the supplying of punctuation and capitalization in the critical editions of these texts was done only to provide some clarity and order to an otherwise unwieldy and abnormally long sentence. This aid is inaccurate and should not be allowed to influence the scholarly analysis of the grammatical structure of the text. Dropping these additions makes it quite clear that the dominical words function as part of the petition requesting the acceptance of the sacrifice and not as an isolated narrative or independent sentence.

SOME THEOLOGICAL CONSEQUENCES

Once the misleading periods and capitalizations are eliminated, the text in question can be translated thus:

---

[50] *Ibid.,* fol. 39 recto.

[51] *Trento, Castello del Buonconsiglio, Cod. 1590,* fol. 17 verso.

[52] *The Bobbio Missal (Paris, Bibliothèque Nationale, lat 13246),* ed. E. A. Lowe, Henry Bradshaw Society 53 (London, 1917) fol. 13 recto–13 verso; *The Stowe Missal (Dublin, Library of the Royal Irish Academy, codex D. II.3),* ed. G. F. Warner, Henry Bradshaw Society 31 (London, 1906) fol. 27 verso.

[53] *Vat. Reg. lat. 316,* fol. 181 recto.

". . . which oblation, we beg you O God, be pleased to make blessed, approved, ratified, reasonable, and acceptable, so that it may become for us the Body and Blood of your beloved Son, our Lord Jesus Christ, who on the day before he suffered took bread in his holy and venerable hands, lifting his eyes to heaven to you, O God, his almighty Father, giving you thanks, he blessed, broke, and gave (it) to his disciples saying, take and eat of this all of you, for this is my body. . . ."[54]

Although the supper account retains a certain narrative style, it functions grammatically as a subordinate clause within a petition for the acceptance of the offering and for the consequent transformation of the elements. The dominical words, as they appear in the Roman Canon, function not as a declarative statement about the bread and the wine on the altar but rather as a warrant for God's acceptance of the petition for their transformation. The words of Christ within the canon are addressed not to the assembly (as once they were addressed to the disciples) and not to the bread and wine, but to God in petition; they are supplicatory rather than anamnetic.

On the other hand, in the anaphoras of the Antiochene Family, the dominical words do function grammatically as a declaration within the christological thanksgiving; they are anamnetic rather than supplicatory. Yet the theological tradition of the Christians who use such prayers resists assigning a consecratory significance to this declaration, preferring to think of the dominical words as incomplete without the epicletic supplication. In this way the East seeks to preserve the Holy Spirit's role in the sacrament as the agent who makes our christological anamnesis both effective for the present and proleptic of the eschatological gifts.

The theological position of the West emphasizes the christological anamnesis of the supper account but pays little attention to the importance of the epicletic supplication. It assumes that the dominical words are an anamnetic declaration despite the evidence to the contrary. This eucharistic *lex credendi* is simply contradicted by the Canon's *lex orandi*. The latter is established by sixteen hundred years of unswerving practice in which the Lord's words are not a christological anamnesis of the Last Supper but rather a part of the supplication for the transformation of the elements. The theological

---

[54] My trans.

position that places so much emphasis on the declarative nature of the dominical words seems to have no support from the euchological *lex orandi*. This fact alone may not refute the usual Western theological position concerning the dominical words, but it cannot be ignored.

When we note that both the Roman Canon's anamnetic offering *(Unde et memores)* and its supplication for the acceptance of the sacrifice *(Supra quae)* for the good of the communicants *(Supplices te rogamus)* follow and complete the prayer, a further important element comes to light. The dominical words do indeed complete and support the petition for the acceptance of the oblation and for the transformation of the gifts, but they also look forward to the offering and to the supplication for the fruits of communion in the prayers that follow. Thus we can conclude that the dominical words in the Roman Canon function not only as warrant for the preceding petitions for the acceptance of the oblation and for the consequent transformation of the elements. They are as well a warrant for the acceptance of the anamnetic offering and its consequent effects upon the communicants sought in the *Supplices te rogamus*. In this way they are truly the very center of the eucharistic supplication.

The *Quam oblationem* and the *Supplices te rogamus* often have been described as non-pneumatic epicleses for transformation and for the effects of communion respectively, and the dominical words appear to separate these two petitions producing a declarative hiatus in the petitioning. This interpretation gave rise to the deliberate insertion of explicit epicleses for transformation and communion before and after the narrative in the three eucharistic prayers approved for the Roman Rite in 1968. The desire to maintain the structure and syntax of the Roman Canon in these new prayers can be seen in the grammatical devices which unite the clauses from epiclesis to epiclesis. Despite the inexplicable periods, it is as if this entire section of the prayer functions as a single long sentence. Eucharistic Prayer II can serve as an example:

Vere Sanctus es, Domine, fons omnis sanctitatis. Haec ergo dona quaesumus, Spiritus tui rore sanctifica ut nobis Corpus et Sanguis fiant Domini nostri Iesu Christi. Qui cum Passioni voluntarie traderetur, accepit panem et gratias agens fregit, deditque discipulis suis, dicens:	Holy indeed are you, Lord, the fountain of all holiness, therefore, we beg you, sanctify these gifts with the dew of your Spirit so that they may be for us the Body and Blood of our Lord Jesus Christ, who when he was to be handed over to a voluntary Passion, took bread and giving thanks, broke it, gave it to

Accipite et manducate ex hoc omnes: Hoc est enim Corpus meum, quod pro vobis tradetur. Simili modo, postquam cenatum est, accipiens et calicem. . . . Memores igitur mortis et resurrectionis eius, tibi, Domine, panem vitae et calicem salutis offerimus, gratias agentes quia nos dignos habuisti astare coram te et tibi ministrare. Et supplices deprecamur ut Corpus et Sanguinis Christi participes a Spiritu Sancto congregemur in unum.[55]

his disciples, saying: Take and eat of this all of you: this is my Body, which is handed over for you. Likewise after supper, taking the cup. . . .

Therefore, remembering his death and resurrection, we offer to you, Lord, the bread of life and the cup of salvation, giving thanks because you have held us worthy to stand before you and to minister to you, and we humbly pray that participating in the Body and Blood of Christ, we may be gathered as one by the Holy Spirit.[56]

Proper attention to the words that connect the various clauses in this section of the prayer will make it plain that the dominical words do not separate two distinct epicleses but are in fact absorbed by the epicletic petition with its two elements. The structure of the Roman Canon, once its eucharistic supplications are made explicitly pneumatic in the new Eucharistic Prayers of the Church, seems to encapsulate the dominical words within the epiclesis rather than to divide the epiclesis in two by the intrusion of a declarative statement. If the *Quam oblationem* and the *Supplices te rogamus* may be called respectively a consecratory and communion epiclesis, then we can view the dominical words as part of the epicletic supplication which begins seeking the transformation and concludes petitioning for fruitful communion. This fruitful communion depends upon the acceptance of the sacrifice, which is based upon the transformation, which in turn is justified by reference to what the Lord said at the Last Supper.

Enrico Mazza's theory proposes that the Roman Canon actually did exist for a time without the dominical words *(Qui pridie)* and without the anamnesis/offering *(Unde et memores)* which is a natural outgrowth of the words. If he is correct, the *Quam oblationem,* the *Supra quae propitio,* and the *Supplices te rogamus* would follow one another immediately. Obviously, the resulting petitions would parallel the petitions of the usual epicletic prayers of the other texts such as those belonging to the Antiochene Family of Eucharistic Prayers.

[55] *Missale Romanum 1975,* 457–58.
[56] My trans.

They seek the action of God upon the offerings so that they would become the Body and Blood of the Lord for the purpose of sanctifying those who will receive them in communion. The addition of the supper narrative and its subsequent anamnesis does not merely divide the two petitions for consecration and communion but actually amplifies them by noting that this prayer can be expected to be efficacious because it conforms to the will of the Lord himself.

DECLARATIVE OR DEPRECATIVE CONSECRATION

Theologians of the West have often preferred to grant sacramental efficacy to declarative statements over deprecative euchological texts. Louis-Marie Chauvet links this preference with the Thomist concern to see the sacraments as achieving their ends by way of an instrumental efficient causality and to an exaggerated sense of the christological source of sacramental power.[57] He laments that in such a narrow view of the sacrament, supplication cannot cause a sacramental effect and must be judged insufficient.[58] Thomas sees instrumental efficient causality at the center of each sacrament and the hypostatic union as the source of sacramental power. Thus, for example, he mistakenly locates the core of the sacramental action of ordination in the *porrectio* with its accompanying declarative form rather than in the imposition of hands and prayer of consecration.[59] This preference for the declarative form is evident in baptism and in penance and as well in the Eucharist.

Thomas insists that the words of Christ are spoken by the priest as a declarative statement during the Canon. As such they take on a significance even beyond that of the like formulas of other sacraments. In baptism, for instance, the priest says, "I baptize you . . . ," meaning that he, the minister, acts in his own name as his actions and words supply the matter and form of the sacrament so that, through this instrumental efficient causality, baptism may be accomplished by the power of Christ. However, in the unique sacrament of the Eucharist, the priest declares, "This is my body," in such a manner as to take on the identity of Christ. If he were not to do so, then the words would mean that the bread is transformed into the priest's body and

[57] Louis-Marie Chauvet, *Symbol and Sacrament: A Sacramental Reinterpretation of Christian Existence,* trans. Patrick Madigan and Madeleine Beaumont (Collegeville: The Liturgical Press, 1995) 453–76.

[58] *Ibid.,* 473.

[59] *Ibid.,* 471.

not Christ's. Thus the consecrating priest acts in this sacrament *in persona Christi* when he says, "This is my body," otherwise he would have to say, "This is the Body of Christ."[60]

This is why Thomas must disagree with Peter Lombard who said a century earlier that an excommunicated priest cannot confect the Eucharist validly because he makes the offering in the plural form as he acts *in persona ecclesiae*.[61] Cut off from the Church by excommunication, the censured priest is unable to act *in persona ecclesiae* and thus is incapable of confecting the Eucharist. Thomas insists rather that the determining action of the priest in the Eucharist is not the prayer of supplication or of offering but only the speaking of the words of the Lord, in which case he must act *in persona Christi*. He explains his point of view thus:

"In reciting the prayers of the mass the priest speaks in the person of the Church. In consecrating the sacrament, however, he speaks in the person of Christ, whose role he plays by the power of Holy Orders. If, therefore, a priest cut off from the unity of the Church celebrates mass, since he has not lost the power of Holy Orders, he consecrates the true body and blood, but because he is apart from the unity of the Church, his prayers have no effectiveness."[62]

Elsewhere, Thomas goes further still and claims that the words of the Lord are sufficient by themselves to effect the consecration and that all the other words of the canon are not absolutely necessary to this end. He says:

"Some theologians say that this sacrament could not be validly celebrated by reciting the aforementioned words only, leaving out the others, especially those found in the canon of the Mass. But this is obviously not the case. . . . We must then conclude that if a priest were to say these words only, with the intention of effecting the sacrament,

---

[60] *ST* III, q. 78, a. 1 and a. 2.

[61] Bernard D. Marliangeas, *Clés pour une théologie du ministère: In persona Christi, In persona Ecclesiae*, Théologie historique 51 (Paris: Beauchesne, 1978) 55–56. Marliangeas quotes Peter Lombard, *Libri IV Sententiarum:* "Illi vero qui excommunicati sunt, etc. . . . non videntur hoc sacramentum posse conficere, licet sacerdos sint: quia nemo dicit in ipsa consecratione, offero, sed Offerimus, quasi ex persona Ecclesiae; et ideo cum alia sacramenta extra Ecclesiam possint celebrari, de hoc non videtur."

[62] *ST* III, q. 82, a. 7 ad. 3m. English trans. from *Summa Theologiae*, trans. Thomas Gilby, vol. 59 (New York: McGraw Hill, 1964) 121.

it would be validly consecrated; his intention would suffice to make the words mean that they were spoken in the person of Christ, even if this were not stated by reciting the foregoing words. But a priest so consecrating would gravely sin in not keeping the rite of the Church."[63]

This way of understanding the Eucharistic Prayer, as an important but not entirely necessary setting for the formula of consecration spoken by a priest *in persona Christi,* is perhaps the strongest expression of the christomonistic conception of sacramental causality.[64] The expressions of supplication and offering in the Roman Canon are not central to the sacramental action but merely provide an apt setting for the consecration. In fact, Thomas will say that the entire sacrament of the Eucharist is present in the one moment of the consecration of the two species. This act contains the entire sacrament in that it effects the Real Presence and simultaneously makes present the sacrificial death of the Lord.[65] The prayers of the offering in the canon do not make the sacrifice of Christ present, but rather are the prayers by which the priest offers that sacrifice for the good of the Church.[66]

The priest acts *in persona Christi* when he confects the sacrament by reciting the dominical words. This action effects the Real Presence in which Christ's sacrificial death is signified by the separate consecration which portrays the separation of the Body and Blood of the Lord at the moment of his death. This sacrifice of the Lord's death, now present sacramentally, is offered by the priest speaking the offertorial prayers of the Canon. In these the priest offers *in persona ecclesiae* the sacrifice of Christ already present in the sacrament.[67] This is the offering nullified by excommunication. A censured priest cannot act in the person of the Church from which he is excommunicated, but he continues to act in the person of the Christ to whom he is

[63] *ST* III, q. 78, a. 1 ad. 4m. English translation from *Summa Theologiae,* vol. 58, trans. W. Barden (New York: McGraw-Hill, 1965) 169. Not only is Thomas saying that the words of the canon are not absolutely necessary, but even the "foregoing words" of the supper narrative, "Take and eat . . .," are not required for a valid consecration.

[64] See Chauvet's discussion of this designation originated by Congar in Chauvet, 463–64.

[65] This is more thoroughly discussed in David N. Power, *The Eucharistic Mystery: Revitalizing the Tradition* (New York: Crossroad, 1992) 228–30.

[66] Power, 229.

[67] *Ibid.*

united by means of ordination. Such a division was not part of Peter Lombard's view.

Thomas's preference for the declarative form is clearly at the heart of the definition of sacramental matter and form in the "Decree for the Armenians," which was produced during the Council of Florence.[68] Though created and signed during the council, it is not universally recognized as dogmatically binding because of its erroneous insistence that the *traditio instrumentorum* and its accompanying declarative formula are the matter and form for ordination.[69] An outline of the matter and form of each of the seven sacraments is presented for the Armenians to accept as part of their proposed union with Rome. With the exception of the anointing of the sick, each sacrament is associated with its declarative form.[70] Only in regard to the Eucharist, however, is the form said to be expressed by the priest *in persona Christi*.[71] Such is the understanding of sacramental efficacy in place in the West throughout the fourteenth century and formalized in the fifteenth-century "Decree for the Armenians." No mention is made of the epiclesis, for it, like the deprecative words of the canon, can have no sacramental effect.

Part of Nicholas Cabasilas's mid-fourteenth-century *Commentary on the Divine Liturgy* was written in opposition to this Thomistic approach to the Eucharist. He complains that the Latins criticize the Eastern reverence for the epicletic petition because it shows that they (the Greeks) "rely more on their own prayer than on God's word . . . they make the holy sacrament dependent on something uncertain,

---

[68] *Bulla unionis Armenorum,* Council of Florence, Session 8, 22 November 1439. The original and its English translation are from Norman P. Tanner, ed. and trans., *Decrees of the Ecumenical Councils,* 2 vols. (Washington, D.C.: Georgetown University Press, 1990) 1:534–59. Tanner notes that the sacramental definitions are based on Thomas Aquinas, *De articulis fidei et ecclesiae sacramentis* (Turin, 1954) 141–51. See Tanner, 1:541, n. 1.

[69] McKenna, *Eucharist and Holy Spirit,* 80.

[70] Tanner, 1:542. For baptism, it is conceded that two other formulas, one of which is optative, may be used. The decree states, "But we do not deny that true baptism is conferred by the following words: May this servant of Christ be baptized in the name of the Father and of the Son and of the holy Spirit; or, This person is baptized by my hands in the name of the Father. . . ." A similar optative form is given for the anointing of the sick. No such concession is made in regard to the declarative forms for confirmation, penance, matrimony, holy orders, and the Eucharist.

[71] "Forma huius sacramenti sunt verba Salvatoris, quibus hoc confecit sacramentum. Sacerdos enim in persona Christi loquens hoc confict sacramentum," Tanner, 1:546.

namely, human prayer . . . it does not follow that he who prays will necessarily be heard, even if he has the virtue of Paul."[72]

Cabasilas points out that it is precisely the opposite impulse that marks the Greek epicletic petition. Participation in the eucharistic mystery is completely a gift from God and thus sought after in fervent petition. Such supplication expresses the human reliance upon God as the sole source of sacramental efficacy. Nor does Cabasilas abide the criticism that the divine response to such supplication is uncertain. Can any supplication be more certain of a positive hearing than one in which the object of prayer is known to be God's will for the petitioner? The epicletic supplication must achieve its end because, Cabasilas says, "We are assured of the result, not by reason of man who prays, but by reason of God who hears; not because man has made a supplication, but because the Truth has promised to grant it."[73]

In the next section of his commentary, Cabasilas points out that the Latins do in their canon precisely what they criticize the Greeks for doing in their anaphoras: they pray, after the supper narrative, that the offering will be acceptable to God and achieve its purpose. He says:

"That which silences our adversaries decisively is the fact that the Latin Church herself, to whom they refer themselves, does not cease to pray for the offerings after the words of consecration have been pronounced. This point has escaped them, no doubt, because the Latins do not recite this prayer immediately after pronouncing Christ's words, and because they do not ask explicitly for consecration and the transformation of the elements into the Body of the Lord, but use other terms, which, however, have exactly the same meaning. . . .

"Since Christ is at one and the same time priest, altar, and victim, the consecration of the offerings by this priest, their transformation into this victim, and their carrying up to the heavenly altar are all one and the same thing. Therefore, if you pray that any one of these things come to pass, you pray for all; you possess that for which you pray and you have accomplished the sacrifice."[74]

The prayer to which he refers is the *Supplices te rogamus* of the Roman Canon. A Western theologian would never imagine that such

[72] Nicholas Cabasilas, *Commentary on the Divine Liturgy*, trans. J. M. Hussey and P. A. McNulty (Crestwood, N.Y.: St. Vladimir's Seminary Press, 1977) 72.
[73] Ibid., 73–74.
[74] Ibid., 76, 78–79.

a prayer for the transfer of the offerings to the heavenly altar and for their efficacy for the communicants could possibly be interpreted to be a consecratory epiclesis. Cabasilas, however, cannot imagine a prayer for the fruitfulness of the offering and its benefits for communicants which did not imply the consecration of the elements. Here we have a central issue that divides East and West which simply goes unnoticed. The West, since Thomas, has thought it possible to separate sacramental efficacy in the Eucharist from the achievement of the *res tantum* of the sacrament. An excommunicated priest can act *in persona Christi* to participate in the instrumental efficient causality which makes Christ and his sacrifice present, yet at the same time cannot act *in persona ecclesiae* to petition for the fruitfulness of that presence, the *res tantum,* for those who receive.[75] This is simply an incomprehensible division for the Greeks, as Cabasilas's argument makes clear.

The separation of what Thomas calls the *res et sacramentum* from the *res tantum* of the Eucharist and of the action done *in persona Christi* from that done *in persona ecclesiae* is not only incomprehensible to Cabasilas but it is not supported by our study of the structure and syntax of the Roman Canon. That structure upholds both the unity of the consecration of the elements with their efficacious reception by the communicants, and the unity of the actions of Christ with those of the Church by embracing all these within the action of the offering. As was pointed out earlier, the acceptance of the offering sought in the *Quam oblationem* along with the promise of Christ expressed in the *Qui pridie* have the effect of making Christ present in the elements of the meal, and the union of that offering with the offertorial action of Christ at the heavenly altar make the eating and drinking the very source of "grace and heavenly blessing" for the communicants *(Supplices te rogamus).* As Peter Lombard noticed, the priest makes the offering *in persona ecclesiae* in perfect conformity to the will of Christ at the Last Supper. This action is united to that of Christ at the right hand of the Power in heaven. The action of the priest *in persona Christi* is one with his action *in persona ecclesiae.* The text of the Roman Canon gives no reason to think of these as separable.

My purpose here is not to refute the theological positions by which these separations are defined, but merely to suggest that the text of

[75] See a discussion of this in a different context in Chauvet, 465–68. He notes that it is the separation of the eucharistic body of Christ from the ecclesial body of Christ that is at issue here. It is a result of the Church's portrayal as the "mystical body" rather than as the true Body of Christ.

the Roman Canon cannot be enlisted as a source or as a support for such a theology. If modern sacramental theology cannot afford to ignore the *lex orandi,* then the theology implicit in the structure and syntax of the Roman Canon cannot be ignored in the development of eucharistic theology.

CONCLUDING OBSERVATIONS

This study began with the expectation that the text of the Roman Canon would provide further insight into the epiclesis question which has divided East and West, that it would suggest a relationship between the actions done *in persona Christi* and *in persona ecclesiae,* and that the relationship between the dominical words and the eucharistic offering would be clarified. Let us review each in turn.

THE EPICLESIS QUESTION

It has been shown that the Western preference for the declarative over the deprecative sacramental texts is connected to the Thomist idea of instrumental efficient causality and to an exclusively christocentric foundation for sacramental efficacy. This approach leaves little room for a sacramental form that is deprecative. Supplicatory expressions lack the decisiveness which seems required by instrumental efficient causality.

It has likewise been shown that the dominical words in the Roman Canon function as part of the supplication and not as an independent declarative statement. The supper narrative appears in the Canon as a relative clause in a sentence which pleads for the acceptance of the offerings so that they may become what the Lord promised at the Last Supper, the Body and Blood of Christ. If such a supplication is judged insufficient to effect the sacrament, the venerable text of the Roman Canon cannot be enlisted as a strong support for this conclusion. Theologians must search elsewhere to justify the necessity of a declarative formula.

A second facet of the epiclesis question concerns the placement of the epicletic supplication in relation to the dominical words. If the declarative expression of the Lord's words effects the sacramental transformation, as the common Western opinion states, then a petition for the same cannot make sense after the narrative, where it appears in the anaphoras of the Antiochene Family. For this reason, the consecratory epiclesis of the post-Vatican II Eucharistic Prayers precedes the narrative and is thought to reflect the *Quam oblationem* of the Roman Canon. Again following the perceived structure of the Canon, a communion epiclesis is made to follow the narrative and its anamnesis/offering, a parallel to the Canon's *Supplices te rogamus.* The result is commonly called a split epiclesis, with the dominical words often thought to be a declarative hiatus in the petitioning.

Our study of the structure and syntax of the canon has suggested that there is, in fact, no declarative hiatus between the consecratory and communion petitions. Rather, the dominical words are absorbed into the supplications to provide the warrant both for making the petitions and for the hope that they would be answered. This bears a striking similarity to the Eastern explanation of the efficacy of the epicletic petition expressed above in the quotations from Nicholas Cabasilas. In fact, it is more accurate to say that the Roman Canon possesses a single supplication for both the transformation of the elements and the fruitfulness of their reception joined by the supper narrative as warrant. One cannot exist without the other. On this, the Roman Canon and Cabasilas seem to agree.

IN PERSONA CHRISTI AND *IN PERSONA ECCLESIAE;* THE CONSECRATION AND THE OFFERING

The first of these issues, the relationship between *in persona Christi* and *in persona ecclesiae* is an enormously complex question and its solution is far beyond the scope of this article. There are, however, a few insights from the structure of the Canon that offer some light for further study.

For Thomas, the priest's reiteration of the Lord's words at the Last Supper over bread and wine produces both the consecration of the elements and the presence of Christ's sacrificial death in the sacramental separateness of the species associated with his Body and Blood. This is a ministerial action done *in persona Christi.* The offering of the sacrifice of Christ present in the consecrated species and the supplications for its acceptance and fruitfulness are not strictly part of the sacrament and are expressed by the priest acting *in persona ecclesiae.* This division depends upon the distinction between the declarative form of the narrative and the deprecative nature of the offering and petitions. It has been shown that such a distinction is not supported by the syntactical structure of the Roman Canon. Further, it has been seen that the dominical words are part of the sentence in which supplication is made for the acceptance of the offering *(Quam oblationem).* The syntax of the Roman Canon tends to support Peter

Lombard's view that the priest acts in the Eucharist *in persona ecclesiae* because he makes the offering in the first person plural.

The priest does not shift from one mode to the other during the recitation of the Canon, but in giving voice to the prayer of the Church, acts *in persona ecclesiae* in that obedience by which the Church's prayer is conformed to the prayer of Christ, the heavenly high priest, so that the one presiding at the Eucharist acts simultaneously *in persona Christi*. This is the meaning of the transfer of the gifts to the altar on high. It is not a spatial movement that is at issue here, it is the unity of the Church's eucharistic sacrifice to the sacrificial life of the ascended, glorified Christ. The union of the Church's prayer with Christ's makes the eucharistic sacrifice effective, so that all who partake at this altar partake proleptically of the banquet in the reign of God.

In the end, it appears that the Roman Canon's offertorial language unites the epicletic supplication with the dominical words and reveals the unity of the actions of priest and congregation as the actions of a Church united with those of its high priest, the ascended and glorious Christ.

Robert F. Taft, S.J.

8. *Ex Oriente Lux?* Some Reflections on Eucharistic Concelebration[*]

The following notes on concelebration do not pretend to offer a complete study of the Eastern tradition, nor definitive solutions to the growing dissatisfaction with the restored Roman rite of eucharistic concelebration. But they may help to clarify the *status quaestionis,* rectify misinterpretations of early eucharistic discipline, and dispel misconceptions concerning the antiquity and normative value of Eastern usage. I'll begin with the latter and work backwards.

It has long been a theological device to turn eastwards in search of supporting liturgical evidence for what one has already decided to do anyway. Something like this was at work in certain pre-Vatican II discussions on the possibility of restoring concelebration in the Roman rite. The underlying presupposition seems to be that Eastern practice will reflect a more ancient—indeed *the* ancient—tradition of the undivided Church. Let's review the evidence.

1. CONCELEBRATION IN THE EAST TODAY

The information on contemporary Eastern forms of eucharistic concelebration given by McGowan and King[1] is generally accurate, with a few exceptions that will be corrected here.

The *Armenians* practice eucharistic concelebration only at episcopal and presbyteral ordinations, a custom they may have borrowed from the Latins.[2] *Catholic Armenians* have begun to practice eucharistic concelebration since Vatican II, in imitation of the new Latin usage.

---

[*] Reprinted from *Beyond East and West.* Second Edition (Rome: POI, 1997). Revised from *Worship* 54 (1980) 308–25, with additional material from my commentary referred to in n. 44 below.

[1] J. McGowan, *Concelebration: Sign of the Unity of the Church* (New York: Herder and Herder, 1964) 39–53; A. King, *Concelebration in the Christian Church* (London: A. R. Mowbray, 1966) 102–32. The basic general study is A. Raes, "La concélébration eucharistique dans les rites orientaux," *LMD* 35 (1953) 24–47.

[2] On Latin influence in Armenia, see G. Winkler, "Armenia and the Gradual Decline of its Traditional Liturgical Practices as a Result of the Expanding Influence

The *Maronites,* also influenced by the Latins, probably owe their practice of verbal co-consecration to scholastic theology of the Eucharist. Before the seventeenth century, concelebration without co-consecration was in use.[3]

In the *Coptic Orthodox* Church several presbyters participate in the common Eucharist vested, in the sanctuary. Only the main celebrant (who is not the *presiding* celebrant if a bishop is present) stands at the altar, but the prayers are shared among the several priests. Some prayers, but not necessarily the "consecratory" part of the anaphora, are the preserve of the main celebrant at the altar.[4] *Catholic Copts,* like the Maronites, have adopted a type of verbal co-consecration. This could represent the revival of an older usage. In several ancient Alexandrian manuscripts, diaconal admonitions at the words of institution exhort the concelebrants to join with the main celebrant at this solemn moment of the anaphora.[5] Though not necessarily a proof of *verbal* co-consecration, this certainly implies "concelebration" even in the narrow modern sense of the term.

Among the *Syrian Orthodox* it is customary for several presbyters to join with the bishop in the celebration of the liturgy. Only the bishop is fully vested. The assisting presbyters wear just the stole over their clerical gown, a garment similar to the Byzantine *rason,* but at the beginning of the anaphora one of them puts on the *phaino* (Greek *phainolion,* the principal outer vestment) and joins the bishop at the altar for the anaphora. Though the bishop shares the various prayers of the anaphora with the presbyters, he alone recites the words of institution and the epiclesis up to and including the blessing of the gifts,[6] at which point he retires to his throne while the presbyter in the *phaino*

---

of the Holy See from the 11th to the 14th Century," in *Liturgie de l'église particulière et liturgie de l'église universelle* (BELS 4, Rome: Edizioni Liturgiche, 1976) 329–68.

[3] Cf. P. Daou, "Notes sur les origins de la concélébration eucharistique dans le rite maronite," *OCP* 6 (1940) 233–39. Daou (236–39) denies that the Maronite practice arose in imitation of Latin liturgical usage, but it is certainly the result of Latin eucharistic theology, of which his very article is the perfect example.

[4] Information from my colleague, Samir Khalil, S.J., a priest of the Coptic rite.

[5] See R.-C. Coquin, "Vestiges de concélébration eucharistique chez les melkites égyptiens, les coptes et les éthiopiens," *Le Muséon* 80 (1967) 37–46; also J.-M. Hanssens, "Un rito di concelebrazione della messa propria della liturgia alessandrina," *Studia orientalia christiana. Collectanea* 13 (Cairo 1968–1969) 3–34, and the Coptic sources cited in ch. 7, where only one of the officiating priests is said to be the celebrant.

[6] That is up to the "Amen" in F. E. Brightman, *Liturgies Eastern and Western* (Oxford: Clarendon, 1896) 89, line 11.

takes over at the altar to complete the epicletic prayer and share the rest of the anaphora with the other presbyters. At the end of the anaphora the bishop again takes his place at the altar, and the assisting priest retires to remove the *phaino*. It is necessary only for the bishop to communicate, but of course the concelebrants may if properly disposed. Though this form of concelebration is not mentioned in most descriptions of the *West Syrian* rite,[7] I have assisted at such a celebration and, on inquiring, was assured that it is common usage. In addition, both Orthodox and Catholic Syrians practice a rite of "synchronized Masses," each celebrant having his own bread and cup.[8]

The *Ethiopians* have a similar rite of "synchronized Masses" as well as a form of eucharistic celebration in which several presbyters—ideally, thirteen—take active part with various functions and prayers distributed among them, that is, not done simultaneously by all as in verbal co-consecration.[9] Indeed, this is the normal form of Eucharist among the Ethiopian Orthodox, and at least five presbyters, and preferably seven, are considered essential if the Eucharist is to be celebrated at all. These presbyters must all communicate at the celebration.

In the traditional *East-Syrian* Eucharist, the bishop surrounded by his presbyters presides over the liturgy of the word from the bema in the middle of the nave.[10] When the time for the anaphora approaches, one of the presbyters is selected to read it. He alone "consecrates." In this tradition *all* services and sacraments are "concelebrations" in which all the various orders of ministers participate according to their rank: singers singing, lectors reading, deacons proclaiming, presbyters sharing the prayers. But they do not *all* say the *same* prayers. Distribution is the principle.

Apparently the early *Byzantine* tradition followed a similar rite in which only one celebrant recited the anaphora, but later we see, as in

[7] An exception is A. Cody, "L'office divin chez les Syriens Jacobites, Leurs eucharisties épiscopales et leurs rites de pénitence. Description des cérémonies, avec notes historiques," *Proche-Orient chrétien* 19 (1969) 1–6.

[8] Cf. King, *Concélébration* 121–22. Personal inquiry among Syrian Orthodox clergy has confirmed that this rite is still in use.

[9] My information on Ethiopian usage is from Abba Tekle-Mariam Semharay Selim, *Règles speciales de messe éthiopienne* (Rome: École typographique "Pie X," 1936) 10–13.

[10] See W. F. Macomber, "Concelebration in the East Syrian Rite," J. Vellian (ed.), *The Malabar Church* (OCA 186, Rome: PIO, 1970) 17–22; S. Y. H. Jammo, *La structure de la messe chaldéenne du début jusqu'à l'anaphore. Étude historique* (OCA 207, Rome: PIO, 1979) *passim*; R. Taft, "On the Use of the Bema in the East-Syrian Liturgy," *Eastern Churches Review* 3 (1970) 30–39.

the West, the inexorable growth in the verbalization of eucharistic concelebration, with the same prayers being said by all concelebrating ministers.[11] In this as in other traditions one must distinguish Orthodox from Eastern-Catholic practice. Many Eastern-Catholic priests, under Western influence, say Mass daily out of devotion, even when there is no pastoral need for them to officiate, so for them concelebration is much the same as for their post-Vatican II Latin confreres: a means of satisfying their private devotion, their desire to "say Mass" every day, while avoiding the dissolution of eucharistic *koinonia* represented by that curious counter-symbol of ecclesial communion, the so-called "private Mass."[12]

Among the *Byzantine Orthodox*, concelebration is normally practiced only when a bishop is celebrating solemnly, or to solemnize a festive presbyteral liturgy. Thus in a monastery on an ordinary day, one priest would celebrate and the others assist *modo laico*, unvested,

---

[11] On the earlier form of Byzantine concelebration, see R. Taft, "Byzantine Liturgical Evidence in the *Life of St. Marcian the Oeconomos:* Concelebration and the Preanaphoral Rites," *OCP* 48 (1982) 159–70. The best general study on Byzantine concelebration is H. Brakmann, "Καί ἀναγινώσκουσι πάντες οἱ Ἱερεῖς τὴν εὐχαρισήριον Εὐχήν. Zum gemeinschaftlichen Eucharistigebet byzantinischer Konzelebranten," *OCP* 42 (1976) 319–67. Note that each concelebrant says the prayers to himself. There is no common choral recitation as in Latin usage, except among some latinized Byzantine Catholics at some parts of the liturgy.

[12] This discomfort with the private Mass is based not on the Reformation critique of medieval eucharistic theology, but on ancient elements within the Catholic tradition of East and West. The point is not whether only two or three can constitute a Christian community to celebrate the Lord's Supper, but rather the multiplication of individual, private Masses ("divisive Mass" would be a more accurate term) *within the same community at the same time and place.* Hence the evidence sometimes advanced to demonstrate the existence of "private Mass" in antiquity is beside the point. Such celebrations were what we would call "small-group Masses," which are another matter entirely. The issue is not the "head count," but the weakening of *koinonia* by placing it second to the devotional desires of individual presbyters to say "their" Mass. This would have been inconceivable in antiquity. Relics of a more traditional approach were retained by the Latin Church until recently. The absolute prohibition of private Masses on Holy Thursday, at papal conclaves, at the opening of a synod (cf. McGowan, *Concelebration* 55 ff.) shows that when the Church wished to manifest in its fullness the eucharistic sign of ecclesial communion, eucharistic dispersion into individual Masses was forbidden. If the multiplication of Masses or the devotional desires of the individual celebrant to say "his" Mass was truly of more spiritual value, a source of more grace and glory to God, then what possible right could the Church have had to limit God's grace and glory in this way?

in the nave or in the sanctuary. On feasts a few concelebrating presbyters would join the principal celebrant. A bishop is usually joined by numerous concelebrating presbyters, and even by other bishops.

Byzantine Catholics and those Orthodox that follow the Russian usage in this matter practice verbal co-consecration. This was once thought to be the result of Western influence in the sixteenth century, but recently scholars have challenged successfully this theory.[13] Besides, A. Jacob has shown that verbal concelebration was in use in Constantinople by at least the tenth century,[14] and it is hardly possible to postulate the adoption of Latin usage there during that period of growing estrangement and ritual dispute between the Byzantine and Latin Churches.[15]

Among the *Greek Orthodox,* however, there appear to be conflicting usages coexisting in peaceful competition. One priest whom I questioned assured me that all concelebrants should say all the priestly prayers, including the words of institution and epiclesis; another informed me that only the main celebrant consecrates. The 1951 Athens *Hieratikon* contains a rubric for the beginning of the anaphora that "all the priests read the eucharistic prayer,"[16] but the same edition gives the impression later in the text that only the main celebrant says the institution narrative and epiclesis.[17] H. Brakmann, however, has shown that these rubrics refer to the main celebrant's role and cannot be interpreted restrictively as excluding the recitation of the consecratory prayers by the concelebrating presbyters.[18] Nevertheless, the 1962 *Apostolikḗ Didakonia* edition of the *Hieratikon* makes it quite clear that only the first priest consecrates.[19] Here we seem to

[13] Cf. Brakmann, "Zum gemeinschaftlichen Eucharistiegebet" 321 ff., 337–67, and A. Jacob, "La concélébration de l'anaphore à Byzance d'après le témoignage de Léon Toscan," *OCP* 35 (1969) 249–56.

[14] Cf. the previous note.

[15] Cf. O. Rousseau, "La question des rites entre Grecs et Latins des premiers siècles au concile de Florence," *Irénikon* 22 (1949) 248 ff.

[16] In the appendix *Hieratikon sylleitourgon* 170.

[17] *Ibid.,* 170–71.

[18] "Zum gemeinschaftlichen Eucharistigebet" 324–34.

[19] Appendix *Hieratikon sylleitourgon* 248–49, rubrics 15–16. The final rubric (no. 25, 250) could not be more explicit: if the first celebrant concedes to the concelebrants the parts that are proper to him, especially the blessings (the consecratory blessings of the epiclesis, undoubtedly), this would not be a sign of courtesy and humility on his part, but a high-handed violation of ecclesiastical discipline regardless of the pretext! Such admonitions are of course usually meant to counteract existing practice.

have a case where verbal concelebration is in use *except for* the consecration! But we must not immediately conclude that this practice is in direct continuity with ancient tradition. It may be the result of the teaching of Nicodemus the Hagiorite (1749–1809), who held that in order to preserve the unity of the offering, only one priest should say the prayers.[20] But it is obvious from Nicodemus's polemic against "certain concelebrants . . . each of whom has his separate book of the Divine Liturgy and recites the prayers privately" that he was arguing against an existing practice.[21]

It is worth noting that in the Byzantine, as in other traditions, concelebration is not limited to the Eucharist. The same norms apply to other services. When a bishop celebrates vespers, a vigil, a requiem, he always has concelebrants, and the same is true of more solemn services even when there is no bishop celebrating. In such concelebrations, various parts are reserved to the main celebrant, others parceled out. The anointing of the sick is done (ideally) by seven presbyters. But except for the blessing of the oil in this rite, and the prayers of the eucharistic liturgy, the concelebrants do not all recite the *same* prayers in these services. Rather, *distribution* is the norm. But the anointing of the sick is a real "sacramental" concelebration, since even the anointings are shared. A similar rite is found among the Copts and Armenians.[22]

We do not yet have the studies at our disposal to evaluate the reasons for the appearance and spread of verbal concelebration in the East. But it does not represent the practice of the primitive Church.

2. EUCHARISTIC CELEBRATION IN THE ANCIENT CHURCH: CELEBRATION OR CONCELEBRATION?

In 1 Corinthians, our earliest witness to the Eucharist, St. Paul presents the ideal form of this service as one fraternal banquet which the whole community "celebrates" together (11:17-34; cf. 10:16-17). I presume that one community leader presided over the celebration and said the prayer of table blessing, after the manner of Jewish repasts.[23]

[20] On Nicodemus, see Brakmann, "Zum gemeinschaftlichen Eucharistiegebet" 334 ff. Cf. the similar objection in Thomas Aquinas, *ST* III 82, 2.
[21] *Heortodromion étoi herméneia eis tous asmatikous kanonas tôn despotkôn kai theométorikôn heortôn* (Venice: N. Glykei, 1836) 576, n. 1.
[22] Cf. H. Denzinger, *Ritus orientalium coptorum, syrorum et armenorum in administrandis sacramentis* . . . vol. 2 (Würzburg: Stahel, 1864) 483ff., 519 ff.
[23] Cf. L. Bouyer, *Eucharist. Theology and Spirituality of the Eucharistic Prayer* (Notre Dame: University of Notre Dame, 1968) 80 ff.

Paul seems to imply this in 1 Corinthians 14:16-17: ". . . if you bless with the spirit, how can any one in the position of an outsider say the 'Amen' to your thanksgiving when he does not know what you are saying? For you may give thanks well enough, but the other one is not edified." And his insistence on unity in 1 Corinthians 11 would seem to demand one blessing of the shared food.

To speak of "concelebration" in this context would of course be tautological, implying a clergy-laity division that had not hardened so early. Paul speaks of a variety of roles and ministries at the common services (1 Cor 12 and 14), and of the need for order in the community (1 Cor 12:27-30) and in its assemblies (1 Cor 14, esp. 26-40). But one certainly does not get the impression of a community divided into "celebrants" and "congregation." Rather, the whole problem in 1 Corinthians 12 and 14 is that everyone got into the act without due regard for one another, thereby provoking disorder and disunity in the (ideally) one celebration.

This same concern with unity runs through the Last Supper discourse in John (13:3-16, 34-35; 15:1-12; 17:11, 20-23) and descriptions of the primitive ecclesial assembly in Acts (1:14; 2:1, 42-47; 4:32-35; 20:7). And it is uppermost in the mind of the Apostolic Fathers. Ignatius of Antioch at the beginning of the second century is the classic witness:

"Take care, then, to use one eucharist, for there is one flesh of our Lord Jesus Christ, and one cup of union in His blood, one altar just as there is one bishop together with the presbytery and the deacons, my fellow servants. . . . (*Philadelphians* 4; cf. 6.2).

". . . All of you to a man . . . come together in one faith and in Jesus Christ . . . to show obedience to the bishop and presbytery with undivided mind, breaking one bread . . . (*Ephesians* 20.2; cf. 5.1-3).

". . . Strive to do all things in harmony with God, with the bishop presiding in the place of God, the presbyters in the place of the council of the apostles, and the deacons . . . entrusted with the ministry of Jesus Christ. . . . Love one another at all times in Jesus Christ, let there be nothing among you that could divide you, but be united with the bishop and those presiding. . . . Just as the Lord did nothing without the Father, being one with Him . . . so neither should you undertake anything without the bishop or presbyters. Do not try to make anything private appear reasonable to you, but at your meetings [let there be] one prayer, one supplication, one mind, one hope in love, in the blameless joy that is Jesus Christ, above whom there is nothing. Come together all of you as to one temple of God and to one altar, to one Jesus Christ . . . (*Magn.* 6–7; cf. *Smyr.* 8)."

Barnabus (*Ep.* 4.10) and Clement of Rome (*Ep.* 34.7) reflect the same concern.[24] But in this literature we see more than a continuation of the Pauline preoccupation with unity at Corinth. By the end of the first century a more articulate ministerial structure has emerged to serve this unity, and is reflected in the order of services. The presiding minister or "high priest" is joined in the celebration by other ministers. They are distinguished from the "layman"—the term first appears at this time[25]—by role and seating in the assembly. If such a system cannot yet be considered general, the *Letter of Clement* testifies to it at least for Rome and Corinth by around A.D. 96:

"40.1. . . . We should do with order *(taxis)* all that the Master has prescribed to be accomplished at set times. 2. Now He ordered that the offerings *(prosphorai)* and public services *(leitourgiai)* be done not haphazardly or irregularly, but at fixed times and hours. 3. And He has himself determined by his supreme will where and by whom He desires this to be done. . . . 4. Thus those who make their offerings *(prosphorai)* at the appointed times are accepted and blessed. . . . 5. For the High Priest *(archiereus)* is assigned the services *(leitourgiai)* proper to him, and to the priests *(hiereis)* has been designated their proper place *(topos)*, and on the levites [i.e., deacons] have been imposed their proper ministries *(diakoniai)*. The lay person *(laikos anthropos)* is bound by the regulations for the laity. 41.1. Let each of us, brothers, be pleasing to God in his own order *(tagma)* . . . without infringing the prescribed rule of his service *(leitourgia)*. . . ."[26]

Here we see at least an adumbration of the system that emerges in documents of the third century: presbyters other than the assembly president cannot be said to have participated in the services simply "as laity." They were not just "in attendance" at the service, albeit with "reserved seats"; they also performed liturgical actions.[27] But

---

[24] Barnabus, *Ep.* 4:10 PG 2, 733–34; Clément de Rome, *Épitre aux corinthiens*, ed. A. Jaubert (SC 167, Paris: Cerf, 1971) 156.

[25] Our first witness is the text of Clement (40.5) cited below. Cf. I. de La Potterie, "L'origine et le sens primitif du mot 'laïc,'" *Nouvelle Revue Théologique* 80 (1958) 840–53.

[26] My translation from the edition of Jaubert, 166.

[27] Cf. *Apostolic Tradition* 4, ed. B. Botte, *La tradition apostolique de s. Hippolyte. Essai de reconstitution* (LQF 39, Münster: Aschendorff, 1963) 11; *Didascalia* II, 57,

any attempt to interpret this participation as "concelebration" in the sense of consciously exercising in common some sort of sacramental "power" proper to their order, seems to go beyond the evidence. Rather, one gets the impression of a single common assembly at which each category of laity as well as clergy had its special place and role. Indeed, most sources say far more about the role of the deacons and people in the eucharistic celebration than they do about the role of the presbyters, yet no one would think of calling them "concelebrants" in the narrow, contemporary sense of the term!

Since the fourth century, Eastern evidence generally concurs that the full-blown Eucharist involved the bishop surrounded by his presbyters, who were not merely "in attendance" in the presbyterium but actively participated in the ritual in a manner reserved to their order.[28] This is clear from canonical literature such as Canon 1 of the Council of Ancyra (c. 314) or the *Second Canonical Letter* of St. Basil (d. 379), which envisage the case of a presbyter under ecclesiastical sanction preserving his seat in the presbyterium while suspended from all ministerial functions, including the right to "offer" the Eucharist.[29] Here a clear line is drawn between presbyters in attendance

---

R. H. Connolly, *Didascalia apostolorum* (Oxford: Clarendon, 1929) 119–20 = F. X. Funk, *Didascalia et Constitutiones apostolorum* (Paderborn: F. Schoeningh, 1905) I, 158–66.

[28] Cf. *Apostolic Constitutions* (late 4th c.) II, 57 and VIII, 11.12; 12.3–4, *SC* 320, 310–20; 336, 76–178, and later related literature: *Didascalia arabica* 35, Funk II, 124–125; *Ex constitutionibus capitula* 14, *ibid.* II, 139; *Constitutiones ecclesiae aegyptiacae* I (XXXI) 10, 31, *ibid.* II. 99, 102; Theodore of Mopsuestia (ca. 388–392), *Hom. 15*, 42; *Hom. 16*, 24, ed. R. Tonneau and R. Devreesse, *Les homélies catéchétiques de Théodore de Mopsueste* (Studi e testi 145, Vatican: Bibliotheca Apostolica Vaticana, 1949) 527, 569; the Synod of Mar Issac (A.D. 410), J.-B. Chabot, *Synodicon orientale* (Paris: Imprimerie nationale, 1902) 268; *Testamentum domini nostri Iesu Christi* (5th c.) I, 23, ed. I. E. Rahmani (Mainz: F. Kirchheim 1899) 34–36; Ps.-Denys (end 5th c.) *Ecclesiastical Hierarchy* 3, 2, *PG* 3, 425; Narsai (d. 502) *Homily 17, The Liturgical Homilies of Narsai*, trans. R. H. Connolly (Texts and Studies 8.1, Cambridge: University Press, 1909) 4–5, 9, 27; the 6th c. *Ordo quo episcopus urbem inire debet*, ed. I. E. Rahmani (Studia Syriaca, fasc. 3, Charfeh 1908) 3–4 [22], trans. G. Khouri-Sarkis, "Réception d'un évêque syrien au VIe siècle," *L'Orient syrien* 2(1957) 160–62, R. Taft, *The Great Entrance. A History of the Transfer of Gifts and other Preanaphoral Rites of the Liturgy of St. John Chrysostom* (OCA 200, Rome: PIO, 1978²) 40–41; Canon 11 of the Letter of Išoʿyahb I to the Bishop of Darai (A.D. 585), Chabot, *Synodicon* 430; Gabriel Qatraya bar Lipah (ca. 615), ed. Jammo, *La messe chaldéenne* 33ff.; and the later sources adduced in Jammo, *passim*, and Taft, *Great Entrance* 166–68, 197–98, 201–6, 210–13, 264ff., 291–310.

[29] Basil, *Ep.* 199, 27 *PG* 32, 724; Ancyra, canon 1, Mansi 2, 514 (cf. Neocaesarea, canon 9, *ibid.* 542).

at the Eucharist and those who "offer." But one cannot press the theological significance of this for concelebration. A similar situation was envisaged for laity in the final stages of penance: they were *consistentes,* allowed to "attend" the whole liturgy without, however, participating in the "offering."[30]

So it is not easy to know what theological meaning should be attached to such evidence without seeming to read history backwards. Where the evidence is clear, as in the Syrian traditions, it favors the conclusion that only the main celebrant "consecrated" the gifts.[31] But by then sacrificial theology is in bloom, and we find texts which say that concelebrating ministers of at least presbyteral rank "offer" *(prospherein, offerre),* even "as priests" *(hierourgein)* the common Eucharist.[32] Now though we must be wary of reading our later theological presuppositions into texts that seem to affirm what we hope to find; we must also avoid giving a minimalist interpretation to texts just because they do not meet modern Roman requirements for "true, sacramental" concelebration. The homilies of Theodore of Mopsuestia, for example, make it quite clear (1) that the concelebrants "offer" the Eucharist, (2) that this involves the exercise of a ministry proper to their order not shared with the laity, and (3) that only the bishop says the Eucharistic Prayer.[33]

Two conclusions seem obvious: (1) From the fourth century we see a growing consciousness that presbyters celebrating the Eucharist together with the bishop are doing something that the laity cannot do, something only they have the mandate to perform. (2) This cannot be interpreted, without further evidence, to mean that they were "co-consecrating" verbally, that they recited in common the prayer of blessing of the gifts. Such a presumption would be anachronistic,

[30] Basil, *Third Canonical Letter* (= *Ep.* 217, 56, 75, 77, PG 32, 797, 804–5).

[31] Theodore of Mopsuestia, see below, n. 32; Narsai, *Homily* 17, in Connolly 4, 7ff., 12 ff., 18 ff., but esp. 27; Ps.-Denys, *Eccles. Hier.* 3 PG 3, 425; *Test. domini* I, 23, ed. Rahmani, 38 ff.

[32] Council of Neocaesarea (ca. 315) canons 13–14, Mansi, 2, 542–42; Theodore of Mopsuestia, *Hom.* 15, 42, ed. Tonneau-Devreesse, 527; the letter of Presbyter Uranius describing the Eucharist celebrated on his deathbed by Paulinus of Nola (d. 431) together with two visiting bishops Symmachus and Acindynus: ". . . una cum sanctis episcopis oblat sacrificio" (*Ep* 2, PL 53, 860); Evagrius Scholasticus's account of the visit of Bishop Damnus of Antioch to Symeon Stylites (d. 459) and the Eucharist they celebrated together: ". . . *To achranton heirougésantes sôma . . .*" (*Hist. eccl.* I, 13, PG 86[2], 2453).

[33] *Hom.* 15 *passim,* esp. 36, 41, 44, *Hom.* 16, preface and 2, 5–16, 20; ed. Tonneau-Devreesse 517–19, 525, 529, 531–35, 537–59, 563.

based on the later identification in scholastic theology of the "essence" of the eucharistic sacrifice with the "consecration" of the gifts. This theory is coherent and may even be true. But it is not primitive, and that is the point at issue here.

G. Dix thought this growing consciousness that "concelebrating" presbyters "co-offer" the sacrifice with the bishop reflects the extension to presbyters of what had once been the preserve of bishops.[34] When the episcopal system of church order described by Ignatius of Antioch first appears on the scene, it seems that only the bishop presided over the eucharistic assembly, except when he would depute a presbyter to preside in his name over the assembly of some outlying community. But I would suggest that the origins of our "concelebration" are to be sought elsewhere, not in this expression of the *koinonia* of the local church, celebrated by the bishop together with the presbyters, deacons, deaconesses, widows, virgins, and so on, but rather in the "eucharistic hospitality" accorded visiting bishops as a sign of communion among sister churches. There are several clear historical instances of this in the case of visiting bishops or bishops in synod.[35] On the local level the same privilege was allowed "chorbishops" (i.e., suffragan, country bishops) by their superior, the town bishop.[36] It is precisely in the latter instance that we first see the term "concelebrants" *(sylleitourgoi),* and it is this that Canon 13 of the Council of Neocaesarea (ca. 315) explicitly forbids to country presbyters.[37] But as it became more and more common for presbyters to be assigned the eucharistic presidency, perhaps a consciousness grew that even at the bishop's liturgy they too could "co-offer," just as visiting bishops were wont to do.

What is certain is that however it happened, this consciousness did indeed grow, to the extent that a few centuries later the Eastern

[34] *The Shape of the Liturgy* (London: Dacre, 1945) 34.

[35] Several examples in McGowan, *Concelebration* 24 ff., 40 ff. But even in the earliest of such cases there is no evidence of "co-consecration," though the *episcopé* of the assembly was shared and this was called a "concelebration." Those texts that are clear on the matter seem to indicate that in such cases the guest bishop was "conceded" the blessing of the gifts. Cf. Eusebius, *Hist. eccles.* V, 24, 17, *Eusebius Werke* II, 1, ed. E. Schwartz (GCS, Leipzig: J. C. Hinrichs, 1903) 496 = *PG* 20, 508; *Didascalia* II, 58, ed. Funk I, 168 = Connolly 122.

[36] Neocaesarea, canon 14, Mansi 2, 542–543. "Chorbishop" is from the Greek *chôra* meaning "country" as opposed to town.

[37] *Loc. cit.*

167

sylleitougein had become, for the Latins at least, "co-consecrate,"[38] and we are on the threshold of "concelebration" identified as the verbal co-consecration of the same eucharistic elements by more than one minister of at least presbyteral rank. In the West we find it in a seventh-century passage of *Ordo romanus* III.[39] Our earliest Eastern evidence is a rubric from a tenth-century Byzantine *diataxis* or rubric book incorporated into Leo Tuscan's version of the Chrysostom Liturgy.[40]

Interestingly enough, this latter text witnesses to another innovation previously unheard of: a eucharistic concelebration of *presbyters alone,* without the presidency of the bishop. Just what ecclesiology such a service is meant to represent has been questioned by the late Russian-Orthodox ecclesiologist N. Afanas'ev in his slender but valuable study *The Lord's Table.*[41]

3. REFLECTIONS

The above evidence reveals at least this much: that there is no one "Eastern" tradition to turn to for support, nor, as both Jungmann and Dix showed a generation ago, can one simply presume that "Eastern" equals "ancient."[42] The presbyteral co-consecratory concelebration practiced in most Eastern-Catholic traditions has nothing to do with ancient usage, but is derived from more recent developments and is colored by later scholastic sacramental theory of individual priestly

[38] Cf. the letter of Pope John VIII to Photius (A.D. 879), *Ep.* 248, *PL* 126, 871: "tecum . . . consecrare" = *sylleitourgesai soi* in the Greek version in Mansi 17[1], 413 B.

[39] III, 1, *Les "Ordines romani" du haut moyen-âge,* ed. M. Andrieu, vol. 2 (Spicilegium sacrum Lovaniense. Études et documents, fasc. 23, Louvain: Université Catholique, 1960) 131. On the question of dating and on the inclusion of this text in *Ordo I,* cf. *ibid.,* 127.

[40] Jacob, "Concélébration"; cf. Taft, *Great Entrance* 124 ff.

[41] *Trapeza Gospodnja* (Pravoslavie i sovremennost, 2–3, Paris: Izdanie Religiozno-Pedagogicheskogo Kabineta pri Pravoslavnom Bogoslovskom Institute v Parizhe, 1952) 64 ff. A. calls such a concelebration a "liturgical paradox," for the *raison d'être* of concelebration was to represent the unity of the local church: bishops, presbyters, deacons, people. Presbyters celebrated the Eucharist when sent to a segment of the local community as representative of the bishop, but they did not "concelebrate" with one another in the bishop's absence.

[42] J. A. Jungmann, "The Defeat of Teutonic Arianism and the Revolution in Religious Culture in the Early Middle Ages," in his *Pastoral Liturgy* (New York: Herder and Herder, 1962) 9–15; *The Place of Christ in Liturgical Prayer* (New York: Alba House, 1965) part 2 *passim,* Dix, *Shape* 264 ff. In fact the Roman rite has preserved important primitive elements long obscured in the East.

sacrifice and the "special grace" (plus stipend) accruing therefrom. And this is what was instituted for the Roman rite at Vatican II. What is ancient about Eastern eucharistic practice is not its various modes of concelebration, some quite admirable, others less so, but its preservation, by and large, of the ancient ideal of eucharistic unity: one community, one altar, one Eucharist. This is the crux of the matter as I see it today: the Eucharist as sacrament of the *koinonia* that is the Church. This is the real issue and it is an ecclesiological one.

The Council Fathers, in restoring concelebration at Vatican II, were aware of this issue (*Orient., eccl.* 15; *Presbyt. ordinis* 7). But they were more concerned with the (for me) secondary question of concelebration as a manifestation of the unity of the ministerial priesthood (*Sacrosanctum concilium* 57). From that standpoint the restored rite must be declared a marked success. Catholic priests have learned once more to pray together. No longer are religious communities of priests faced with the supreme irony of a community prayer-life in which everything is done in common except the one thing Christ left them as *the* sacrament of their unity in him.

It was to such largely clerical concerns that much of the Vatican II preparatory literature on concelebration was dedicated. Rereading some of this material, I was struck by how totally foreign the concerns of these authors are from those of the present. Much of their discussion is focused on whether a presbyter who does not verbally co-consecrate can be said to "offer the sacrifice" by intending to "exercise his priestly power" in gesture and intention, through the voice of the main celebrant. Even Rahner's articles, among the most sane interventions in the whole pre-Vatican II debate, are overly concerned with the celebrant and what he gets out of it.[43]

I see the present crisis as a healthy sign that, having benefited immensely from the priestly unity in prayer fostered by the restored rite of concelebration, we are now ready for a broader perspective. Excessively narrow clerical concerns are now rejected as irrelevant, and the actual rite is more and more perceived as a celebration of division— no longer the eucharistic division among priests caused by the private Mass, but the division of the community into those "celebrating" and those who "attend." I do not think that concelebration necessarily manifests *division* rather than the *hierarchic structure* of the ecclesial

---

[43] K. Rahner and A. Häussling, *The Celebration of the Eucharist* (New York: Herder and Herder, 1968).

community. But when one thinks of those top-heavy mob concelebrations that have become common coin; of the confusion of roles created by having the laity join the concelebrants around the altar for the anaphora and even recite it with them; or worse, when one suddenly sees a hand shoot out from the pews, and a priest attending Mass with the faithful begins to mumble the words of institution— when one has been subjected to such aberrations, it is difficult not to share the growing malaise.

What we are dealing with here (in addition to plain ignorance and bad taste) is a conflict of theologies. It is my own conviction that only a balanced theology of Church can be the guiding norm for the shape of our celebration, and not the "devotion" or desire or supposed "right" to "exercise one's priesthood" or to "offer sacrifice" or whatever of anyone, priest or otherwise. A 1980 commentary on "interritual concelebration"—ordained ministers concelebrating at a Eucharist celebrated in a rite other than their own—issued by the Congregation for the Eastern Churches shows, I believe, that the official Catholic thinking on concelebration is beginning to move in this direction.[44] Respect for the integrity of the tradition of the local worshiping community as the concrete expression of ecclesial communion is the leitmotif of the document. The rite to be used is preferably that of the host church, contrary to previous legislation that always gave precedence to the rite of the *celebrant*.[45] And the document shows a far better sense of the basics than is usual in discussion of clerical concelebration: namely, that the Eucharist is a *communio*, a celebration of unity, not a ritualization of division; that any liturgy is the service of a local church, not a private clerical devotion; that, consequently, its norms are determined by the broader ecclesial and pastoral demands of this *communio*, not by the devotional needs of the ministers, who are there to serve the Church, not themselves.

Even more basic than ecclesiology, perhaps, is a fundamental problem in Roman Catholic liturgical theology: the classic distinction between Eucharist *ut sacramentum* and Eucharist *ut sacrificium*, with the reduction of the former to a discussion of the "real presence," and the

---

[44] *Servizio informazione per le Chiese orientali*, vol. 45, nos. 409–10 (Rome, July–August 1980) 8–18. See R. Taft, "Interritual Concelebration," *Worship* 55 (1981) 441–44. These and other excellent norms and principles governing concelebration have been incorporated into no. 57 of the *Instruction for Applying Liturgical Prescriptions of the Code of Canons of the Eastern Churches* (Vatican: Libreria Editrice Vaticana, 1996).

[45] Canon 2.1 of the motu proprio *Cleri sanctitati* (1957).

overwhelmingly predominant role until recently of the latter in the theology of the eucharistic celebration. As sacrifice, the Eucharist is effected by the priest in the consecration. Even if done privately, it is still said to be "public," offered, like the offering of Christ on the cross, for the salvation of the whole world. The Mass is the sign of this offering, and as such shares its impetratory and satisfactory value. Further, the priest offers acting *in persona Christi,* and every priestly offering involves a "separate act" of Christ the High Priest (Pius XII).[46] Since this is true of five private Masses, or of one verbal co-consecration by five priests, but *not* true (again, Pius XII[47]) of Mass said by one priest with four others attending or only "ceremonially concelebrating," not "sacramentally," then the conclusion for Catholic priests formed in this theory is ineluctable: everybody should "co-consecrate." Helping to sustain this is the notion that somehow "more sacrifice," "more glory," is thus offered to God, and "more grace" acquired for the co-consecrator and those for whom he offers. For someone who believes that this is what the Eucharist is all about, I see no way around the problem.

We need to return to a saner theology, such as that of St. Thomas Aquinas, who said that the fruit of the Eucharist is the unity of the mystical body of Christ (*ST* III, 82, 9, ad. 2), and that "the Eucharist is the sacrament of the unity of the Church, which results from the fact that many are one in Christ" (*ST* III, 82, 2, ad. 3). It was this *koinonia,* and it alone, that determined the shape of the Eucharist in the early Church.[48] One community, one table, one Eucharist was the universal rule. And it remains so still in much of the Christian East. A recovery of this vision is the only way out of the devotional narcissism prevalent in Latin priestly spirituality. What is important is that the gifts *be* blessed so that all may share them. Whether or not I am the presbyter that says the prayer of blessing is irrelevant: to do so is a ministry, not a prerogative.

It is this sacramental manifestation of ecclesial communion, more than the choreography of who stands where and says what, that is the substance of the matter as I see it, in function of which all the other issues are to be decided. In this, history can be instructive, but not determinative, for each generation manifests its own shifts in

---

[46] *Magnificate dominum,* 2 November 1954, *AAS* 46 (1954) 668 ff.

[47] *Loc. cit.*

[48] See L. Hertling, *Communio: Church and Papacy in Early Christianity* (Chicago: Loyola University, 1972).

ecclesial consciousness with corresponding adjustments in the liturgical models by which this is expressed.

What history shows us is that the external shape of the eucharistic celebration changed according to what people thought the Church and its service were all about. When the Church was a somewhat amorphous society, the Eucharist had a less structured shape. As orders and structures emerge and harden, these quite naturally find expression in the assembly: elders and deacons have special places and ceremonial roles at the worship presided over by the bishop, and visiting ministers are invited to take the place befitting their rank. Those who today are distressed by the presence of numerous vested presbyters in the sanctuary will find little comfort in history!

But somewhere along the line a turn in the road is taken, and the service begins to appear less the common celebration of all, each according to his or her rank and role, and more and more that which is done *by* the ministers *for* the rest. From high priest (bishop) presiding over a whole priestly people as the model, we have shifted to high priest/priests (presbyters)/laity.[49] I suspect that the breakup of effective eucharistic unity through the fourth-century decline in communion and division of the community into several non-communicating categories (catechumens, *energoumenoi, illuminandi,* penitents) were at the origins of this process. The Eucharist was no longer able to sustain an ideology of *koinonia* which the service in fact no longer expressed, so the ideology collapsed and the rite (ritual always outlasts theory) was forced to find ideological support elsewhere.[50]

This occurred in both East and West. The West alone, with that inexorable logical consistency with which it drives everything into the ground, took the next step of concluding (implicitly, at least) that the *laos* could be dispensed with, and private Mass was off and running. But even before that, we see a growing consciousness that "concelebrating" ordained ministers "co-offer" the Eucharist in a way different from that in which the whole Church can be said to offer, a consciousness that eventually finds its liturgical expression in co-consecratory concelebration.

[49] Dix, *Shape,* 33 ff.; H.-M. Legrand, "The Presidency of the Eucharist according to the Ancient Tradition," *Worship* 53 (1979) 422.

[50] I discuss this in my article, "The Liturgy of the Great Church: an Initial Synthesis of Structure and Interpretation on the Eve of Iconoclasm," DOP 34–35 (1980–1981) 68 ff.

I doubt very much whether an *in persona Christi* theology of the eucharistic minister had anything to do with the origins of this practice in the East. But that is surely what keeps it alive in the Catholic Church today. What priest wants to give up the right to exercise this privileged role, especially when it is the basis for his whole priestly spirituality and devotion?

Let me stress that the above remarks are not to be construed as an attack on the theology of Eucharist as sacrifice. My concern is liturgical: whose sacrifice of what, offered by whom, for what purpose, and how expressed? Some years ago Aelred Tegels expressed where the answer to what should be the form of concelebration lies:

"God is worshiped in the liturgy to the extent that the worshiping people are sanctified and they are sanctified to the extent that 'conscious, active and full participation' is procured. Liturgy is essentially pastoral. The ideal form of celebration is that which will most effectively associate this congregation, at this time and in this place, with Christ's own act of worship."[51]

Such a norm provides little justification for visiting priests who would simply use the worship of a local church as a convenient way of "saying their Mass," with no concern for the wider issues. This is not to exclude the legitimate demands of clerical devotion: priests are also people, and should be able to ritualize significant realities of their religious life. But this cannot be isolated from the ecclesial norms governing concelebration and, indeed, any liturgy: *Nisi utilitas fidelium . . . hoc impediat*—"unless the good of the faithful stands in its way."[52] Before this norm all discussion of how this or that priest gets more or less devotion, how many "acts of Christ" or "sacrifices" are offered, who does or does not "exercise his priesthood," whether one or more "masses are said," becomes totally secondary.

But even if one were to prescind from all ecclesial and pastoral questions and simply accept the fact that Roman Catholic priests must "exercise their priesthood," one can hardly consider the present Roman rite of concelebration ideal from a liturgical point of view. According to the present discipline of the Roman Catholic Church, no presbyter can be said to "validly" concelebrate the Eucharist unless he recites the prayer of consecration, regardless of what else he might do in gesture or

[51] "Chronicle," *Worship* 44 (1970) 183.
[52] *Eucharisticum mysterium,* May 25, 1967, no. 47.

symbol to show that he clearly intends to participate in—that is, concelebrate—the eucharistic liturgy according to his presbyteral rank. Though one may reject the presuppositions of medieval Latin eucharistic and sacramental theology that had led to such a conclusion, one can hardly question the right of the Roman Church to determine the concrete praxis of her ministers in the discipline of concelebration. But to raise such particular disciplinary exigencies to the level of a universal dogmatic principle, and then apply it in judging the practice of other churches or other epochs, is an unjustifiable procedure. If we approach our early and Eastern sources with such presuppositions, we are forced either to conclude that no "real" concelebration ever existed in ancient Christendom, or else to invent for the ancient period a new form of concelebration, never heard of then: "ceremonial" as opposed to "sacramental" concelebration, which is the only one held to be "real."

To maintain that "verbal" concelebration is the only "real" one is also to question much of Eastern tradition.

In fact this whole problematic is foreign to a sane liturgical mentality, in which the whole body of presbyters is the moral subject of the common ministry performed by them *in solidum*. To demand that they all recite certain words together manifests an ignorance of the hierarchical and symbolic nature of sacrament expressed in presence and gesture and witness, as well as in word.[53] Concelebration even in the narrow clerical sense is the common act of a *collegium*, not the synchronization of the sum of the acts of several individuals. Hence even for one with purely "clerical" concerns, the present Roman rite of verbal co-consecration seems more a denial than a manifestation even of the collegial unity of the presbyterium.[54]

And for one with broader pastoral concerns for the liturgical expression of the unity of the whole church-*koinonia* in the eucharistic rite, presbyteral concelebration in some of the forms presently in use leaves much to be desired as a symbol of our unity, and not of what separates us.

---

[53] Thus for centuries the three bishops that imposed hands at episcopal ordination were rightly considered true "co-consecrators." It would be a distortion of the whole tradition to consider them anything else, though only one said the formula of consecration. But since Pius XII all three co-consecrators have to recite the formula (*Episcopalis Consecrationis, AAS* 37 [1945] 131–32). Cf. McGowan, *Concelebration* 66–67.

[54] See the concluding remarks of B. Schultze, "Das theologische Problem der Konzelebration," *Gregorianum* 36 (1955) 268–71.

Robert F. Taft, S.J.

9. Receiving Communion: A Forgotten Symbol[*]

In popular speech we "receive communion" or "go to communion." Some even speak of "taking communion." I think the differences are more than semantic. "To take communion," like the reflexive in certain modern languages (for example, Italian: *comunicarsi*, Russian: *prichastit'sja*), places the emphasis on communion as an act of the individual believer, a personal exercise of piety; something I *do* rather than something *done to me*; something "taken" rather than a gift *given* and *received*, a sharing of something we have and do and receive in common and from one another—in short, a *communion*.

That this latter was the original sense of eucharistic *koinonia* in the early Church is obvious from the start. In 1 Corinthians 10:17 Paul tells us, "Because there is one bread, we who are many are one body, for we all partake of the one bread." And he then goes on to spell out the implications of this communion. A bit later, at the beginning of the second century, Ignatius of Antioch warns: "Take care, then, to use one Eucharist, for there is one flesh of our Lord Jesus Christ, and one cup of union in his blood, one altar just as there is one bishop together with the presbytery and the deacons, my fellow servants . . ."[1]

This rule of one communion was so strict that initially presbyters— "priests" as we call them—did not "say Mass" without the bishop. As a rule such sacramental ministries were celebrated by the bishop surrounded by his concelebrating church: presbyters, deacons, and people, all in the one *koinonia*. Rome, with its customary liturgical sobriety and respect for tradition, preserved this usage until at least the sixth century, according to the latest research on the topic. On Sundays the bishop of Rome celebrated the full Eucharist for the faithful. In other churches of the city a presbyter celebrated the Liturgy of the Word for the catechumens and penitents, all non-communicants, then he alone received communion from the *fermentum* or eucharistic

---

[*] Reprinted from R. Taft, *Beyond East and West*, Second Edition (Rome: PIO 1997). Expanded from *Worship* 57 (1983) 412–18.
[1] *Philadelphians* 4.

bread consecrated at the pope's Mass. This same rule of one Mass is said to have been operative also at Alexandria and Cathage.[2]

Eucharistic communion, therefore, is not just the sacrament of one's personal communion with the risen Lord. It is rather the sacrament of our communion with one another in the one body of Christ, a body at once ecclesial and eucharistic. That this was the full meaning of eucharistic *koinonia* in the early Church has been shown clearly enough by others.[3] It is also the teaching of St. Thomas Aquinas, who says that "the Eucharist is the sacrament of the unity of the Church, which results from the fact that many are one in Christ."[4]

Contemporary liturgical reforms have once again brought into prominence the *fractio* of the one bread, a pristine ritual expression of this mystery. But historical research into other aspects of the communion rites exposes our failure to carry this thinking through to include the way in which the sacrament is administered. A detailed history of the communion rites in the various traditions would carry us beyond the purpose of these brief notes. But I keep stumbling across texts that I think reflect a more acute liturgical understanding of communion than some of the practices one sees today. The general rule in communion rites right up through the Middle Ages, in both East and West, was that communion is not just *taken,* not even by the clergy, but *given* and *received.* For communion is at once a ministry and a gift and a sharing, and as such is *administered* to the communicant through the hands of another.

1. LATIN SOURCES

For example, in the eighth-century *Ordines romani,* a deacon brings communion to the pope at his throne, the archdeacon or a subdeacon gives him the chalice, then the bishops and presbyters come up to receive the consecrated bread from the pope's hand. One of the bishops or presbyters gives the chalice to the other bishops, presbyters, and deacons, and a deacon in turn gives the chalice to the lesser orders. Then the people receive the bread from the pope or from the bishops and presbyters, and the deacons administer the chalice. In a word,

[2] Report of a recent Sorbonne seminar in patristics and the history of dogma, to be published fully later. See P. Nautin, "Le rite du *fermentum,*" École pratique des Hautes Études, Ve section—Sciences religieuses, *Annuaire* 90 (1981–1982) 338.

[3] See L. Hertling, *Communio: Church and Papacy in Early Christianity* (Chicago: Loyola University, 1972).

[4] *ST* III, 82. 2 ad. 3; cf. 82. 9 ad. 2.

everyone *receives* communion from someone else. No one, not even the pope, just *takes* it.[5]

2. BYZANTINE SOURCES

In early Byzantine sources the only evidence I know of is the Life of St. Marcian the *Oeconomos* which describes a concelebration at Constantinople ca. 468–600. Marcian, though apparently only a presbyter, administers communion to all the other clergy, including, it seems, the archbishop.[6]

Similarly, the oldest (eleventh century) *diataxis* or *ordo* of the Byzantine partriarchal liturgy, which I edited a few years ago from the twelfth-century codex *British Library Add 34060*, gives this complicated set of rubrics for the communion of the patriarch:

"X.1 . . . [the patriarch] descends from the platform and bows three times to the east . . . 2. With him bows the priest who is supposed to give him communion, and both mount the platform and kiss the holy altar. 3. And first the bishop, having stretched forth his hands, receives. 4. Then holding the bread in the last two fingers, with the other three he takes the other particle and gives it to the one that gave communion to him . . . 8. And the archdeacon gives the chalice to the priest, and the bishop, after turning to him and bowing, communicates . . . 10. And after kissing the holy altar, he turns, and the chalice is taken from the priest, and [the bishop] communicates him."[7]

Then the two of them go off to administer the bread and chalice to the rest of the clergy and people. Not only does the patriarch receive communion from a "priest" (*hiereus,* probably one of the concelebrating bishops: in Byzantine Greek *hiereus* is used indiscriminately for anyone in "priestly" orders), he even waits until that minister also has received the host in his hand so both can consume the holy food together. This usage was the rule of Byzantine pontifical concelebrations for as long as the rubrics of the *diataxis* of Demetrius Gemistos

[5] See for instance *Ordo* I 106–121, in M. Andrieu, *Les "Ordines romani" du haut moyen âge,* vol. 2 (Spicilegium sacrum Lovaniense. Études et documents, fasc. 23, Louvain: Université Catholique, 1960) 101–6; *Ordo XV,* 54–65, *ibid.,* vol. 3 (fasc. 24, Louvain 1961) 106–9.

[6] R. Taft, "Byzantine Liturgical Evidence in the *Life of St. Marcian the Oeconomos:* Concelebration and the Preanaphoral Rites," *OCP* 48 (1982) 159–70, esp. 161–66.

[7] R. Taft, "The Pontifical Liturgy of the Great Church according to a Twelfth-Century Diataxis in Codex *British Museum Add. 34060,*" part I *OCP* 45 (1979) 300–3.

(ca. 1380) remained in force.[8] They were abandoned by the time of the *diataxis* of Patriarch Athanasius III Petelaras, composed in Moscow in 1653 for the reform of Nikon and later confirmed by Patriarchs Paisius of Alexandria and Macarius of Antioch at the Synod of Moscow in 1667.[9] In these latter rubrics we see today's usage: the bishop gives himself communion, then administers it to the concelebrating presbyters.[10]

But the older usage was not determined by rank—that is, by whether or not the main celebrant was higher up the hierarchical ladder than his concelebrants. For we see the same thing in the rubrics of Byzantine presbyteral concelebrations. For example, the eleventh-century euchology codex *Grottaferrata Gb II* (f. 20r-v) has these rubrics at communion:

"And the priest bows three times before the holy altar, and one of the concelebrating priests gives him one piece of the particles. And he in turn gives another piece to the priest. And they receive in like manner from the chalice, giving it to each other, and they kiss each other. And the second communicating priest stands to the right side of the holy altar holding the chalice, and the rest of the priests come up and receive and kiss him. Likewise the deacons, but the subdeacons and the rest of the clergy and the laity receive in the mouth and do not give the kiss. Likewise from the chalice."[11]

Leo Tuscan's version of the Chrysostom liturgy based on a Greek euchology manuscript of 1173–1178 has a like practice, though if the presbyter is celebrating alone he communicates himself, the rubrics specify:

---

[8] Text in A. Dmitrievskij, *Opisanie liturgicheskikh rukopisej khranjashchikhsja v bibliotekakh pravoslavnago vostoka*, vol. 2 (Kiev: Tipografia N. T. Korchak-Novitskago, 1901) 315–16. Seventeenth-century Slavonic *Trebniki* frequently have illustrations showing a bishop receiving communion from another bishop (Kiev, 1646, Lvov, 1682 and 1695). I am grateful to Sr. Sophia Senyk for bringing these sources to my attention.

[9] On this document see Taft, "Pontifical Liturgy" (n. 7 above), part II, *OCP* 46 (1980) 94.

[10] *Dejan[i]ja moskovkikh soborov 1666–1667 godov, II: Kniga sosbornykh dejanij 1667 goda* (Moscow, 1893) 59r ff.

[11] J.-M. Hanssens, "De concelebratione missae in ritibus orientalibus," *Divinitas* 10 (1966) 512. A similar use is found in Slavonic mss. from the 12–13[th] centuries. See A. Pétrovski, "Histoire de la rédaction slave de la liturgie de S. Jean Chrysostome," *XPYCOCTOMIKA. Studi e ricerche intorno a S. Giovanni Chrisostomo* (Rome, 1908) 870, 877.

"Then if he is alone he receives the Lord's body. But if there are several priests, the first among them, having received communion, gives it to the others, who kiss his hand and cheek. And he likewise receives the Eucharist from one of the others. And in like manner they give the chalice to one another, so that they can drink the blood of the Lord."[12]

3. MEDIEVAL COPTIC SOURCES

We have no evidence for early Egyptian usage in this matter, but the medieval Coptic communion rites are described by Patriarch Gabriel II ibn Turaïk (1131–1145):

"Rules (rubrics) for the priest who celebrates the liturgy. He receives communion first. Then he communicates the body to those priests officiating with him. But it is they who take the chalice and give it to him to receive. Then they give the chalice to one another in communion. Then the celebrating priest gives communion to the non-officiating priests in attendance in church, and he gives them the chalice, either himself or the priests officiating with him. . . ."[13]

The rubrics in chapters 6–7 of the *Book of the Guide* by Patriarch Cyril III ibn Laklak (1235–1243), a sort of rubrical primer for celebrants found in codex *Vatican Arabic 117*, has the celebrating priest give communion even to bishops in attendance at the service, except in the case of the local ordinary, who precedes the celebrant in giving himself communion.[14]

4. EAST-SYRIAN USAGE

But as is often the case in matters liturgical, it is the East-Syrian (Assyrian) Church of Persia that reflects the earliest usage and best understanding of what communion is all about. Canon 2 of Catholicos

---

[12] A. Jacob, "La traduction de la Liturgie de s. Jean Chrysostom par Léon Toscan," *OCP* 32 (1966) 160.

[13] L. Villecourt, "Les observances liturgiques et la discipline du jeûne dans l'Église copte," *Le Muséon* 37 (1924) 201.

[14] G. Graf, "Liturgische Anweisungen des koptischen Patriarchen Kyrillos ibn Laklak," *Jahrbuch für Liturgiewissenschaft* 4 (1924) 125. The same usage is found in the *Liturgical Order* of Patriarch Gabriel V (1409–1427), regulations that still govern the Coptic rite today. See A. 'Abdallah, *L'ordinamento liturgico di Gabriele V–88° Patriarca Copto, 1409–1427* (Studia orientalia christiana: Aegyptiaca, Cairo: Edizioni del Centro Francescano di Studi orientali cristiani, 1962) 381.

Mar Išoʿyahb I (518–596) prescribes the rite of communion of the ministers. The presbyter who has been chosen to consecrate the sacrament receives first, even before the bishop:[15]

". . . The bishop, if he is present, gives it [= the consecrated bread] to him; if he is not present, the senior priest in order of precedence gives it to him. And in turn, he who consecrates gives it to the one who gave it to him. And it should be done likewise for the chalice of the Lord. He who has consecrated gives communion to the priests and deacons who are in the sanctuary. . . . Then the priests distribute communion. . . ."[16]

The anonymous ninth-century *Commentary on the Ecclesiastical Offices* attributed to George of Arbela has the same usage, and tells us why: salvation is something mediated to us by Our Lord. So even the priest, who as the Lord's image is himself a mediator of salvation to others, must receive it from another.[17]

Most interesting of all is the following Syriac text from the end of the ninth century, in the canonical collection of the Nestorian Gabriel of Basra:

"*Question 19:* When there is only one priest and one deacon, what should they do, for in one canon it prescribes that the deacon should not give communion to the priest.

"*Answer:* In this matter the Catholicos Išoʿyahb has determined as follows.[18] It is not allowed that the deacon give communion to the priest, who is distinguished from the deacon by his higher rank. So if no other priest is there to give communion, but only a deacon, the situation should be handled according to a fine custom, namely: the priest takes the 'coal' [= consecrated particle] from the altar and puts it in the hands of the deacon. Then he bows before the altar, takes the 'coal' from the deacon's hands with the fingers of the right hand, places it on the tips of the two fingers of the left hand, and brings it

---

[15] In the traditional East-Syrian Eucharist, one of the concelebrating presbyters was chosen to say the anaphora. See *"Ex Oriente Lux,"* sect. 1 above.

[16] Letter of Išoʿyahb I to the bishop of Darai, A.D. 585, in J.-B. Chabot, *Synodicon orientale ou recueil des synods nestoriens* (Paris: Imprimerie nationale, 1902) 429–430.

[17] Chap. IV, 25, R. H. Connolly (ed.), *Anonymi auctoris Expositio officiorum ecclesiae Georgio Arbelensi vulgo adscripta,* vol. 2 (CSCO 76 = scr. syri. 32, ser. 2, tom. 92, Rome: C. de Luigi, 1915) 70–71 in the Latin trans.

[18] The reference is to canon 3 of Išoʿyahb I, Chabot, *Synodicon* (n. 16 above) 430.

back to his right palm. The deacon says only, 'The Body of our Lord.' Likewise the chalice: he gives it into the hands of the deacon, and after he has prostrated himself and bowed, he rises and takes the chalice with both hands, while the deacon holds the foot of the chalice with one hand. When the priest receives the deacon says: 'The Blood of our Lord.' Then the deacon puts the chalice on the altar. . . ."[19]

The point of the document is clear enough: if eucharistic communion, sacrament of our shared ecclesial communion in the one mystical body of Christ, is a food shared, a gift received from the hand of another as from Christ, with only one priest celebrating there was a real *problem:* who would give him communion? The fact that it would never cross our minds to consider this a problem is the precise point I am trying to make: there has been a decided shift in mentality, and with it a change in ritual.

A concern for preserving hierarchical precedence seems to be at least one reason for this shift. Bar Hebraeus (d. 1286), Mesopotamian Jacobite Maphrian of Tikrit in present-day Iraq, says in his *Nomocanon* IV, 5 that a deacon may not give communion to a priest, nor a priest to a bishop.[20] At any rate, rank eventually wins out over symbolism, and the older usages do not survive into the modern period except in more conservative traditions such as the Coptic and Nestorian.

5. PRESENT USAGE AND SOME REFLECTIONS

Today in the Byzantine tradition, concelebrating or communicating presbyters give themselves communion except when the main celebrant is a bishop. But as we have seen, the earlier tradition of receiving from the hand of another was in no way dependent on such differences of rank. Other churches have retained at least something of the original usage. In the Armenian Orthodox Church, presbyters or even a bishop communicating at the eucharistic liturgy receive the intincted host from the celebrating bishop or presbyter after he has

---

[19] H. Kaufhold, *Die Rechtssammlung des Gabriel von Basra und ihr Verhältnis zu den anderen juristischen Sammelwerken der Nestorianer* (Münchener Universitätsschriften, Juristiche Fakultät, Abhandlungen zur rectswissenschaftlichen Grundlagenforschung, Bd. 21, Berlin: J. Schweitzer Verlag, 1976) 242–43.

[20] P. Bedjan (ed.), *Nomocanon Gregorii Barhebraei* (Leipzig: Harrassowitz, 1898) 45–46 (= Syriac text); Latin trans. by J. A. Assemani in A. Mai, *Scriptorum veterum nova collectio* X.2 (Rome: Typis Collegii Urbani, 1838) 24. The Maphrian was a sort of exarch or metropolitan who was primate of the Syrian Jacobite Church in Mesopotamia.

received.[21] Among the Coptic Orthodox the chief concelebrating presbyter gives communion to the other presbyters after communicating himself. I do not know what their custom is at a pontifical liturgy. In the Ethiopian tradition the main celebrating presbyter gives the consecrated bread first to himself, then to the assisting priest, who in turn administers the chalice first to the main celebrant then to himself.[22] In the Syrian Orthodox liturgy the celebrant takes communion first, followed by the bishop if he is in attendance and wishes to receive. Other presbyters may either take communion themselves or request the celebrant to administer it to them.[23] To the best of my knowledge only the Assyrians have preserved their ancient usage: the celebrant receives the consecrated bread from another presbyter; the chalice is handed to him by the deacon.[24]

I am not well enough acquainted with Protestant liturgical uses to comment on them. In the reformed Roman usage there are various possibilities provided by the instructions in the missal: the main celebrant communicates himself, then the other concelebrants can come up and do the same; or the bread and chalice can be brought to them at their places; or they can receive communion by intinction. One also sees less than ideal uses in the communion of the eucharistic ministers: at least for the communion of the chalice, they sometimes line up to take it rather than have it administered to them. Similar practices are not unknown in Masses when the chalice is administered to the laity (as of course it should always be): the chalices are arranged on the altar at strategic points, and everyone comes up to help themselves.

Some traditions are, for the moment at least, stuck with a ritual heritage in this matter which they are at present unwilling or unable to change for a variety of reasons that need not concern us here. But that is not true of the present Roman usage, which has acquired a certain flexibility since Vatican II. What the logistics of the communion rites should be today cannot, of course, be solved by historical scholarship or by universally applicable rubrics. There are too many

[21] I am grateful to Archbishop Khajag Barsamian for this information.

[22] Abba Tekle-Mariam Semharay Selim, *La messe éthiopienne* (Rome: École typographique "Pie X," 1937) 92.

[23] I am grateful to Bishop Mathews Mar Severios of Kottayam, India, for this information.

[24] See G. P. Badger, *The Nestorians and their Rituals* (London: J. Masters, 1852) vol. 2, 238, where the modern usage is described.

variables involved: the number of communicants, the liturgical disposition of the church, local traditions. . . . But from the sources we have studied, at least one thing is clear: the Eucharist, ideally at least, is not something one *takes*. It is a gift received, a meal shared. And since sacraments by their very nature are supposed to symbolize what they mean, then self-service, cafeteria-style communion rites just will not do.

Bishop Kallistos (Ware) of Diokleia

10. Communion and Intercommunion[*]

"The Church is a meeting place of human persons dead, alive and yet
to be born, who, loving one another, come together around the rock
of the Altar to proclaim their love of God."

Iulia de Beausobre (1893–1978)

EUCHARISTIC REVOLUTION?

During the past fifty years, there has been a startling change in attitude towards intercommunion. In 1952, as part of the preparations for
the Lund Conference on Faith and Order, a four-hundred-page study
was published under the title *Intercommunion*. This contained a lengthy
appendix on "Existing Rules and Customs."[1] Here the standpoint of
the Roman Catholic Church was briefly summarized: "Roman Catholics are forbidden to receive Communion in other Churches, nor are
members of other Churches allowed to receive Communion in the
Roman Catholic Church."[2] The attitude of the Orthodox Church was
described in basically the same terms, but in this case the possibility of
exceptions was mentioned: "There can be no canonical or regular intercommunion between the Orthodox Churches and others. Some members of the Orthodox Churches uphold this position in its strictness,
and regard even occasional unofficial acts of intercommunion as unjustifiable breaches of Church order. . . . Other Orthodox churchmen,
while emphasizing the canonical position, not only admit that occasional exceptions to the rule take place but are prepared to justify them
in cases of emergency on the principle of Economy."[3]

---

[*] Originally published as "Church and Eucharist, Communion and Intercommunion," *Sobornost* 7 (1968) 550–67. This is the 1980 revised edition. A glossary of terms
begins on p. 207 below.

[1] J. P. Hickenbotham, "Existing Rules and Customs of the Churches," in D. Baillie
and John Marsh (eds.), *Intercommunion. The Report of the Theological Commission appointed by the Continuation Committee of the World Conference on Faith and Order together
with a Selection from the Material presented to the Commission* (London, 1952) 361–87.

[2] *Ibid.*, 384.

[3] *Ibid.*, 380.

Writing today, one could no longer describe the Roman Catholic standpoint in such simple and uncompromising terms. Indeed, even before the Second Vatican Council, the rules were somewhat more flexible than the sentence quoted above would suggest. Latin canon law officially permitted certain exceptions: for example, a dying Catholic had always been permitted to receive absolution from an Orthodox priest if no priest of his own Church was available.[4] Now, however, Vatican II has greatly mitigated the previous rules,[5] while the actual practice of Catholics in many places goes far beyond anything that the council envisaged. Theologically and canonically, there has been nothing short of a revolution in the Roman Catholic view of intercommunion. This in its turn has had a profound influence on the theory and practice of High Church Anglicans and Old Catholics.

What of the Orthodox? Most of them stand today where they did in 1952. But they find themselves increasingly isolated. In adopting a "strict" attitude towards intercommunion, the Orthodox could in the past count on the understanding and support of Roman Catholics and of many Anglicans. Now this is no longer the case. Here, as so often, we find ourselves saying to our Western brethren, "We are your past"—in this instance, the very recent past! The grave theological arguments urged in support of the "traditional" view are now very largely forgotten or misunderstood, even by some of the very people who not long ago found such arguments convincing.

Let us take another look at these arguments.[6] Going back to the first principles, let us view intercommunion in the light of "eucharistic ecclesiology." Bearing in mind the connection that exists between the Eucharist and the faith, on the one hand, and between the Eucharist and the visible structure of the Church, on the other, let us ask: Is intercommunion admissible? And if it is not, is this solely on disciplinary or practical grounds? Or is it because the very notion of intercommunion is somehow inconsistent with the nature of the Church as a eucharistic society?

[4] See *Codex Juris Canonici . . . Benedicti Papae XV auctoritate promulgatus* (Rome, 1918), canon 882; and compare C. Journet, *The Church of the Word Incarnate,* vol. 1 (London, 1955) 508.

[5] See my article, "The Ecumenical Directory: An Orthodox Comment," *Eastern Churches Review* 1, 4 (1967–8) 410–12.

[6] Here I shall attempt to carry further some ideas that I put forward in my article, "Intercommunion: The Decisions of Vatican II and the Orthodox Standpoint," *Sobornost,* series 5, no. 4 (1966) 258–72.

What is the distinctive and unique function of the Church—that which the Church does, and which nobody and nothing else can do? What function does the local parish fulfill, which cannot be fulfilled by a voluntary community center, a youth association, or an old peoples' club? What human needs does the priest meet, which cannot be met, perhaps with greater professional expertise, by the social worker, the marriage counselor, the child care officer, or the psychiatrist?

We reply: The Church is here to preach the Gospel of Christ, to announce the good news of the Son of God, crucified and risen. Such an answer is true but incomplete. For our task as Christians is more than to preach and to announce; we are here not merely to *say* but to *do*. To do what? "The tradition which I handed on to you came to me from the Lord himself: that the Lord Jesus, on the night of his arrest, took bread and, after giving thanks to God, broke it and said: 'This is my body, which is broken for you; do this as a memorial of me'" (1 Cor 11:23-4, NEB). Not "say this" but "do this." The tradition which St. Paul and the other Apostles received from Christ, and which they in their turn have handed on to the Church, consists not in words but in an action, the action of the Eucharist—in what Charles Williams used to term the *operation* of the Mass. Primarily and fundamentally, Holy Tradition is the Eucharist. It is in the Eucharist that all the various expressions of the Tradition find their source and their *Sitz im Leben*. Here is the life-giving fountain from which everything else springs.

This, then, is what the Church is here for; this is its distinctive and unique function—to eat the bread of the Eucharist and to drink from the common cup, "until the Lord comes again" (1 Cor 11:26). The Church is in its essence eucharistic. It is a society founded upon the action of the Eucharist, an organism that lives and breathes the liturgy, that fulfills itself visibly in time and space through the continuing celebration of the Lord's Supper. It is the Eucharist that holds the Church in unity. When the Church offers the Eucharist, then and only then does it become truly what it is. In Iulia de Beausobre's words, the Church is a eucharistic place of meeting round the "rock of the Altar."[7]

Fixed vividly in my memory is a conversation that I had with a Russian priest in the center of Moscow during August 1976. "Our sufferings," he said to me, "have brought us back to the essentials.

[7] I. de Beausobre, *Creative Suffering* (London, 1940) 44.

Now, as never before, we understand that the Church exists in and for the Eucharist. So much else has been taken away from us, but the celebration of the liturgy remains; and in this one thing we have everything." His words made me think of the story of the origins of Russian Christianity. When the envoys of Prince Vladimir arrived at Constantinople to inquire about the Christian faith, the Greeks did not offer them a verbal explanation but took them to the Church of the Holy Wisdom, to witness the celebration of the liturgy. It was the action of the Eucharist that converted them.[8]

The eucharistic essence of the Church is indicated by the fact that the other sacraments, such as baptism or marriage, were originally performed as part of the celebration of the Eucharist. As a reminder of this ancient practice even now the Orthodox services of baptism and marriage begin with the initial blessing specifically associated with the Eucharist: "Blessed is the kingdom. . . ." In the Orthodox Marriage Office today, the couple drink from a cup of wine; in earlier times, before drinking from this common cup, they would first have received communion together. Fortunately, it is now becoming more frequent in the Orthodox Church to celebrate marriage as part of the liturgy, according to the ancient pattern.[9]

Fortunately also, the sacrament of ordination to the episcopate, priesthood, or diaconate has never ceased to be performed invariably as part of the Eucharist. This is of fundamental importance for any right understanding of, for example, the episcopal office itself. The bishop is a eucharistic person. His primary ministry is to preside at the Divine Liturgy, and all his other functions as teacher or administrator are to be interpreted in terms of his role as celebrant at the Eucharist. The bishop's *cathedra* is not to be regarded as the throne of a ruler or judge, or as a professor's chair; all such models are misleading. His *cathedra* is the seat that he uses as eucharistic president. By the same token, an *ex cathedra* pronouncement is not an arbitrary or

[8] See *The Russian Primary Chronicle (Laurentian Text)*, trans. S. H. Cross and O. P. Sherbowitz-Wetzor (Cambridge, Mass., 1953) 111.

[9] On the connection between Baptism and the Eucharist, see A. Schmemann, *Of Water and the Spirit* (Crestwood, N.Y.: St. Vladimir's Seminary Press, 1974), especially 115–21; on that between Marriage and the Eucharist, see J. Meyendorff, *Marriage: An Orthodox Perspective* (Crestwood, N.Y.: St. Vladimir's Seminary Press, 1970), esp. 23–27. On the common cup and Holy Communion, see A. N. Smirensky, "The Evolution of the Present Rite of Matrimony and Parallel Canonical Developments," in *St. Vladimir's Seminary Quarterly* viii, 1 (1964) 41.

arrogant statement, based on an appeal to authority, but the kind of thing that a bishop says when talking pastorally to his flock during the Eucharist. Trouble starts as soon as the bishop himself, or others around him, cease to view him in a eucharistic context, and start to think of him as a prelate, prince, or bureaucrat.

The all-important link between Church and Eucharist is plainly indicated in the culminating moment of the Byzantine Liturgy, the epiclesis of the Holy Spirit. There is a double invocation: the celebrant prays to God, "Send down thy Holy Spirit *on us* and *on these gifts* here set forth." The people standing around the holy table and the gifts lying upon it are both consecrated together, so that each may become the body of Christ.

THE EUCHARIST AND THE UNITY OF THE CHURCH

As a eucharistic organism, the Church realizes and maintains its unity through the act of Holy Communion. It is the Eucharist that creates the oneness of the Church. Unity is to be understood not in juridical but in eucharistic terms. Unity is not imposed from above by some hierarch or administrative center endowed with supreme power of jurisdiction, but it is *created from within* by the celebration of the liturgy.

This is precisely what St. Paul affirms. "The bread that we break is a communion with the body of Christ. The fact that there is only one loaf means that though there are many of us, we form a single body because we all share in this one loaf" (1 Cor 10:16-17, Jerusalem Bible). For ecclesiology there is no biblical text more decisive than this. Between communion in the one eucharistic loaf and membership in the one body of Christ, St. Paul is asserting not just an analogy but a causal connection. *Because* we eat from the one loaf, *therefore* we are made one body in Christ. Expounding this text, Professor George Galitis of Thessalonika University remarks: "Communion . . . makes us according to Paul one body, the Body of Christ. And this Body of Christ . . . is the Church. Consequently, participating in the Body of Christ, that is in the Church, and partaking of . . . the Body of Christ through the Eucharist are two ways of saying the same thing. . . . Thus, the Eucharist is the *Sacrament of the Church itself*. It is through this Sacrament that the Church realizes itself, that the Body of Christ is built and held together."[10]

---

[10] G. Galitis, *The Problem of Intercommunion from an Orthodox Point of View. A Biblical and Ecclesiological Study* (Athens, 1968) 14–16.

Such also is the standpoint of the second and third generations of Christians, as can be seen, for example, from what is perhaps the most ancient liturgical text that we possess, the Eucharistic Prayer in *The Teaching of the Twelve Apostles* [the *Didache*] (late first or early second century). The prayer perhaps has in mind the Syrian uplands, with the wheat growing on the hillsides: "As this broken bread was scattered over the mountains, and was then brought together and became one, so may thy Church be gathered together from the ends of the earth into thy kingdom."[11] Precisely the same link is affirmed here as in 1 Corinthians 10:16-17, between the *oneness of the eucharistic loaf* and the *oneness of the Church*.

The interdependence of Eucharist and Church is a dominant theme throughout the letters of St. Ignatius of Antioch (martyred c. 107). "Be careful to have but one Eucharist," he writes to the Philadelphians. "For there is one flesh of our Lord Jesus Christ, and one cup for union with his blood, one altar, just as there is one bishop with the presbytery and the deacons my fellow-servants."[12] The repetition of the word *one* shows very clearly how Ignatius envisages Church unity: ". . . one Eucharist . . . one flesh . . . one cup . . . one altar . . . one bishop." The unity of the Church is manifested as a specific and objective reality at each local celebration of the Eucharist, when the faithful, gathered around the bishop *epi to auto*, "in the same place"—a favorite phrase of Ignatius—receive communion in the one Christ from one loaf and one chalice. There is an integral connection in Ignatius's mind between the shared communion in Christ's body and blood, and the unity of the local church gathered round the bishop.

Summarizing Ignatius's view of the Church, Fr. John Romanides writes: "The visible Church—both visible and invisible Church constitute one continuous reality for Ignatius—. . . is composed of those baptized faithful who conduct an intense war against Satan, and the consequences of his power rooted in death, by their unity of love with each other in the life-giving human nature of Christ; and who manifest this unity and love in the corporate Eucharist, in which their very life and salvation is rooted. . . . At each gathering *epi to auto*, by means of each Eucharist, the body of Christ, the Church this side of

---

[11] *Didache* ix, 4. See R. C. D. Jasper and G. J. Cuming (eds.), *Prayers of the Eucharist: Early and Reformed* (London, 1975) 15.

[12] *To the Philadelphians* 4; compare *To the Ephesians* 20 and *To the Magnesians* 7.

death, is in the process of formation—the Word made flesh is being formed in the faithful by the Holy Spirit (1 John 3:23-4), and thus the Church, although already the body of Christ, is continuously becoming what she is."[13]

Ignatius's understanding of Church unity has important consequences for the meaning of the term "catholic." The eucharistic celebration is something that can only happen locally; and at each local celebration of the Eucharist it is the *whole* Christ that is present, not just a part of him. So, according to the ecclesiology of Ignatius, when we speak of the "Catholic Church," we should think first of all of the local church, celebrating the Eucharist. The local eucharistic center is not to be regarded merely as a small unity within some vast and all-embracing federation: on the contrary, the local eucharistic center *is* the Catholic Church in its fullness, for at each Eucharist, Christ is present in his entirety. The various local eucharistic centers are related to each other, not as parts of a whole, but on the principle of *mutual identity:* each local church is one with every other local church, and all together they form a single worldwide communion, because in each local church there is celebrated the one, unique, and indivisible Eucharist. "Wherever Jesus Christ is, there is the Catholic Church";[14] and Jesus Christ is fully present whenever "two or three" (Matt 18:20) are gathered for the eucharistic offering.

EUCHARIST-FAITH-BISHOP

Using in particular St. Ignatius as their basis, a number of Orthodox theologians, both Russian and Greek, have given much emphasis to this notion of the Church as a eucharistic community. Indeed, "eucharistic ecclesiology" forms one of the most creative themes in contemporary Orthodox thinking. The same type of ecclesiology has also been developed independently in the West.[15] Among the Russians "eucharistic ecclesiology" is associated in particular with the late Fr. Nicolas Afanassieff (1893–1966).[16] His name was frequently

[13] J. Romanides, "The Ecclesiology of St. Ignatius of Antioch," *The Greek Orthodox Theological Review* vii (1961–1962) 63, 64–65.

[14] *To the Smyrnaeans*, 8.

[15] See, for example, the monograph by L. Hertling, S.J., *Communio: Church and Papacy in Early Christianity*, trans. J. Wicks, S.J. (Chicago, 1972).

[16] The best introduction to Afanassieff's theology is his article, "The Church which Presides in Love," in J. Meyendorff and others, *The Primacy of Peter* (2nd ed., Crestwood, N.Y.: St. Vladimir's Seminary Press, 1992) 91–143. For a full

mentioned in discussions at Vatican II, and he exercised an indirect but significant influence on the council's decrees. The same eucharistic understanding of the Church, but expressed in more carefully qualified terms, is to be found in the writings of his pupil, Fr. Alexander Schmemann.[17] A pioneer contribution on the Greek side is the article by Fr. John Romanides, "The Ecclesiology of St. Ignatius of Antioch," quoted above, which is relatively brief yet surprisingly complete.[18] A detailed and balanced survey of the Patristic evidence up to Nicaea (325) is provided by Metropolitan John (Zizioulas) of Pergamon in his doctoral dissertation.[19] Only at a late stage in the writing of this did Metropolitan John become aware of Father Afanassieff's work; in important ways, however, Metropolitan John supplies a much-needed corrective to the Russian theologian's one-sided treatment of the material.[20]

This stress upon the centrality of the Eucharist in the Church's life is greatly to be welcomed. But as Metropolitan John indicates, it is not to be carried to extremes. It is indeed true to say that the Eucharist creates the Church. It would be misleading, however, to infer from this, "Wherever the Eucharist is celebrated, there is the Church." Such an affirmation is not unconditionally true. For there are schismatic Eucharists (or pseudo-Eucharists) that are celebrated

---

development, see his *magnum opus,* published posthumously, *L'Eglise du Saint-Esprit* (Paris, 1975).

[17] See, for instance, his article *Theologia kai Evcharistia* ["Theology and Eucharist"] in Ilias Mastrogiannopoulos (ed.), *Theologia Alitheia kai Zoi [Theology, Truth and Life]* (Athens: Zoi Publications, 1962) 91–127: also "The Idea of Primacy in Orthodox Ecclesiology," in *The Primacy of Peter,* 145–71.

[18] *The Greek Orthodox Theological Review* vii (1961–1962) 53–77 (originally written in 1955). But Fr. Romanides has more recently expressed reservations about "Eucharistic ecclesiology": See Andrew J. Sohko, *Prophet of Roman Orthodoxy: The Theology of John* (Synaxis Press, Dewdney, B.C., 1998) 150–301.

[19] J. Zizioulias, *I Enotis tis Ekklisias en ti Theia Evcharistia kai to Episkopo Kata tous treis protous aionas [The Unity of the Church in the Holy Eucharist and the Bishop during the first three centuries]* (Athens, 1965). See also his *Being as Communion: Studies in Personhood and the Church* (Crestwood, N.Y.: St. Vladimir's Seminary Press, 1985), esp. chapter 4. For an excellent presentation of Metropolitan John's views, see Paul McPartlan, *The Eucharist Makes the Church: Henri de Lubac and John Zizioulas in Dialogue* (Edinburgh, 1993) which contains a full bibliography.

[20] Thus, for example, as Zizioulas shows, Afanassieff exaggerates the contrast between the "Eucharistic ecclesiology" of Ignatius and the "universal ecclesiology" of Cyprian (Zizioulas, *I Enotis,* 110, 123–24, 139–40, 157, 178–79).

outside the Church. The Eucharist should not be isolated, for it presupposes a particular context or structure. The unity of the Church in the Eucharist cannot be truly made manifest and realized, unless there are present at the same time two other kinds of unity: unity in the faith, and unity in the local bishop. These three forms of unity—oneness of eucharistic communion, dogmatic oneness, oneness around the bishop—are complementary and interdependent, and each loses its true meaning if divorced from the other two.

Eucharistic unity, then, presupposes in the first place *unity in faith*. In the words of Fr. Georges Florovsky, "Communion presupposes 'one mind,' no less than 'one heart'."[21] Mere brotherly feeling is not enough; there can be no true oneness in sacramental life for those who are not one in faith. But unity in faith is not the same as total agreement in theological opinions. There always has been room in the Church on earth, and until the Second Coming there always will be room, for a diversity of *theologoumena*. Of course, it is never easy to draw the line between dogma and private opinion, between the essential and the nonessential; this is precisely the question that we face in all our "ecumenical dialogues." But, wherever the line is in fact drawn, it is always unity in *faith* that is required when we meet around the eucharistic table: nothing more than this—yet nothing less. For, as Fr. Dumitru Staniloae has observed, "The Divine Liturgy is not just a service of consecration and communion, but at the same time an emphatic and insistent public confession of faith."[22] "By the very fact of approaching the chalice," writes Lev Zander, "an Orthodox Christian confesses the faith of the Church, the faith of the fathers."[23] Because of this vital link between communion and faith, at every celebration of the Eucharist in the Orthodox Church, before the start of the *anaphora,* we recite the Creed. The order is significant. We do not first receive communion together, and then affirm our unity in faith; but the proclamation of the one faith comes *first*. And this

[21] G. Florovsky, "Confessional Loyalty in the Ecumenical Movement," in Baillie and Marsh, *Intercommunion*, 201.

[22] D. Staniloae, *Gia ena Orthodoxo Oikoumenismo: Evcharistia-Pisti-Ekklisia. To Provlima tis Intercommunion [Towards an Orthodox Ecumenism: Eucharist-Faith-Church. The Problem of Intercommunion]*, with an introduction by Panagiotis Nellas (Piraeus, 1976) 68–69. We still need an English translation of this timely work.

[23] L. Zander, "Intercommunion and Co-celebration," in Baillie and Marsh, *Intercommunion,* 352. While agreeing with the first part of this article, I cannot accept the conclusions drawn at the end.

proclamation of our faith in the words of the Creed should be understood in an inclusive and not a minimal sense; we proclaim our acceptance, not just of the doctrines explicitly mentioned in the Creed, but of the whole Catholic faith in its fullness.

Eucharistic unity presupposes in the second place *unity in the bishop*. The episcopal president at the Eucharist acts as a sign and sacrament of our ecclesial unity. St. Ignatius is particularly vehement about the connection between bishop and Eucharist. "Let no one do any of the things that concern the Church without the bishop," he says. "Let that Eucharist be considered valid which is celebrated by the bishop, or by one whom he appoints. Wherever the bishop is, there let the people be. . . . He who does anything without the bishop's knowledge is serving the devil."[24] It will be remembered that in Ignatius's day, and indeed until at least the middle of the third century, the parish system with which we are familiar did not as yet exist; the normal celebrant at every Eucharist was the bishop. Even today, whenever a priest presides at the liturgy, he does so not in his own right but as the bishop's delegate. That is why he commemorates the name of his bishop—not as a gesture of courtesy but as an ecclesiological necessity; and that is also why, in the Byzantine rite, the priest cannot celebrate the Eucharist unless he has on the altar an *antiminsion* bearing the bishop's signature.

"Eucharistic ecclesiology" implies therefore a threefold unity: *Eucharistic* unity, that is, unity in the one loaf and the one cup of Holy Communion; *dogmatic* unity, that is, unity in the one faith; and *ecclesial* unity, that is, unity in the bishop. Together they form a threefold cord. Let us take care to keep the three strands intertwined.

THE PROBLEM OF INTERCOMMUNION

If the Church is eucharistic by its very essence, what implications does this have for the question of intercommunion?

There are two preliminary points to be made. First, if the Church is indeed a eucharistic community, which realizes its true nature through the act of Holy Communion, then there is nothing in our present condition as divided Christians that should cause us sharper anguish than the fact that we communicate at separate tables. The very thing that should actualize our oneness has become the sign of our division. It is not enough to deplore schisms because they are

[24] *To the Smyrnaeans*, 8 and 9.

wasteful in money and manpower, and create a bad "public image." We need to go deeper than that. Our separation at the Lord's table is a contradiction of the Church's very essence, as a sharing from the one loaf and the one cup. Eucharistic division strikes at the very heart of the Church's life. This was felt most acutely by pioneers in the work for Christian unity such as Fr. Sergius Bulgakov.[25]

Second, the technical term "intercommunion"—which I take to signify sharing in the sacraments, on an occasional or even a regular basis, by Christians belonging to ecclesial communities that are still officially separated—is a word of modern coinage, not to be found in the Bible, the Fathers, or the Holy Canons. The Bible, the Fathers, and the Canons know of only two possibilities: communion and non-communion. It is all or nothing. They do not envisage any third alternative such as "partial intercommunion." "In brief," says Fr. Georges Florovsky, "there was no problem of intercommunion (in the modern sense of the term) in the undivided Church. . . . There was simply the question of 'full communion,' i.e., of membership in the Church. And there were identical terms of this membership for all."[26] As Professor George Galitis observes, summarizing the evidence from the Early Church: "It is impossible to allow any approach to divine communication by way of 'hospitality,' or in [the] case of need, because *admitting one to communion and to church membership are identical; to what church one belongs is manifested by where he receives communion, or by where he is admitted to communion.* So the concept of intercommunion is unknown to the ancient church, as it is to the NT also: there is only communion and non-communion."[27]

To this some will object that, since the contemporary "ecumenical movement" has created a situation without precedent, fresh terminology must be devised to deal with it. But is the contemporary situation so very novel? Schisms existed already in New Testament times,

---

[25] See Henry Hill, "Father Sergius Bulgakov and Intercommunion," *Sobornost,* series 5, no. 4 (1966) pop. 272–76. Fr. Sergius's views are briefly expounded in his article, "By Jacob's Well: On the Actual Unity of the Divided Church in Faith, Prayer and Sacraments," *Journal of the Fellowship of St. Alban and St. Sergius,* no. 22 (December, 1933) 7–17; reprinted in J. Pain and N. Zernov (eds.) *A Bulgakov Anthology* (London, 1976) 100–13. While it is possible to question the theological basis of Fr. Sergius's proposals, no one can doubt his fiery sincerity.

[26] G. Florovsky, "Terms of Communion in the Undivided Church," in Baillie and Marsh, *Intercommunion,* 50.

[27] G. Galitis, *The Problem of Intercommunion,* op. 24–25 (italics in the original).

and the Apostles struggled to heal them. Church leaders in the fourth century, such as St. Athanasius or St. Basil, were concerned throughout their lives with questions of disunity and reconciliation. We do the Fathers a strange injustice when we assume that we in the twentieth century are the first people to work seriously for peace and unity. Faced by the inveterate anomaly of Christian division, most Orthodox today believe that the concepts and terminology of the New Testament and the Fathers still remain valid; and for this reason they cannot but feel uneasy about the non-biblical and non-patristic notion of "intercommunion," regarded as a halfway house on the road to full communion.

Let us turn now to our main question. What attitude towards intercommunion is implied by a eucharistic doctrine of the Church? At first sight it would appear that "eucharistic ecclesiology" can be used as a powerful argument in support of intercommunion. Such certainly is the way in which it was applied by Father Afanassieff, especially at the end of his life, with particular reference to Orthodox-Catholic relations.[28] In bare outline the case might be stated as follows (here I put the argument in my own words, not drawing directly on Father Afanassieff). It is the Eucharist that creates the unity of the Church. Despite our outward divisions, then, let us join in communion from the one loaf, setting our hope in the healing power of the sacrament. Let us share in the sacrament, and so discover at the deepest level our unity with each other—a unity not manufactured but given, not brought about by human ingenuity but conferred by Christ himself in the Eucharist. Our sharing in Holy Communion will bring us to a genuine unity of faith and life, such as we shall never achieve simply through doctrinal discussions.

The method here proposed is to some extent that of "assuming the conclusion as given." To solve a problem in mathematics, sometimes we have to regard the problem as if it were already solved, and by going forward on that basis we actually discover the solution. May we not apply this to our efforts towards unity? Although we are not fully reunited (so the argument runs), let us act as if we were and receive communion together, trusting God to do the rest. A great strength in this approach is that it proposes not just words but action.

[28] See, for example, his articles "Una Sancta" *Irenikon,* xxxvi (1963) 436–75, and "L'eucharistie, principal lien entre les catholiques et les orthodoxes," *Irenikon* xxxviii (1965) 337–39.

196

As we all recognize, it is spiritually dangerous for us to continue talking together indefinitely, without actually *doing* anything.

It is sometimes said that this approach treats eucharistic communion not as an end but merely as a means towards unity. The advocates of intercommunion, however, do not see the matter in this light. It is their contention that, on a deep but genuinely effective level, divided Christians are *already* one. As Fr. Sergius Bulgakov affirms, "Unity is simultaneously something already given and something that we must attain to."[29] There is an important truth here. We should regard Christian unity in developing and dynamic terms. It is not something that can be achieved once and for all, as a fixed reality within the historical process; but up to the Second Coming of Christ our unity will always be incomplete, always in the process of growing to fulfillment. When appealing to the unity that is already an existing fact, the supporters of intercommunion place particular emphasis upon the sacrament of baptism, as a bond linking divided Christians in one.

Yet, by no means do all the Orthodox theologians who accept the standpoint of "eucharistic ecclesiology" see it as justifying intercommunion. Father Schmemann and Father Romanides and Metropolitan John (Zizioulas) all differ from Father Afanassieff in this regard. Indeed, the historical evidence presented by Metropolitan John seems to point against intercommunion, not in favor of it. It is true that the Eucharist creates the unity of the Church. But the Eucharist is indissolubly bound to the whole content of the faith, and likewise to the visible structure of the Church. Those who advocate intercommunion on the basis of "eucharistic ecclesiology" often fall into the mistake of treating the Eucharist too much in isolation. They separate the strands of the threefold cord. While rightly stressing the unifying power of the Eucharist, they do not integrate this unity sufficiently with dogmatic unity (unity in faith) and with ecclesial unity (unity in the bishop). In celebrating the Eucharist together, and in receiving communion together from the one loaf, we proclaim our faith; we sum up and express in visible form the dogmatic truth that we share. In celebrating and communicating together, we also actualize and manifest in visible form our membership in the one church. But what if we do not in fact share one faith? What if we are not in fact gathered around one bishop? How then can we receive communion together?

[29] "By Jacob's Well," *art. cit.*, 8.

It is not adequate to reply that communion together in the Eucharist will bring us to the oneness of faith that at present we lack. This is to put things in the wrong order: at the liturgy the confession of a common faith comes *before* communion, not afterwards. Love and truthfulness in Christ compel me to say, as an Orthodox, that there are serious differences on matters of faith between Orthodoxy and the West, whether Catholic, Anglican, or Reformed. With all my heart I pray that these differences may be overcome by the fire of the Spirit. But unless and until this has happened, it would be *unrealistic*—even *untruthful*—for me as an Orthodox to receive communion with the non-Orthodox. As Father Staniloae justly observes, "I cannot understand how communion in the Holy Eucharist can somehow compensate for non-communion in faith."[30]

And besides this need for unity in faith, there is also a need for unity in the bishop. How can we have communion together, if I do not acknowledge your bishop, nor you mine? It is no answer to reply that the Eucharist is Christ's, not the bishop's. For Christ has entrusted his sacraments to the Church, and the Church, as a visible reality existing locally, is centered around the bishop. If, then, I cannot in honesty as an Orthodox recognize as my chief bishop the pope of Rome or the archbishop of Canterbury—if I cannot recognize as my local bishop the nearest Catholic or Anglican hierarch—how am I to receive communion with Roman Catholics and Anglicans? As a Christian, I cannot dissociate myself from the whole burden of Christianity's past and present. I have no right to participate in the Eucharist on a personal basis with certain individuals of another ecclesial community if my Church and theirs are still in separation. Once more, such communion is *unrealistic*—a failure properly to confront the bitter fact that we are at this moment still divided. In the wise words of Father Florovsky, "It is indeed a dreadful thing that Christians cannot join together at one and the same altar. But it is exactly what should have been expected. For they are *really* divided. . . . The Ecumenical Movement is primarily a fellowship in search. It is a venture or an adventure, not an achievement. It is a way, not the goal. And therefore an open communion would compromise the whole endeavor. It would be to pretend falsely that Christendom has already been reunited. We know only too well that it has not."[31]

30 D. Staniloae, *Gia ena Orthodoxo Oikoumenismo*, 23.

31 G. Florovsky, "Confessional Loyalty in the Ecumenical Movement," in Baillie and Marsh, *Intercommunion*, 198, 202.

Nor (alas!) do we meet the difficulty by appealing to baptism as proof of an already existing unity. For at once the question arises: Baptism into which Church? It is not sufficient to respond: "Into the one Catholic Church of Christ." For this one Catholic Church does not exist simply as an abstract idea, but is visibly manifested in time and space *as the local church*. One cannot be baptized into the Catholic Church without belonging at the same time to a local church, and here at once the problem of disunity confronts us: for it is precisely as members of local church communities that we are separated.

This point applies equally to the Eucharist. To quote Father Staniloae once more: "The members of one Church, who receive the sacraments from another Church—to what Church do they belong? Of what spiritual reality do they form part? They no longer belong completely to their own Church, since they receive Holy Communion from another Church; nor do they belong to the other Church in which they occasionally receive the Eucharist, since they do not hold the faith of that other Church."[32] It is not convincing to say in answer to his question, "They belong to the Catholic Church of Christ, which is invisibly one." For the Eucharist is something that happens visibly and locally, and so in receiving communion we cannot ignore the fact of our visible divisions. In general the supporters of intercommunion often incline unconsciously towards a "Nestorian" type of ecclesiology, which underestimates the bond between the invisible and the visible aspects of the Church.

A sound eucharistic ecclesiology, then, so far from involving the acceptance of intercommunion, implies rather its repudiation. As Father Staniloae insists: "Ecclesiastical unity, unity in faith, and unity in the Holy Eucharist are all three inseparable and interdependent. . . . Consequently, the Orthodox Church cannot accept 'intercommunion,' which separates communion in the Holy Eucharist from unity in faith and ecclesiastical unity. More exactly, such intercommunion is a danger that threatens to destroy the Church."[33] But, in common with many other Orthodox theologians who are opposed to intercommunion, Father Staniloae is prepared to allow a partial relaxation in regard to the "non-Chalcedonian" Churches (the "Monophysites"), such as the Coptic Church of Egypt or the Syrian Church of India. In this case, however, there already exists a genuine unity of faith, more

---

[32] D. Staniloae, *Gia ena Orthodoxo Oikoumenismo*, 33.
[33] D. Staniloae, *op. cit.*, 29.

or less officially recognized on either side, and the problems of church order (e.g., the number of ecumenical councils) seem well on the way towards a solution.[34]

The observant reader will have noticed that, throughout the foregoing discussion, nothing was said about the "validity" or "non-validity" of non-Orthodox sacraments. This omission was deliberate. The issue of intercommunion, while connected with that of validity, is by no means identical with it. Needless to say, for those Orthodox who consider invalid all sacraments outside their own Church, there can be no question whatever of intercommunion. But on the other hand, it is possible to reject intercommunion as unacceptable, without thereby necessarily condemning the sacraments of other church communities as totally null and void. We may refrain from intercommunion because of our insistence upon the bond between the Eucharist and the faith, and between the Eucharist and church order; but we may at the same time leave the problem of validity as an open question. That is exactly the standpoint of many Orthodox.

REPRESENTATIVE ORTHODOX STATEMENTS

Turning now from theological principles to specific evidence, let us pass in review five representative statements by Orthodox hierarchs or synods during 1965–1976. Three of these favor a more liberal policy as regards intercommunion, while two reaffirm the traditional rules.

In favor of a more lenient policy there is, first of all, the decision made by the Holy Synod of the Russian Church at Moscow on December 16, 1969: "In cases where Old Believers and Catholics ask the Orthodox Church to administer the holy sacraments to them, this is not forbidden."[35] No explicit reference is made to the reverse situation— to the possibility of Orthodox receiving the sacraments from Old Believer or Roman Catholic clergy. The Moscow decision gave rise to sharp controversy within the Orthodox Church, and was variously interpreted. Spokesmen for the Moscow Patriarch in Western Europe, such as Metropolitan Anthony (Bloom) in London and Bishop Pierre (L'Huillier) in Paris, took the view that it applied only to the Soviet Union, where exceptional conditions prevailed, and not to the West. Within the main part of the USSR, outside the Baltic provinces, there

[34] D. Staniloae, *op. cit.,* 42–43.

[35] On this decree and the ensuing controversy, see the full discussion in *Eastern Churches Review* iii, 1 (1970) 91–93; iii, 2 (1970) 217–18; iii, 3 (1971) 324. The 1969 decision has now been revoked by the Church of Russia.

were then extremely few Catholic Churches still functioning. The decree, so it was argued, had therefore in view the problems of Roman Catholics, permanently cut off from their own Church; it aimed to meet a situation of pastoral emergency within Russia, and was not to be interpreted as an "ecumenical gesture" aiming to promote *rapprochement* in the Western world. On the other hand, the late exarch of the Moscow Patriarchate for Western Europe, Metropolitan Nikodim of Leningrad, gave the decree a far broader "ecumenist" application.[36] At the opposite extreme, there were bishops in the Soviet Union who refused altogether to apply the decision in their own dioceses, and who adhered to the traditional rules. Unfortunately, the Moscow Patriarchate never issued an official clarification of the 1969 decree, indicating its precise purpose and scope.

Among the other Orthodox Churches, the Church of Greece strongly and on an official basis condemned the Moscow decision.[37] The Holy Synod at Athens appealed to the Ecumenical Patriarchate to intervene, but to the best of my knowledge, Constantinople never made any official pronouncement on the matter, either in support or in condemnation of the Moscow decision.

It would have been presumptuous for Orthodox who did not live under conditions of persecution to pass judgment about the pastoral problems of the Orthodox Church within the USSR. Nevertheless, the Moscow decision raised ecclesiological difficulties which cannot be passed over in silence. We are bound to ask the question posed by Father Staniloae. If a Roman Catholic in the USSR was permanently cut off from the ministrations of his own Church, to such an extent that there was little prospect during the rest of his life that he would ever be able to receive communion from a Catholic priest (such cases certainly existed); and if this Roman Catholic for the rest of his life

---

[36] We may recall Metropolitan Nikodim's action in giving communion to Catholics in Rome on 12 October 1969: *Eastern Churches Review*, iii, 1 (1970) 92–93: obviously there was no question in this case of the Catholics being cut off from their own Church! In Leningrad he admitted visiting Catholic clergy to celebrate with him at the Orthodox Liturgy. For a typical case, see the experience of a Canadian Redemptorist priest in the USSR: E. Briere, *I Met the Humbled Christ in Russia* (New Jersey, 1977), reviewed in *East-West Digest* xiv, 4 (February, 1978) 157. Once more there was no question of Fr. Briere being cut off from his own Church, for there was always a functioning Catholic parish in Leningrad.

[37] See the statement issued by the Holy Synod at Athens on February 25, 1970: *Eastern Churches Review* iii, 1, 91, and its subsequent letter to the Ecumenical Patriarch dated 24 March 1970 (*ibid.*, iii, 3, 324).

received communion regularly at the Orthodox liturgy—then to what Church did he belong? In what sense was he still visibly and effectively a member of the Roman Catholic Church? In the words of Professor Galitis, already quoted: "To what Church one belongs is manifested by where he receives communion." Would it not have been realistic, therefore, and more theologically correct to conclude that the Catholic, in thus seeking communion in the Orthodox Church, had to all intents and purposes become an Orthodox?

Although the Holy Synod at Constantinople remained silent, two leading hierarchs of the Ecumenical Patriarchate made statements which indirectly implied agreement with the Moscow decision. Archbishop Athenagoras of Thyateira, until 1979 the head of the Greek Orthodox Church in Great Britain, had this to say in *The Thyateira Confession* about communion between Orthodox and Catholics: "When they are not near a Roman Catholic Church, Roman Catholics are permitted to receive Holy Communion in Orthodox churches; and the same is also extended to Orthodox when they are not near an Orthodox church."[38] Here the archbishop goes beyond the Moscow standpoint, for he suggests reciprocity: in his view, not only may Catholics receive communion in Orthodox churches, but the reverse is equally permitted. There is, however, a certain ambiguity in the passage just cited. The archbishop says that communion between Orthodox and Roman Catholics is "permitted," but he does not make clear *by whom* this is permitted. If the archbishop means "permitted, in certain situations by the Roman Catholic authorities," then the statement is entirely correct. But if he means "permitted by the Orthodox," the question arises whether this permission is official and explicit, or unofficial and tacit; and, if the permission is official and explicit, the further question arises when and by whom it was granted. On all this Archbishop Athenagoras sheds no light. Personally, I know of no decision by the Ecumenical Patriarchate officially permitting communion between Orthodox and Catholics; but, as we shall note shortly, there does exist an encyclical issued by the Phanar in March 1967, explicitly *forbidding* such communion.

Archbishop Athenagoras goes on to discuss relations with the Anglicans. Here he observes: "On account of friendly relations it has become customary for the Orthodox to perform funerals for the

[38] *The Thyateira Confession. The Faith and Prayer of Orthodox Christians* (Leighton Buzzard, 1975) 69.

Anglicans and offer them the Holy Eucharist in places where there is no Anglican clergyman available. This is reciprocated for the Orthodox Christians wherever there is no Orthodox clergyman available. This is done both officially and unofficially and in various localities it is a necessary practice expressing Christian sacramental hospitality."[39] That such sharing in the Eucharist between Anglicans and Orthodox happens *unofficially* is undoubtedly true; but how far has it received *official* sanction from the Orthodox side, and more specifically from the Holy Synod of the Ecumenical Patriarchate? The archbishop cites no evidence in support of his statements.

A viewpoint similar to that of *The Thyateira Confession* was expressed shortly afterward by Metropolitan Meliton of Chalcedon, at that time the senior hierarch in the Ecumenical Patriarchate after the then Patriarch Dimitrios. Under the chairmanship of Metropolitan Meliton, the diocesan bishops of the Ecumenical Patriarchate in Western Europe held a consultation at Chambésy, Geneva, on February 1–3, 1976. Among the matters discussed was that of "eucharistic hospitality." When non-Orthodox approach for communion at an Orthodox liturgy, what should the celebrant do? Metropolitan Meliton is reported as saying, "Communion is a crowning of unity and not a means of advancing towards it" (this, as we have seen, is the traditional Orthodox view); but, he added, "One should not crush the ardour and the thirst of a Christian who comes to ask for communion in the Orthodox Church."[40]

No one would dispute the extreme delicacy of the situation to which the metropolitan alludes, when non-Orthodox approach in all good faith to receive Orthodox communion, under the impression that this is fully permitted from the Orthodox side. There is a need on such an occasion for the utmost tact and pastoral gentleness on the part of the Orthodox celebrant. Yet the assumption underlying the metropolitan's words is theologically disturbing. He seems to be saying that the responsibility in such a case rests exclusively with the conscience of the person approaching for communion, and that the priest has no right to come between that person and our Lord. Yet in fact, from the very start, the Church has held that the priest does have a direct responsibility for the way in which he administers the sacraments. The sacraments are Christ's, but Christ has entrusted them

[39] *Op. cit.*, 70.
[40] *SOP*, no. 5 (February, 1976) 2.

to the Church; and the priest who celebrates the liturgy has been appointed by the Church as minister of Christ's sacraments. He is therefore responsible before God under what conditions he gives communion and to whom. If he refuses communion to anyone, his responsibility is very grave; but it is no less so when he gives communion.

Alongside these three statements—from the Moscow Synod, Archbishop Athenagoras, and Metropolitan Meliton—let us set two other pronouncements pointing in the opposite direction. The first is a statement entitled *The Discipline of Holy Communion,* approved unanimously by SCOBA (The Standing Conference of Orthodox Bishops in America) at New York on January 22, 1965. Archbishop Iakovos, head of the Greek Archdiocese (Ecumenical Patriarchate), was in the chair. The statement is of particular interest to us, since it has in mind the situation of the Orthodox Church in the West, and was drawn up in the period immediately following Vatican II. The central passage reads:

"It is, all of her faithful children are aware, the ancient, unvarying and unalterable teaching of the Orthodox Church that the reception of Holy Communion is the final end and goal of the Christian life, the very fulfillment of unity. It is the last step in that earthly progress which unites the faithful to Christ the Lord and to each other in Him. To Holy Communion the Church admits only her baptized and chrismated children who confess the full Orthodox faith, pure and entire, and by it she shows forth their oneness with her and with her Divine Spouse. Holy Communion is the sign and evidence of right belief and of incorporation in the Israel of God. Further, the Church teaches that the Eucharist cannot be found, and must not be sought, outside of her covenanted mysteries. It is the achievement of unity.

"The standing Conference would at this time remind the children of the Church as they pray, study and work for Christian reunion that the Eucharistic Mystery is the end of unity, not a means to that end, and therefore, decisions regarding Holy Communion reached by Christian bodies outside of the Orthodox Church have no significance of [sic][41] validity for the Orthodox Church or her members. Holy Communion will not be sought by Orthodox Christians outside of the Church, nor will it be offered to those who do not yet confess the Orthodox Church as their mother."[42]

[41] Perhaps read "or."

[42] Full text in R. Stephanopoulos (ed.), *Guidelines for Orthodox Christians in Ecumenical Relations. Published by the Standing Conference of Canonical Orthodox Bishops*

It is noteworthy that the SCOBA statement nowhere suggests the possibility of exceptions by virtue of Economy. To my knowledge, there has been no subsequent pronouncement by SCOBA modifying the above decision of January 1965.

Similar in its conclusions, although less austere in its phrasing, is an encyclical letter issued by the Ecumenical Patriarch Athenagoras on March 14, 1967. He makes it clear that he is writing not just in his own name but in that of the Holy Synod, following an official discussion. He expresses joy at the remarkable progress achieved in recent work for Christian unity, and states that he "looks with love towards Simon Peter of the Old Rome." This progress, he continues, has given to many the impression "that it is now permissible from henceforward for Christians to go to Confession and receive the Holy Eucharist indiscriminately, that is, that our Orthodox people may go to Roman Catholic churches and clergy as well as to those of other Confessions and vice-versa." It is true, the patriarch continues, that where there is no Orthodox church building, the Orthodox use for the Divine Liturgy a place of worship belonging to some other church community. "However, this does not signify in any way that Orthodox may receive the grace of the sacraments from a non-Orthodox priest, for neither has any such decision been taken on this matter, nor does sacramental communion exist between the Orthodox Church and other Churches, as yet."[43]

The words "as yet" appear in the Greek text at the end of the sentence, and the patriarch clearly wishes them to be emphasized. While excluding communion for the present, he extends a hope for the future. So far as the present situation is concerned, however, the patriarch's encyclical is unambiguous. Communion between Orthodox and non-Orthodox is not permitted at the moment. As in the SCOBA statement, no mention is made of possible exceptions by virtue of economy, in cases of emergency, or prolonged isolation. Perhaps such exceptions are not excluded, but they are not mentioned. Whatever the personal convictions and hopes of the late Ecumenical Patriarch Athenagoras, here he is speaking formally in the name of his Church.

---

in America and commended to the clergy for guidance (no place, no date [?1973]) 52–53.

[43] Patriarchal Letter, Protocol no. 98 (1967), cited in *Eastern Churches Review* i, 3 (1967) 303; full text in Greek and English in *The Orthodox Herald*, no. 27–28 (March–April, 1967) 2, 10.

So far as I know, this encyclical has not been officially cancelled by any subsequent encyclical from Constantinople.

It is important to note the date of the encyclical. It was issued some fifteen months *after* the revocation of the anathemas between Constantinople and Rome on December 7, 1965. In the view of the patriarch and Synod at Constantinople, this revocation did not by itself restore the two Churches to sacramental communion. Here the encyclical endorses the opinion expressed at the time of the revocation by an Orthodox theologian closely linked to Patriarch Athenagoras, Archimandrite André Scrima. The act of December 7, 1965, he said, has removed a "preliminary obstacle"; but he added: "It would be particularly incorrect to see in it an invitation to sacramental intercommunion."[44]

In these two official statements from SCOBA and from the Ecumenical Patriarchate, so I am strongly convinced, we hear the authentic voice of the Orthodox tradition. And the SCOBA declaration indicates what is the fundamental reason for the Orthodox standpoint: sacramental communion between divided Christians is doctrinally and spiritually incorrect, because of the intimate link existing between the Eucharist and the Church's faith and order. Here the SCOBA statement reflects a sober and balanced "eucharistic ecclesiology." If the phrasing sounds outspoken, even harsh, this must be seen as the strictness of Christian love.

"UNITE US ALL . . ."

Intercommunion is an emotive topic. Profound feelings are involved, and convictions are deeply divided. It touches the mysterious heart of the Church's life and the Church's unity, and it touches this not theoretically but practically, in a way that we feel and see. We need on either side to respect the consciences of those who differ from us. Above all we should resist the temptation to accuse others of a want of seriousness or an insufficiency of love. We are not to assume that those who practice intercommunion are lacking in theological seriousness; but equally we are not to assume that those who regard intercommunion as impossible are lacking in love. God alone knows who among us suffers the most because of Christian disunity, and who has the greatest love.

Whatever our views on intercommunion, we can join in this prayer from the Liturgy of St. Basil, said immediately after the consecration

[44] *Eastern Churches Review* i, 1 (1966) 25.

of the Holy Gifts: "Unite us all, who partake together from the one loaf and cup, one with another in the communion of the one Holy Spirit; and let no one among us receive the body and blood of thy Christ for judgment or condemnation, but may we find mercy and grace with all thy saints since the beginning of time."

GLOSSARY

Lund Conference on Faith and Order	International conference of the Faith and Order Commission of The World Council of Churches on "The Church, Ways of Worship and Intercommunion," August 15–28, 1952.
Economy = ὀικονομία	a theological/pastoral principle by virtue of which pastoral accommodations are made according to people's needs and circumstances
The Divine Liturgy	the eucharistic liturgy
The Teaching of the Twelve Apostles	the *Didache*—Διδαχὴ κυρίου διὰ τῶν δώδεκα ἀποστόλων
ἐπὶ τὸ ἀυτό	"all together in the same place," "all together in one place," Ig. *Eph* 5:3
theologoumena	"theological explanations" or "theological opinions"
Non-Chalcedonian Churches	Churches, such as the Coptic and Armenian Churches, which have never accepted the Council of Chalcedon (451)
the Holy synod of the Russian Church	the permanent synod of bishops which governs the Russian Church together with the Patriarch of Moscow
Metropolitan	an archbishop with jurisdiction over a metropolitan province of the Church
Exarch	a bishop lower in rank than a patriarch, but having rights over the metropolitans of a particular area
the Holy synod at Athens	the permanent synod of bishops governing the Orthodox Church of Greece together with the Archbishop of Athens

the Ecumenical Patriarchate	the Patriarch of Constantinople (Istanbul)
the Phanar	the official residence and center of the Ecumenical Patriarchate in Constantinople
the Holy Synod of the Ecumenical Patriarchate	the permanent synod of bishops which advises the Ecumenical Patriarch and helps him govern the Orthodox churches
Archimandrite	a title of honor which may be given to a monk who is a priest

John Zizioulas

11. Eucharist and Catholicity*

The lines that follow represent an attempt to see the concept of the catholicity of the Church in the light of the eucharistic community. It is not an accident that in adopting the term "catholic" from Aristotelian language,[1] the early Christians did not conceptualize it, but instead of speaking of "catholicity," as we do today,[2] they spoke of a "catholic Church" or even—and this is more significant—of "catholic churches" in the plural.[3] This means that we cannot speak of "catholicity" and ignore the concrete local Church.

*Chapter 4 of John Zizioulas, *Being as Communion, Studies in Personhood and the Church* (Crestwood, N.Y.: St. Vladimir's Seminary Press, 1985) 143–69.

[1] The Aristotelian use of the term καθόλου as contrasted with the κατὰ μέρος or καθ᾽ ἕκαστον survived at the time of the primitive Church mainly under the form of the adjective καθολικὸς (see e.g., Polybius, VI, 5, 3; Dionysius Halicarn, *Comp.*, 12; Philo, *Vita Moesis* II, 32, etc.).

[2] Such conceptualizations have occurred not only in western theology, but also within that of the Orthodox Church, as we see, for example, in the well-known idea of *sobornost,* which appeared in nineteenth-century Russian theology, mainly through the works of Khomiakov. This idea is a conceptualization made on the basis of a translation of καθολικὴ by *sobornaia* in the Slavonic Creed and under the influence of eighteenth-century philosophical trends. It would be very interesting to study the exact meaning of this Slavonic term at the time of its first appearance, because it is possible that at that time the word meant precisely the *concrete gathering together,* i.e., a σύνοδος not in the technical sense of the councils but in that of συνέρχεσθαι ἐπὶ τὸ αὐτὸ as we find it in Paul (1 Cor 11:20 ff.) and Ignatius (*Eph.,* 5:2-3), and as it was explicitly used even in the time of Chrysostom when σύνοδος could simply mean the eucharistic gathering (see Chrysostom, *De Proph. obsc.,* 2, 5, PG 56:182; cf. below, n. 22). If that is the case, then it is interesting to note that not only ideas such as the identification of "catholic" with "universal" as it developed in the West but even that of *sobornost* as it developed in the East did nothing but obscure the original *concrete* meaning of the καθολικὴ ἐκκλησία.

[3] During the first three centuries at least, the term "catholic Church" was applied almost exclusively to the local church. Ignatius in his well-known passage in *Smyrn.*, 8, where the term appears for the first time in our sources, seems to contrast the local episcopal community with the "catholic Church" in a way that has led many scholars (Zahn, Lightfoot, Bardy, etc.) to identify the latter with the "universal Church." But there is not a single indication in the text that would suggest this

Already in the book of the *Didache* in the later first or early second century the idea was clearly expressed that in the celebration of the Eucharist the Church experiences that which is promised for the *Parousia*, namely, the eschatological unity of all in Christ: "Just as this loaf was scattered all over the mountains and having been brought together was made one, so let your Church be gathered from the ends of the earth in your Kingdom."[4] This conviction was not irrelevant in the application of the term "catholic Church" to the local community. It was a clear indication that, although the catholicity of the Church is ultimately an eschatological reality, its nature is revealed and realistically apprehended *here and now* in the Eucharist. The Eucharist understood primarily not as a *thing* and an objectified means of grace but as an *act* and a *synaxis* of the local Church,[5] a

---

identification. It is clear from Ignatian ecclesiology as a whole that not only does a "universal Church" not exist in Ignatius's mind but, on the contrary, an identification of the whole Christ and the whole Church with the local episcopal community constitutes a key idea in his thought (cf. below at n. 24). In the *Martyrium Polycarpi* the expression ἡ κατὰ τὴν οἰκουμένην καθολικὴ ἐκκλησία has led scholars to similar conclusions in a way which seems to overlook the fact that, if one translated καθολικὴ by "universal" in this text one would be confronted with an impossible tautology which would read something like: "The universal Church which is in the universe"! That in this document there is no such contrast between "local" and "universal" is shown by the fact that it speaks of Polycarp as being the bishop "of the catholic Church which is in Smyrna" (16, 2) precisely because the local Church is the "dwelling place" (παροικία) of the whole Church (*inscr.*). In the same way Tertullian can use the term "catholic Churches" in the plural (*Praescr. Haer.*, 26, 4, *PL* 2, 38: see comments by Labriolle-Refoulé in the edition "Sources Chrétiennes" 46, 1957, 126, n. 4), while Cyprian can write "on the unity of the catholic Church" having in mind probably the Church of Carthage (see Th. Camelot, "Saint Cyprian et la primauté" in *Istina* 2 [1957] 423, and M. Bevenot, *St. Cyprian: The Lapsed—The Unity of the Catholic Church* [Ancient Christian Writers 25, 1957] 74–75, and the Roman confessors in the middle third century can speak of "one bishop in the catholic Church" (Cyprian, *Ep.*, 49 [46] 2–4; Eusebius, *Hist. Eccl.*, VI 43, 11). It was probably only in the fourth century and out of the struggle of such theologians as Optatus of Milevis (*Adv. Parm.*, 2, 1) and Augustine (*Ep.*, XCIII, 23; *De Unit.*, 6, 16, etc.) against the provincialism of the Donatists that the term "catholic" came to be identified with "universal." Cf. P. Battifol, *Le Catholicisme de Saint Augustin* (1929) 212. During the same century in the East catholicity receives a synthetic *definition*, in which "universality" is one of the elements that constitute catholicity. See Cyril of Jerusalem, *Catech.*, 18, 23, *PG* 33:1044.

[4] *Didache*, 9, 4. Cf. 10, 5. For the fact that these are eucharistic texts see J. P. Audet, *La Didache: Instruction des Apôtres* (1948) 407.

[5] This aspect of the Eucharist had been forgotten for a long time. It has been emphasized in the West by such scholars as O. Casel, G. Dix, etc. For the ecclesio-

"catholic" act of a "catholic" Church, can therefore be of importance in any attempt to understand the catholicity of the Church.

In the following lines we shall first briefly study the eucharistic community as it developed in the early Church with attention fixed on those aspects which were related to catholicity. We shall then try to draw from this study some general conclusions concerning our discussions about catholicity today.

1. THE "ONE" AND THE "MANY" IN THE EUCHARISTIC CONSCIOUSNESS OF THE EARLY CHURCH

In his First Letter to the Corinthians (10:16-17) and in connection with the celebration of the Lord's Supper Paul writes: "The cup of blessing which we bless, is it not a communion (κοινωνία) of the blood of Christ? The bread which we break, is it not a communion of the body of Christ? Because there is one bread, we who are many are one body, for we all partake of the one loaf." This is not the only time that Paul speaks of the "many" as being "one" in Christ, and not just a neuter "one" but a masculine "one."[6]

The idea of the incorporation of the "many" into the "one," or of the "one" as a representative of the "many" goes back to a time earlier than Paul. It is an idea basically connected with the figures of the "Servant of God" and the "Son of Man."[7] But what is significant for us here is that this idea was from the beginning connected with the eucharistic consciousness of the Church. Paul in writing those words to the Corinthians, was simply echoing a conviction apparently widely spread in the primitive Church.

Thus with regard to the tradition of the Servant of God the texts of the Last Supper, in spite of their differences on many points, agree on

---

logical implications of the Eucharist see also H. Fries, "Die Eucharistie und die Einheit der Kirche," in *Pro Mundi Vita: Festschrift zum eucharistischen Weltkongress* (1960) 176; J.-M. R. Tillard, *L'Eucharistie, Pâque de l'Eglise* (*Unam Sanctam*, no. 44, 1964); J. J. von Allmen, *Essai sur le repas du Seigneur* (1966) 37 ff.; and the works of N. A. Afanasiev, A. Schmemann, and J. Meyendorff (the latter's *Orthodoxy and Catholicity*, 1966).

[6] Gal 3:28. Cf. 2 Cor 11:2; Eph 2:15, etc.

[7] This contributed to the appearance of the well-known theory of "corporate personality" in the Bible. On this theory cf. among others: S. Pedersen, *Israel: Its Life and Culture* (1926); H. Wheeler Robinson, *The Hebrew Conception of Corporate Personality* (1936) 49 ff.; A. R. Johnson, *The One and the Many in the Israelite Conception of God* (1942); and J. de Fraine, *Adam et son lignage: Etudes sur la "personalité corporative" dans la Bible* (1959).

the connection of the Supper with the "many" or "you," "for," or "in the place of " (᾽αντί, περί) whom the one offers himself.[8] This relation of the Eucharist to the tradition of the Servant of God in whom the many are represented established itself in the liturgical life of the Church already in the first century. In the most ancient liturgical prayer of the Roman Church, which is found in *1 Clement*, we come across the idea of the Servant of God many times in connection with the Eucharist.[9] The same is true about the *Didache*, where this idea finds its place in an even more explicit manner.[10]

Similar observations can be made about the connection of the Eucharist with the "Son of Man" tradition. If the sixth chapter of the Fourth Gospel refers to the Eucharist, it is significant that the prevailing figure of the Son of Man is connected there with the Eucharist. *He* is the one who gives "the food which remains to eternal life."[11] Unlike the manna which God gave to Israel through Moses, this bread is "the true bread" which, having come down from heaven, is nothing else but "the Son of Man" himself.[12] It is significant that Christ appears here as the Son of Man, and not in another capacity, as he identifies himself with "the true bread." Hence the eating of this bread is called specifically the eating of "the flesh of the *Son of Man*"[13] who takes into himself every one who eats this bread,[14] thus fulfilling his role as the corporate Son of Man.

It is precisely this idea that prevails in chapters 13–17 of the same Gospel, where the eucharistic presuppositions of the Last Supper are so deeply connected with the eschatological unity of all in Christ, finding their climax in the prayer that "they all may be one."[15] It is impossible to see all this outside a eucharistic context in which the idea of the unity of the "many" in the "one" prevails. Because of this the Fourth Gospel not only allows itself to be taken as a eucharistic liturgy,[16] but it is also characterized by such otherwise inexplicable expressions as the strange exchange of first person singular with the

---

[8] See Mark 14:24; Matt 26:28; Luke 22:20; and 1 Cor 11:24.
[9] *1 Clem.*, 59:2–4.
[10] *Didache*, 10, 2; 9, 2. Cf. above, n. 4.
[11] John 6:27.
[12] John 6:27, 51.
[13] John 6:53.
[14] John 6:56.
[15] John 17.
[16] Ph. H. Menoud, *L'évangile de Jean d'après les recherches récents* (1947) 247.

first person plural in 3:11-13—"Truly, truly *I* say unto you, *we* speak of what *we* know and bear witness to what *we* have seen; but you do not receive *our* testimony. If *I* have told you earthly things and you do not believe, how can you believe if *I* tell you heavenly things? No one has ascended into heaven but he who descended from heaven, *the Son of Man.*" It should be noted that it is again a Son of Man text that contains such a philological phenomenon which can only be understood in an ecclesiological sense.[17]

All this shows the early and deep connection of the idea of the unity of the "many" and the "one" with the eucharistic experience of the Church. It would fall outside the scope of this study to discuss here whether or not this connection offers an explanation of the ecclesiological image of "the Body of Christ."[18] But it is certainly true that neither the identification of the Church with the Body of Christ nor the ultimate unity of the "many" in the "one" can be understood apart from the eucharistic word "this is my Body."[19]

The ecclesiological consequences of this can be clearly seen in the sources of the first three centuries. The first of these consequences is that the local eucharistic community receives the name ἐκκλησία or even ἐκκλησία τοῦ θεοῦ already in the letters of St. Paul. A careful study of 1 Corinthians 11 reveals that the term ἐκκλκσία is used in a dynamic sense: "when you come together into, i.e., when *you become,* ἐκκλησία" (v. 18). This implies clearly what in the following verses becomes explicit, namely, that the eucharistic terms "coming together," "coming together ἐπὶ τὸ ἀυτό," "Lord's Supper," etc., are identified with the ecclesiological terms "ἐκκλησία" or "ἐκκλησία of God."

The other consequence which, I think, is of great importance for later developments of the idea of catholicity is that this local community is called ὅλη ἡ ἐκκλησία, i.e., *the whole Church,* already by Paul again.[20] Now, whether this idea had anything to do with the idea of the "catholic Church" to appear a few generations later will not occupy us here, interesting as it is from a historical point of view.[21] What remains a fact,

[17] Cf. E. Schweizer, *Gemeinde und Gemeindeordnung im Neuen Testament* (1959) §11a.
[18] For such an explanation see A. D. J. Rawlinson, "Corpus Christi," in *Mysterium Christi* (ed. G. A. Bell and A. Deissmann, 1930) 225 ff.
[19] Cf. C. T. Craig, *The One Church in the Light of the New Testament* (1951) 21.
[20] Rom 16:23.
[21] This is discussed in my book *The Unity of the Church in the Eucharist and the Bishop during the First Three Centuries* (1965—in Greek). [ET, *Eucharist, Bishop, Church: The Unity of the Church in the Divine Eucharist and the Bishop During the*

in any case, is that, in the literature of the first three centuries at least, the local Church, starting again with Paul, was called the ἐκκλησία τôυ θεοῦ or the "whole Church" or even the καθολικὴ ἐκκλησία, and this not unrelated to the concrete eucharistic community.[22] As the ecclesiology of Ignatius of Antioch makes clear, even the context in which the term καθολικὴ ἐκκλησία appears is a eucharistic one, in which Ignatius's main concern was the unity of the eucharistic community.[23] Instead of trying, therefore, to find the meaning of the "catholic Church" in this Ignatian text in a contrast between "local" and "universal," we would be more faithful to the sources if we saw it in the light of the entire Ignatian ecclesiology, according to which the eucharistic community is *"exactly the same as"* (this is the meaning I would give to ὥσπερ which connects the two in the Ignatian text) the whole Church united in Christ.[24]

Catholicity, therefore, in this context, does not mean anything else but the *wholeness* and *fullness* and *totality* of the body of Christ "exactly as" (ὥσπερ) it is portrayed in the eucharistic community.

First Three Centuries. Tr. Elizabeth Theo Kritoff (Brookline, Mass.: Holy Cross Orthodox Press, 2001) ed.].

[22] It is not accidental that the term "catholic" came to be applied to the *cathedral,* i.e., the main church where the bishop would celebrate and the entire episcopal community would be present (Council of Trullo, canon 59). The terms *ecclesia major, ecclesia senior,* and *ecclesia catholica* became synonymous expressions by which the cathedral was distinguished from the parishes from the fourth century on (such evidence appears for example in the *Etheriae Peregrinatio,* ed. by H. Prétré in *Sources Chrétiennes* 21, 1948; and in the lectionaries of the Church of Jerusalem, ed. by M. Tarchnisvilli in 1959, etc.). It is probably from this use of the word "catholic" that the term *katholikon* came to be applied to the main church in a Byzantine monastery, since this was the place where all the monks would gather for the celebration of the Eucharist. The significance of these usages for the connection between the eucharistic community and the "catholic Church" in the early centuries hardly needs to be emphasized.

[23] *Smyrn.,* 8: ". . . Let that be deemed a valid Eucharist which is under the leadership of the bishop or one to whom he has entrusted it. Wherever the bishop appears let there the multitude of the people be, just as wherever Jesus Christ is there (is) the catholic Church."

[24] Any contrast between the "local" and the "universal" in this text would mean that the "universal" Church is united around Christ whereas the "local" is united *not* around Christ *but* around the bishop. This kind of theology is foreign to Ignatius who, on the contrary, sees no difference between the unity in Christ and the unity in the bishop (e.g., *Eph.,* 5, 1; *Magn.,* 3, 1–2; cf. *Poly. inscr.*), and this not by way of metaphor but in a mystical sense of real identification.

2. THE COMPOSITION AND STRUCTURE OF THE EUCHARISTIC COMMUNITY AS REFLECTIONS OF CATHOLICITY

With such a view of the eucharistic community in the background it would have been impossible for the composition and the structure of this community to be different from what it actually was in the first centuries. A different composition and structure would mean a different ecclesiology. It is, therefore, important for us in order to understand this ecclesiology, especially as it concerns the aspect of "catholicity," to bear in mind this composition and structure.

As a combination of the existing fragmentary liturgical evidence of the first centuries allows us to know, the "whole Church"[25] "dwelling in a certain city"[26] would "come together"[27] mainly on a Sunday[28] to "break bread."[29] This *synaxis* would be *the only one* in that particular place in the sense that it would include the *"whole Church."*[30] This fact, which is not usually noted by historians, is of paramount ecclesiological significance, for it immediately draws the line of demarcation between the Christian and the non-Christian pattern of unity at the time of the early Church.

Coming together in brotherly love was certainly not a Christian innovation. In the Roman Empire it was so common to form "associations" that there was need for special laws concerning such associations signified under the name of *collegia*.[31] The brotherly love which prevailed among the members of the *collegia* was so strong and organized that each one of them would contribute monthly to a common fund and would address the other members by the title

---

[25] Rom 16:23.

[26] 1 Cor 1:2; 2 Cor 1:1; 1 Thess 1:1; Acts 11:22, etc.

[27] 1 Cor 11:20, 33, 34. Cf. Ignatius, *Eph.*, 5:2-3.

[28] The observance of Sunday was almost identical with the eucharistic *synaxis*. Cf. W. Rordorf, *Sunday—The History of the Day of Rest and Worship in the Earliest Centuries of the Christian Church* (1968) 177 ff., and 238 ff.

[29] Acts 2:46; 20:7.

[30] The existence of the "Churches in the household" does not present a problem in this respect, even if these Churches are understood as eucharistic assemblies, for there are strong reasons to believe that—significantly enough—there was no more than one such "Church in the household" in each city. These reasons are presented in my *The Unity of the Church . . .*, 64 ff.

[31] Tacitus, *Ann.*, 14, 17; Plinius, *Ad. Traj.*, 34, 97; Menucius Felix, *Oct.*, 8–9; Origen, *Con. Cels.*, 1, 1. Cf. J. P. Waltzing, *Etude historique sur les corporations professionels des Romains* I, 113–29.

"brethren" *(fratres, sodales, socii)*.[32] Apart from the pagans, the Jews who lived in the Roman Empire were also organized in special communities under their own ethnarch[33] and their brotherly love was so strong that in cases of special groups, like the Essenes, it was based on principles of common property. To speak, therefore, of the unity of the early Christians in terms of brotherly love would be to miss the unique point of this unity and perhaps even to expose it to a comparison from which it would certainly not gain much, especially in the light of such evidence as that provided by texts like Galatians 5:5 and 1 Corinthians 11:21, etc.!

Certainly there was a basic difference in faith that distinguished Christians from their environment.[34] But there was also a certain distinctiveness in the manner of their gathering together, which should not pass unnoticed. This distinctiveness lay in the composition of these gatherings. Whereas the Jews based the unity of their gatherings on race (or, in the later years, on a broader religious community based on this race) and the pagans with their *collegia* on profession, the Christians declared that in Christ "there is neither Jew nor Greek,"[35] "male or female,"[36] adult or child,[37] rich or poor,[38] master or slave,[39] etc. To be sure the Christians themselves soon came to believe that they constituted a *third race,* but this was only to show that in fact it was a "nonracial race," a *people* who, while claiming to be the true Israel, declared at the same time that they did not care about the difference between a Greek and a Jew once these were members of the Christian Church.

This attitude which transcended not only social but *also natural* divisions (such as age, race, etc.) was portrayed in the eucharistic community *par excellence.* It is very significant that, unlike what the

[32] Cf. F. X. Krause, "Fraternitas," in *Realencyclopaedie der christlichen Alterthümer* I (1880), col. 540.

[33] Cf. E. Schürer, *Geschichte des jüdischen Volkes* (1914) 14–17.

[34] Confessions of faith were very early attached to the liturgy so that an interaction between the two was established. Cf. K. Federer, *Liturgie und Glaube—Eine theologiegeschichtliche Untersuchung* (1950) 59 ff.

[35] Gal 3:28; Col 3:11. Cf. 1 Cor 12:13.

[36] Gal 3:28.

[37] Matt 19:13. Cf. 14:21. The question of the participation of children in the eucharistic assemblies of the early Church is, of course, connected with the problem of paedobaptism at that period, on which the work of J. Jeremias, *Die Kindertaufe in den ersten vier Jahrhunderten* (1958) continues to be illuminating.

[38] Jas 2:2-7; 1 Cor 11, 20 ff.

[39] 1 Cor 12:13; Gal 3:28; Eph 6:8.

churches do today in an age marked by a tragic loss of the primitive ecclesiology, there was never a celebration of the Eucharist specially for children or for students, etc., nor a Eucharist that could take place privately and individually.[40] Such a thing would destroy precisely the catholic character of the Eucharist which was *leitourgia,* i.e., a "public work" for all Christians of the same city to which—significantly enough—for a long time and in places as crowded as Rome in the second century even the people from the country would come to participate.[41] The eucharistic community was in its composition a *catholic community* in the sense that it transcended not only social but also natural divisions,[42] just as it will happen in the Kingdom of God[43] of which this community was a revelation and a real sign.[44]

This "catholicity" of the eucharistic community was also reflected in its structure. As far as we can reconstruct this structure from the pieces of evidence that we possess, we can see that in the center of the *synaxis* of the "whole Church"[45] and behind the "one altar"[46] there was the throne of the "one bishop"[47] seated "in the place of God"[48] or

[40] The gradual individualization of the Eucharist with the introduction of private eucharistic prayers into the structure of the liturgy and finally with the prevalence of the "private Mass" in the West represents a historical development which should be examined in close connection with the development of ecclesiology.

[41] Justin, *Apol.,* I 67. Cf. 65. This situation must have lasted at least until the middle of the third century when the first indications of the formation of parishes appear. The entire problem with its ecclesiological implications is discussed in my *The Unity of the Church . . .,* 151–88.

[42] Cf. above, n. 37.

[43] Matt 22:30; Mark 12:25; Luke 20:34 ff.

[44] The presuppositions of faith and love for communion were, of course, creating limitations to this community. It is important to study how a closed liturgical community, which the early Church undoubtedly was, can be related to the "catholic Church." For this a special study would be necessary. Cf. the works of W. Elert, *Abendmahl und Kirchengemeinschaft in der alten Kirche hauptsächlich des Ostens* (1954), and S. L. Greenslade, *Schism in the Early Church* (no date).

[45] See above.

[46] The connection of the "one Church" with the "one Eucharist," the "one bishop," and the "one altar," clearly established already in the teaching of Ignatius (*Philad.,* 4; *Magn.,* 7, 2; *Eph.,* 5, 2; *Tral.,* 7, 2, etc.) continues through Cyprian (*Ep.,* 43 [40], 5; *De unit.,* 17, 14, etc.) well into the fourth century with the idea of μονογενὲς θυσιαστήριον (Eusebius, *Eccl. Hist.,* X, 4, 68) and a number of deeply meaningful liturgical practices like the *fermentum,* the *antimension,* etc.

[47] Ignatius, *Philad.,* 4. Cf. previous note.

[48] Ignatius, *Magn.,* 6, 1; 3, 12; *Tral.,* 3, 1.

understood as the living "image of Christ."[49] Around his throne were seated the presbyters,[50] while by him stood the deacons helping him in the celebration, and in front of him the "people of God,"[51] that order[52] of the Church which was constituted by virtue of the rite of initiation (baptism-chrismation) and considered the *sine qua non* condition for the eucharistic community to exist and express the Church's unity.

A fundamental function of this "one bishop" was to express in himself the "multitude" (πολυπληθεία)[53] of the faithful in that place. He was the one who would offer the Eucharist to God in the name of the Church, thus bringing up to the throne of God the *whole body of Christ*. He was the one in whom the "many" united would become "one," being brought back to him who had made them, thanks to their redemption from Satan by the one who took them upon himself. Thus the bishop would become the one through whose hands the whole community would have to pass in its being offered up to God in Christ, i.e., in the highest moment of the Church's unity.

The decisive preeminence of the bishop in the idea of a "catholic Church" was thus developing from within the heart of the eucharistic community. Not only the multiplicity of the people but also the plurality of orders ought to cease to be a division and be transcended into a diversity like the one given by the Holy Spirit who distributes the gifts without destroying the unity. This was the function of *ordination*. Ordination means *order* and therefore creates *orders*. This was nothing strange to the primitive eucharistic gatherings, which were structured by such orders. But a distribution of gifts and ministries and the creation of *orders* could mean a destruction of unity, as it can

---

[49] The idea that the bishop is "the image of Christ" lasted at least until the fourth century (cf. *Pseudo-Clem. Homil.*, 3, 62). For material see O. Perler, "L'Evêque, représentant du Christ . . ." in *L'Episcopat et l'Eglise universelle* (ed. Y. Congar, *et al., Unam Sanctam* 39, 1962) 31–66.

[50] Rev 4, 4. Cf. Ignatius, *Symrn.*, 8, 1; *Eph.* 20, 2, and the arrangement of the eucharistic assembly presupposed in such sources as Hippolytus, *Ap. Trad.* (ed. Dix, 6 and 40 ff.).

[51] See Justin, *Apol.*, 65, 67, and previous note.

[52] *1 Clem.*, 40, 5; 41, 7. The idea that the "layman" is not a "non-ordained" person but one who through baptism and chrismation belongs to his own order in the church is fundamental in the correct understanding of the eucharistic synaxis and its ecclesiological implications.

[53] Ignatius, *Eph.*, 1, 3; *Tral.*, 1, 1: the "multitude" of Tralles could be seen in the person of their bishop.

in the natural world. By restricting all such ordinations to the eucharistic community and making it an exclusive right of the bishop, *not as an individual but as the head of this eucharistic community,* to ordain, the early Church saved the catholic character of its entire structure. The bishop with his exclusive right of ordination and with the indispensable restriction of ordaining only in the eucharistic context took it upon himself to express the catholicity of his Church. But it was the eucharistic community and the place he occupied in its structure that justified this.

3. THE EUCHARISTIC COMMUNITY AND THE "CATHOLIC CHURCH IN THE WORLD"

But there was a paradox in the way the eucharistic community lent itself to the formation of the "catholic Church" in the first centuries. The paradox lay in the fact that although the eucharistic community, being a *local* entity, led inevitably to the idea of a *catholic local Church,* it led at the same time to a transcendence of the antithesis between local and universal, thus making it possible to apply the term "catholic" both to the local and the universal realms at the same time. This was possible for reasons that are rooted both in the very nature and in the structure of the eucharistic community.

The nature of the eucharistic community was determined by its being "eucharistic," i.e., by the fact that it consisted in the communion of the Body of Christ in its totality and in its inclusiveness *of all*. What each eucharistic community, therefore, was meant to reveal, was not part of Christ but the whole Christ and not a partial or local unity but the full eschatological unity of all in Christ. *It was a concretization and localization of the general,* a real presence of the καθόλου in the καθ᾽ ἕκαστον in the true Aristotelian sense.[54] As it is indicated in the passage of the *Didache* we mentioned earlier,[55] the local eucharistic assembly understood itself as the revelation of the eschatological unity of all in Christ. This meant that *no mutual exclusion* between the local and the universal was possible in a eucharistic context, but the one was automatically involved in the other.

---

[54] The relationship of the καθόλου to the καθ᾽ ἕκαστον in Aristotle is expressed very well in the example he gives: "as 'man' belongs to the καθόλου and Callias to the καθ᾽ ἕκαστον"(*Interpr.,* 7, 17). Thus the καθ᾽ ἕκαστον is not understood as a part of the καθόλου but as its concrete expression. In this way of thinking the dilemma between "local" and "universal" appears to make no sense.

[55] See above, n. 4.

This principle found expression in the structure of the eucharistic community through the fact that the head of this community was related to the other eucharistic communities in the world by his very ordination. The fact that in each episcopal ordination at least two or three bishops from the neighboring Churches ought to take part[56] tied the episcopal office and with it the local eucharistic community in which the ordination to it took place with the rest of the eucharistic communities in the world in a fundamental way.[57] This fact not only made it possible for each bishop to allow a visiting fellow-bishop to preside over his eucharistic community[58] but must have been also one of the basic factors in the appearance of episcopal conciliarity.

The exact place that the "synod" or "council" occupied in the context of the catholicity of the early Church represents one of the most obscure and difficult problems. Were these councils intended, when they first appeared, to form a structure of a "universal catholicity" above the local Churches? Cyprian, one of the persons most involved in such conciliar activity, certainly did not think so. For him the authority of a council was moral and each bishop remained always directly responsible to God for his own community.[59] But the very fact of the gradual acceptance of the "council" as a norm in the life of the Church proves that its roots must have been very deep.

On another occasion too I tried to show that the phenomenon of early councils cannot be understood apart from a primitive conciliarity which preceded the councils and which again was not unrelated to the eucharistic community.[60] It was not an insignificant thing that most, if not all, of the earliest councils were ultimately concerned

[56] Hippolytus, *Apost. Trad.*, 2; Council of Arles, c. 20; I Nicaea, c. 4 and 6, etc.

[57] This is a fundamental point which N. Afanasiev has failed in his eucharistic ecclesiology to see and appreciate, as one may gather from the views expressed, for example, in his article "Una Sancta," *Irénikon* 36 (1963) 436–75, and elsewhere.

[58] This we know, for example, from Polycarp's visit to Rome on the occasion of the paschal controversy (Eusebius, *Eccle. Hist.*, V, 24, 14–17). Cf. Syriac *Didascalia*, 12 (ed. Connolly, 122).

[59] Cyprian, *Ep.*, 55 (52) 21. The significant passage is: "Manente concordia vinculo et perseverante catholicae ecclesiae individuo sacramento, actum suum disponit et dirigit unusquisque episcopus rationem propositi sui Domino redditurus." This makes it difficult to attribute to Cyprian the beginning of a "universalist ecclesiology" as N. Afanasiev has done (cf. his "La doctrine de la primauté à la lumière de l'ecclésiologie," *Istina* 2 [1957] 401–20).

[60] In my article "The Development of Conciliar Structure to the Time of the First Ecumenical Council," in *Councils and the Ecumenical Movement* (World Council Studies, no. 5, 1968) 34–51.

with the problem of eucharistic communion[61] nor that the final admission of supra-local conciliar structures with authority over the local bishop was provoked by the pressing need to solve the problem of eucharistic admission among the local churches.[62] All this meant that behind these developments stood a concept of "catholicity" deeply rooted in the idea of the eucharistic community. The various local Churches had to wrestle—perhaps unconsciously—with the problem of the relationship between the "catholic Church" in the episcopal community and the catholic Church in the world. The moment they would admit a supra-local structure over the local eucharistic community, be it a synod or another office, the eucharistic community would cease to be in itself and *by virtue of its eucharistic nature* a "catholic Church." The moment, on the other hand, that they would allow each eucharistic community to close itself to the other communities either entirely (i.e. by creating a schism) or partially (i.e., by not allowing certain individual faithful from one community to communicate in another or by accepting to communion faithful excluded from it by their own community)[63] they would betray the *very eucharistic nature of their catholicity* and the catholic character of the Eucharist. The council was, therefore, an inevitable answer to this dilemma, and its genesis must be seen in the light of this situation.

Placed in this background, the councils represent in their appearance the most official negation of the division between local and universal, a negation which must be taken in all its implications. The eucharistic mentality which led to this solution would not allow any structure which would deny the fact that each eucharistic community revealed in a certain place *the whole Christ* and the ultimate eschatological unity of all in him. But the same mentality would not allow any provincialism that would fail to see the same reality in the other eucharistic communities. The whole Christ, the catholic Church, was present and incarnate in each eucharistic community. Each eucharistic community was, therefore, in full unity with the rest by virtue *not*

---

[61] Already in the first synods recorded in our sources. See Eusebius, *Eccl. Hist.*, V, 16, 10. Cf. V, 24, 9; 28, 9.

[62] This is for the first time reflected in canon 5 of I Nicaea. This canon is concerned with excommunications which took place in various local Churches. Its deeper meaning lies in the idea that conciliarity is born out of the Church's belief that eucharistic communion in a certain community is a matter that concerns all communities in the world.

[63] See again canon 5 of 1 Nicaea where the problem lies in the historical background.

of an external superimposed structure but of the whole Christ represented in each of them. The bishops as heads of these communities coming together in synods only expressed what Ignatius, in spite of—or perhaps because of—his eucharistic ecclesiology wrote once: "the bishops who are in the extremes of the earth are in the mind of Christ."[64] Thanks to a eucharistic vision of the "catholic Church" the problem of the relationship between the "one catholic Church in the world" and the "catholic Churches" in the various local places was resolved apart from any consideration of the local church as being incomplete[65] or any scheme of priority of the one over the other, and in the sense of a *unity in identity*.[66]

4. SOME GENERAL CONCLUSIONS

In light of this brief study of the "catholic" character of the eucharistic community as it developed in the early Church, the following thoughts may be of some relevance to the present-day ecumenical discussion on the catholicity of the Church.

(1) The primary content of "catholicity" is not a moral but a christological one. The Church is catholic not because she is obedient to Christ, i.e., because she does certain things or behaves in a certain way. She is catholic first of all because she is the Body of Christ. Her catholicity depends not on herself but on him. She is catholic because

---

[64] Ignatius, *Eph.*, 3, 2.

[65] The idea that the local church is a representative of the entire Church and therefore a full Church was a fundamental one in the consciousness of the early Church. Cf. B. Botte, "La collégialité dans le Nouveau Testament et chez les Pères apostoliques" in *Le Concile et les Conciles* (ed. B. Botte, *et al.*, 1960) 14 f., and J. Hamer, *L'Eglise est une communion* (1962) 38: "it is not in adding together the local communities that the whole community which constitutes the Church is born, but each community, however small, represents the whole Church."

[66] The fundamental and crucial problem of the relationship between the "local" and the "universal" catholic Church must be solved apart from any notion of a *unity in collectivity*, and in the direction of a *unity in identity*. Schematically speaking, in the first case the various local Churches form *parts* which are added to one another in order to make up a whole, whereas in the latter, the local Churches are *full circles* which cannot be added to one another but *coincide* with one another and finally with the Body of Christ and the original apostolic Church. It is for this reason that any "structure of the unity of the Church in the Churches" (cf. the suggestion of Professor J.-J. von Allmen, *op. cit.*, 52) renders itself extremely difficult, once it is a *structure*. (It is not an accident that the ancient Church never realized such a *structure* in her life in spite of her conciliar activity.) The problem deserves a fuller discussion. With regard to the sources of the first three centuries, cf. the discussion in my book *The Unity of the Church . . .*, 63–148.

she is where Christ is. We cannot understand catholicity as an ecclesiological notation unless we understand it as a christological reality.[67]

To derive this assertion from a study of the eucharistic community means ceasing to understand it in the context of the problem of whether catholicity is a *given* reality or a *demand*. This problem, which is often presented in the form of a dilemma, is strange to the eucharistic vision of catholicity because in such a vision whatever is given is revealed in *an existential way,* i.e., in the form of a presence *here and now,* a presence so fully incarnate in history that the ontological and the ethical cease to claim priority over each other. For example, to illustrate this from our brief study of the eucharistic community, it is not possible to ask the question whether this community was composed in such a "catholic" way because she was conscious of a certain demand for that, or whether her being composed in such a way led to the consciousness of such a demand or such a concept of "catholicity." History is, in this respect, very instructive because there is perhaps nothing hidden so obscurely in the roots of Church history as the eucharistic structure of the first communities. To ask whether a certain belief preceded this structure, or if this structure led to this or that belief, would be asking a historically impossible question.

When, therefore, we say here that catholicity is not a moral but a christological reality, we are not choosing between a "given" fact and a "demand," for the entire scheme of "given" versus "obtained" is far from being the context of discussion in a eucharistic vision of catholicity. The christological character of catholicity lies in the fact that the Church is catholic not as a community which aims at a certain ethical achievement (being open, serving the world, etc.) but as a community which experiences and reveals the unity of all creation *insofar as this unity constitutes a reality in the person of Christ.* To be sure, this experience and this revelation involve a certain *catholic ethos.* But there is *no autonomous catholicity,* no catholic ethos that can be understood in itself.[68] It is *Christ's* unity and it is *his* catholicity that the Church reveals in her being catholic. This means that her catholicity is neither

---

[67] Christology as the starting point in ecclesiology in general has been stressed by G. Florovsky, "Christ and his Church, Suggestions and Comments," in *1054–1954, L'Eglise et les Eglises II* (1954) 164, and should not be understood as a negation of the pneumatological or the triadological aspect of the Church. For a clarification of this approach see Y. N. Lelouvier, *Perspectives russes sur l'Eglise: Un théologien contemporain, Georges Florovsky* (1968).

[68] Sociological views of catholicity must be only *derived* views and not *vice versa.*

an objective gift to be possessed nor an objective order to be fulfilled, but rather a *presence,* a presence which unites into a single existential reality both what is given and what is demanded, the presence of him who sums up in himself the community and the entire creation by his being existentially involved in both of them. The Church is catholic only by virtue of her being where this presence is (Ignatius), i.e., by virtue of her being inseparably united with Christ and constituting his very presence in history.

(2) To reveal Christ's whole Body in history means to meet the demonic powers of division which operate in history. A christological catholicity which is seen in the context of this encounter with the anti–catholic powers of the world cannot be a *static* but a *dynamic catholicity.* This can happen only if we recognize in the catholicity of the Church a *pneumatological dimension.*

In the celebration of the Eucharist, the Church very early realized that in order for the eucharistic community to become or reveal in itself the wholeness of the Body of Christ (a wholeness that would include not only humanity but the entire creation),[69] the descent of the Holy Spirit upon this creation would be necessary. The offering up of the gifts and the whole community to the throne of God, the realization of the unity of the Body of Christ, was therefore preceded by the *invocation of the Holy Spirit.* "Send down thy Holy Spirit upon *us* and upon the *gifts* placed before thee."[70] For the world to become even symbolically a real sign of the consummation of all in Christ would be an impossibility without the Holy Spirit. The eucharistic community shows by its very existence that the realization of the Church's catholicity in history is the work of the Holy Spirit.

It is important to bear in mind that the Body of Christ, both in the christological (incarnational) and in the ecclesiological sense, became a historical reality *through the Holy Spirit.*[71] For creation to lend itself

[69] This view of the Eucharist has been a fundamental one in the eastern liturgies ever since Irenaeus's teaching, on which see A. W. Ziegler, "Das Brot von unseren Felder. Ein Beitrag zur Eucharistielehre des hl. Irenäus," in *Pro mundi vita: Festschrift zum Eucharistischen Weltkongress 1960* (1960) 21–43.

[70] The liturgy of St. John Chrysostom (prayer of consecration). The same prayer in the liturgy of St. Basil makes it even clearer that the Holy Spirit is invoked not just for the consecration of the gifts but also for the realization of the unity of the community: "And to unite us all as many as are partakers in the one bread and cup, one with another, in the communion of the one Holy Spirit."

[71] See N. Nissiotis, "La Pneumatologie ecclésiologique au service de l'Unité de l'Eglise," *Istina* 12 (1967) 322–40, where a discussion of the role of the Holy Spirit

to the *Logos* of God in order to bring about the incarnation would have been impossible without the intervention of the Holy Spirit. This is a fundamental scriptural assertion,[72] and the same is true about the realization of the community of the Church on the day of Pentecost.[73] To see these events retrospectively through the eyes of the Church means to place them in their pneumatological context, for that which made them a reality *eph hapax,* namely, the Holy Spirit, is that which makes them an existential reality, here and now, again. In this sense the eucharistic *anamnesis* becomes not a mere mental operation but an existential realization, a *re*-presentation of the Body of Christ,[74] thus revealing to us that the Church's existence as the Body of Christ and, therefore, her catholicity constitutes a reality which *depends constantly* upon the Holy Spirit.

This means not only that human attempts at "togetherness," "openness," etc., cannot constitute the catholicity of the Church, but that no plan for a progressive movement towards catholicity can be achieved on a purely historical and sociological level. The eucharistic community constitutes a sign of the fact that the *eschaton* can only *break through* history but never be identified with it. Its call to catholicity is a call not to a progressive conquest of the world but to a "kenotic" experience of the fight with the anticatholic demonic powers and a continuous dependence upon the Lord and his Spirit. A catholic Church in the world, cognizant as she may be of Christ's victory over Satan, lives in humility and service and above all in constant prayer and worship.

(3) The way the catholicity of the Church is revealed in the eucharistic community shows that the ultimate essence of catholicity lies in the transcendence of all divisions in Christ. This should be understood

---

in ecclesiology is found. Cf. O. Clément, "L'Ecclésiologie orthodoxe comme ecclésiologie de communion," *Contacts* 20 (1968) 10–36 (English trans. in *One in Christ* 6 [1970] 101–2).

[72] Luke 1:35; Matt 1:18-20.

[73] Acts 1–2. Ever since, baptism and confirmation were inseparably united in the early Church and understood as the very operation of the Spirit in Christ's baptism and anointing (Luke 4:18) so that each baptized and chrismated Christian would become himself Christ (Tertullian, *De Bapt.,* 7-8; Theophilus of Antioch, *Ad Autol.,* 1, 12, and especially Cyril of Jerusalem, *Cat.,* 21, 1, *PG* 33: 1089).

[74] This idea forms part of the emerging consensus on the Eucharist in the Ecumenical Movement today. See "The Eucharist in Ecumenical Thought" (a Faith and Order document) in *Study Encounter,* vol. IV, no. 3 (1968).

absolutely and without any reservations. It covers all areas and all dimensions of existence whether human or cosmic, historical or eschatological, spiritual or material, social or individual, etc. The dichotomies in which life has been placed and conceived, unfortunately to a great extent by Christian tradition itself,[75] represent a betrayal of the catholic outlook so essential to the Church of Christ. One thinks in this respect, for example, of the dichotomy between the "sacred" and the "secular," or between body and soul. The eucharistic community with its understanding of the Eucharist as *a meal*,[76] with its basic elements being material and not merely spiritual, with its long litanies and supplications in which man's everyday material and physical needs find their place, etc., constitutes a sign of a "catholic" view of existence in which no dualistic dichotomies can be accepted. Man and the world form a unity in harmony and so do the various dimensions in man's own existence. An ecclesiological catholicity in the light of the eucharistic community suggests and presupposes a *catholic anthropology* and a *catholic view of existence* in general.

In such a catholic outlook the entire problem of the relationship of the Church to the world receives a different perspective. The separation and juxtaposition of the two can have no essential meaning because there is no point where the limits of the Church can be objectively and finally drawn. There is a constant interrelation between the Church and the world, the world being God's creation and never ceasing to belong to him and the Church being the community which through the descent of the Holy Spirit transcends in herself the world and offers it to God in the Eucharist.[77]

(4) But how can this view of catholicity be reconciled with the fact that the eucharistic community itself is divided into *orders*, i.e., into categories and classes of people? History shows that there is a real problem here, because the divisions which have occurred on this basis are so deep that the Church is still suffering from

[75] Cf. A. Schmemann, *Sacraments and Orthodoxy* (1965) 14 (now *For the Life of the World* [St. Vladimir's Seminary Press, 2002] ed.).

[76] Cf. again the ecumenical consensus in "The Eucharist in Ecumenical Thought" (n. 74 above).

[77] This transcendence which is possible only "in the Spirit" presupposes a baptismal purification of man and his world and in this sense it is important to bear in mind the "paschal" character of the Eucharist (cf. J.-M. R. Tillard, *op. cit.*, 164) and the intimate relationship between baptism and Eucharist (see J.-J. von Allmen, *op. cit.*, 37 f.).

them.[78] How can the situation which results from ordination into ministries and orders, into clergy and laity, be transcended in the way all divisions are transcended in the eucharistic community?

The fact that all ordinations were at a very early time incorporated in the eucharistic liturgy is, I think, of great importance in this respect. The first important implication of this fact is that there is no ministry which can be conceived as existing *parallel* to that of Christ but only as *identical* with it. In her being the Body of Christ, the Church exists as a manifestation of Christ's own ministry and as a reflection of this very ministry in the world. It is not an accident that the early Church applied to Christ all forms of ministries that existed. He was the apostle,[79] the prophet,[80] the priest,[81] the bishop,[82] the deacon,[83] etc. A christologically understood ministry transcends all categories of priority and separation that may be created by the act or ordination and "setting apart."

Another fundamental implication is that no ministry in the Church can be understood outside the context of the community. This should not be explained in terms of representativeness and delegation of authority, for these terms being basically juridical finally lead to a separation of the ordained person from the community: to act *on behalf* of the community means to stand *outside* it because it means to act *in its place*.[84] But what is precisely denied by this communal dimension, we want to point out here, is that there is no ministry that can stand *outside* or *above* the community.

To affirm that the ministry belongs to the community means, in the last analysis, to place the entire matter of ordination outside the dilemma of choosing between *ontological* and *functional*. It has been for a long time an object of discussion whether ordination bestows

[78] We have in mind the whole issue of clericalism and anti-clericalism which has been a real problem, especially in the West. The East, by having kept for centuries a eucharistic vision of ecclesiology, did not experience this problem. It was only recently that, due to a replacement of this vision by later ecclesiological ideas, the problem appeared threatening in some Orthodox areas.

[79] Heb 3:1.

[80] Matt 23:8; John 13:13.

[81] Heb 5:6; 8:4; 10:21; 2:17.

[82] 1 Pet 2:25; 5:4; Heb 13:13. Cf. Ignatius, *Magn.*, 3, 1-2; *Polyc. inscr.*

[83] Rom 15:8; Luke 22:27; Phil 2:7.

[84] In this sense terminology like that of "vicar," etc. when applied to the episcopate or the ministry in general may suggest a similar representation "outside" or "in the place of" someone who is absent.

something indelible upon the ordained person, something that constitutes his individual possession (permanently or temporarily) or simply empowers him with an authority to function for a certain purpose. In the light of the eucharistic community, this dilemma makes no sense and is misleading, for the terms of reference there, as we have had occasion to stress earlier here, are basically existential. There is no *charisma* that can be *possessed individually*, and yet there is no *charisma* which can be conceived or operated *but by individuals*. How can this statement be understood?

Here, I think, we must seek illumination from a fundamental distinction between the *individual* and the *personal*. The distinction has already been made more than once in philosophy[85] but it has seldom been applied to theological problems such as those presented by ecclesiology. And yet the paradox of the incorporation of the "many" into the "one" on which the eucharistic community, as we have seen, and perhaps the entire mystery of the Church are based can only be understood and explained in the categories of *personal existence*. The individual represents a category that presupposes separation and division. "Individuality makes its appearance by its differentiation from other individualities."[86] The person represents a category that presupposes unity with other persons.[87] The eucharistic community, and the Church in general, as a *communion (koinonia)* can only be understood in the categories of personal existence.

Ordination to the ministry in the context of the eucharistic communion implies that the "seal of the Holy Spirit" which is given cannot exist outside the receiver's existential relationship with the community. It is not a mere function to be exercised outside a deep bond with this community. It is a bond of love,[88] such as every gift of the Spirit is, and its *indelible character* can only be compared with that

[85] The distinction was already made, though from a different standpoint, by Thomas Aquinas and it was developed in modern times by J. Maritain, *Du Régime temporal et de liberté* (1933). Cf. N. Berdyaev, *Solitude and Society* (1938) 168. See also ch. 1, "Personhood and Being," of [my *Being as Communion* (St. Vladimir's Seminary Press, 1985) ed.].

[86] M. Buber, *I and Thou* (1958) 62.

[87] *Ibid.*

[88] The Orthodox service of ordination to the priesthood is in many parts identical with that of matrimony. This does not only suggest an understanding of the ministry as a bond between the ordained, Christ, and the community, but it indicates at the same time the *direction* in which theology should move in its attempts to understand the character of ordination.

which is possessed or given by love. Outside this existential bond with the community it is destined to die, just as the Spirit who gives this *charisma* once, and constantly sustains it, does not live outside this community because he is the bond of love. It is in this sense that the Spirit is exclusively possessed by the Church[89] and that all ministry is a gift of this Spirit.

All this means a transcendence of the divisions created by the variety of ministries and the distinctiveness of orders in the Church. It is in this context that the bishop's exclusive right to ordination must be viewed. If he came to possess such a right it was because of his capacity as the head of the eucharistic community—*hence his inability to ordain outside this community*—and in relation to his role as the one who offers the entire community in the Eucharist to God. His exclusive right to ordain, in fact his whole existence as bishop, makes no sense apart from his role as the one through whom all divisions, including those of orders, are transcended. His primary function is always *to make the catholicity of the Church reveal itself in a certain place.* For this he must himself be existentially related to a community. There is no ministry in the catholic Church that can exist *in absoluto.*

(5) The implications of such a view of the ministry and especially of the episcopate for the understanding of *apostolic succession* are clear. To speak of apostolic succession as a chain of episcopal ordinations going back to the apostolic times, without implying the indispensable bond of these ordinations with the community in whose eucharistic *synaxis* they have taken place, would amount to a conception of the ministry *in absoluto.* But if it is not a mere accident that the early Church knew of no episcopal ordination either outside the eucharistic context or without specific mention of *the place* to which the bishop would be attached,[90] we must conclude that there is no apostolic succession which does not go through the concrete community.

---

[89] E.g., Cyprian, *Ep.,* 69 (66), 11; 75, 4, etc. In this sense the idea that there is no salvation outside the Church appears to be more than a negative statement. A fundamental truth behind it is that there is no possibility for an individualistic understanding of salvation: *unus christianus, nullus christianus.*

[90] Already in the sub-apostolic times the bishop appears to be attached to the inhabitants of a certain city (Ignatius, *Magn.,* 15; *Polyc. Inscr.*). Later on, the existing evidence from acts of councils indicates that the bishop's name was attached to the name of a city (*Patrum Nic. nomina,* ed. by Gelzer, 61). What is most significant is that in the service of episcopal ordination the name of the area to which the bishop is assigned has entered the prayer of ordination: the divine grace . . . ordains this or that person to be bishop of this or that diocese. Even when the in-

To assert that apostolic succession goes through the concrete episcopal community means to free one's mind from the bondage of historicity and place the entire matter in a wider church-historical perspective. It would be impossible and irrelevant to discuss here the problems that are related to the appearance of the idea of apostolic succession in the early Church. It is certainly true that this idea was from the beginning related to attempts at reconstructing episcopal lists, which means that the concern at that time was to prove the survival of orthodox teaching by means of strictly historical reconstruction. But why *episcopal* lists? The bishops were not the only expounders of orthodox teaching—for a long time their primary function was not considered to be that of teaching[91]—while one could use a list of presbyters—they were actually considered at that time to be teachers of the people[92]—to prove the survival of orthodoxy in a certain place at least equally well. Why is it that no attempt has been made for such presbyterial lists? To raise such a question does not mean to ignore the fact that the bishops were, at least at the time of the appearance of the idea of apostolic succession, considered to be the teachers *par excellence* and in any case were the ones that bore ultimate responsibility for the orthodox teaching, especially since the time of Gnostic pressure upon the Church. But even if we put aside the possibility that the idea of apostolic succession goes back to a time earlier than the middle second century and not necessarily in connection with the preservation of orthodox teaching,[93] the fact that

---

stitution of the so-called "titular" bishops—who were essentially bishops without a flock—was introduced, provision was made that the name of the diocese, even from among those which no longer existed, would be attached to the name of the bishop in his ordination. This, of course, amounts to a contradiction between theory and practice in ecclesiology, but it nevertheless reveals that the Church has never admitted in her consciousness an episcopate *in absoluto*.

[91] In Ignatius (e.g., *Philad.*, 1, 2) the bishop was not necessarily the teacher. In Justin (*Apol.*, I, 67) the bishop seems to be giving the sermon in the eucharistic *synaxis,* but it was mainly from the time of the *Martyrium Polycarpi* (16, 2) and afterwards that the stress on the bishop's teaching appears clearly. Cf. G. Dix, "Ministry in the Early Church" in *The Apostolic Ministry* (ed. K. E. Kirk, 1957) 204 f.

[92] Sources like the *Shepherd of Hermas* (Vis. 32, 4), Tertullian (*De Praescr.*, 2), Origen (*In Ezekiel*, 2, 2, *PG* 13, 682 C), etc., indicate that the presbyters had teaching as one of their functions. The same is evident from the prayers of ordination to the presbyterate (Hippolytus, *Apost. Trad.*, 9, ed. G. Dix, 13), and from the existence of famous presbyters known as teachers (Clement of Alexandria, Origen, etc.).

[93] *1 Clem.*, 44, 2–4.

the lists of successions were exclusively episcopal—just as in a similar case of the same period, i.e., in the appearance of the councils, the composition was exclusively episcopal—shows that the idea behind them was grounded on a reality broader than the concern for proving the survival of orthodoxy, or to put it in other terms, that the concern for the survival of orthodoxy was not isolated from the broader reality of the Church's life as a community headed by the bishop. The bishops as successors of the apostles were not perpetuators of ideas like the heads of philosophical schools,[94] nor teachers in the same sense that the presbyters were, but heads of communities whose entire life and thought they were supposed by their office to express. Their apostolic succession, therefore, should be viewed neither as a chain of individual acts of ordination nor as a transmission of truths but as a sign and an expression of the *continuity of the Church's historical life in its entirety,* as it was realized in each community.

Such an understanding of apostolic succession explains why in its first appearance this concept was so concretely conceived that the reference was made not to "apostolic succession"[95] in general but to apostolic "successions" (plural),[96] exactly as in the language of that time the catholicity of the Church was understood in the form of "catholic Churches" (plural). The fundamental implication of this fact is that each episcopal community reflects in itself not only the "whole Church" but also the *whole succession of the apostles.* Indeed, it is quite significant that each bishop was at that time thought to be a successor not of a particular apostle, but of *all the apostles.*[97] This made each episcopal church *fully apostolic*[98] and each bishop an occupant of the *cathedra Petri.*[99] This means that apostolic succession can never be a

[94] Hippolytus, *Philos.,* 9, 12, 21 (*PG* 15, 3386): The "catholic Church" was not a "school" *(didaskaleion).*

[95] It is noteworthy that for some ancient authors (e.g., Tertullian, *De Praescr.,* 20, 2–5) apostolic succession is one "of apostolic churches rather than of apostolic bishops," as it is pointed out by R. P. C. Hanson, *Tradition in the Early Church* (1962) 158.

[96] Hegesippus quoted by Eusebius, *Eccl. Hist.,* I, 22, 3–5: "in each succession and in each city. . . ."

[97] Cf. F. Dvornik, *The Idea of Apostolicity in Byzantium and the Legend of St. Andrew* (1958).

[98] It is noteworthy how Tertullian (*De Praescr.,* 36, 2) refers to the various churches in connection with their apostolicity; in all the places he mentions (Achaia, Macedonia, Asia, Italy, Rome) "the very thrones of the apostles are still preeminent in their places in which their own authentic writings are still read, etc."

[99] Cyprian, *Ep.,* 69 (66) 5 and 43 (40) 5. Cf. *De Unit.,* 4.

result of *adding up* the various episcopal successions. The apostolic college in its succession was not divided into parts so that each bishop would be ascribed to one part and all bishops together to the whole of this college. Episcopal collegiality, therefore, does not represent a *collective* unity, but a *unity in identity,* an organic unity. It is the identity of each community with the body of Christ expressed in historical terms through the continuity of the apostolic presence in the *locus apostolicus* of each episcopal community.

Apostolic succession represents a sign of the historical dimension of the catholicity of the Church. It serves to combine the historical with the charismatic and transcend the divisions caused by time. In an understanding of the apostolic succession stemming from the eucharistic community, where the past and the future are through the Holy Spirit perceived in one and the same reality of the present,[100] history and time are fully accepted and eternal life is not opposed to them but enters into them and transcends them as they affect man's destiny and salvation. Thus the Church is revealed to be in time what she is eschatologically, namely, a catholic Church which stands in history as a transcendence of all divisions into the unity of all in Christ through the Holy Spirit to the glory of God the Father.

[100] Cf. the liturgy of St. John Chrysostom at the prayer of the anaphora: "Commemorating this command of our Savior and all that was endured for our sake, the cross, the grave, the resurrection after three days, the ascension into heaven, the enthronement at the right hand of the Father, and the second and glorious coming again, thine own we offer to thee in all and for all."

Subject Index

allegorical explanations of Mass: 40–41

anamnesis (*see* memorial): 16–17, 20–26, 38, 42, 124, 126–27, 132–33, 141–42, 145, 147, 225

anaphora: 157–59, 161, 169

Anglican Eucharist: 117–28

anointing of sick: 162

anthropology, catholic: 226

apostolic succession: 229–32

Aquinas, Thomas: 55–56, 79, 92–98, 101, 148–51, 162, 171, 176

Aristotelian doctrine of substance and accidents: 98–192

Baptism: 26, 218

Benediction (*see* Blessed Sacrament): 71

Berengarius: 53–56, 62, 79, 93, 98–99; eleventh century controversy, 54; profession of faith, 54, 56, 79

biblical events, character of: 8–10

Blessed Sacrament (*see* eucharistic species): blessings with, 67, 70–71; devotion to, 67–68, 71; exposition of/adoration, 53, 67–70; perpetual adoration, 69–70; processions of, 67–69; services honoring, 69–71; visits to, 67, 70

Byzantine Divine Liturgy (Eucharist): communion rites, 177–79, 181–82; concelebration, 159–62, 177–79; frequency of celebration, 157; patriarchal/pontifical, 179–80; presbyteral, 179–80

catholic: anthropology, 226; unique/distinctive quality of real presence, 91, 95; view of existence, 226

catholicity of Church: Christological, 222–24; eucharistic structure, 223; in Eucharist, 219–22; pneumatological dimension, 224

Church Year: 15–29; purpose of, 21–22, 25–26

chantries: 28–29

communion, ecclesial: 189, 193–94, 196, 221–22; signified by sacramental communion, 162–65, 169–72, 174–76, 181

communion, sacramental: after Mass, 47; almost replaced by adoration, 65; Armenian, 181; at concelebration, 159, 176–83; Byzantine, 177–79, 181–82; confession before, 59–60; Coptic, 179–82; decline of, 157–72; East-Syrian, 179–81; Ethiopian, 182; frequency of, 57, 157–72; from *fermentum*, 176; in hand/mouth, 39, 45; intinction, 46; meaning and symbolism of, 175–83; norms for, 182; of clergy, 176–83; of the dying, 66; of the sick, 50–51; received, not taken, 175–83; rite of, 175–83; Roman, 176–77, 182–83; sacrament of ecclesial communion, 162–65, 169–72, 174–76, 181; separation from

of celebration: in Eastern Churches, 157–62; in Roman tradition, 175–76; one Mass per day per altar, 171; one Sunday Mass in Rome, Carthage, Alexandria, 176

eucharistic controversies: ninth century, 42–44; Paschasius Radbertus, 42–44, 53–54, 108, 126; Ratramnus, 42, 44, 53, 108; eleventh century, 54–56, 108; Berengarius, 54–56; Lanfranc, 54

eucharistic divisions: 195

eucharistic ecclesiology: 186, 188–89, 191–94, 196–97, 199, 206

eucharistic presence (*see* Real Presence)

eucharistic species (*see* Blessed Sacrament): adoration of, 63–64; desecrations of, 55; desire to see, 63–71; devotion to, 63–71; miracles of, 43, 55, 66; reverences toward, 189; solemn showing of before communion, 40; symbolic burial of, 51–52; unique relic, 52; use for private ends, 56

eucharistic/sacramental hospitality: 203

exegesis, patristic and mystagogy: 126

feast, theology of: 15–26

fermentum: 38, 40

Forty Hours adoration: 70

fraction, symbol of eucharistic communion: 176

frequency of Eucharist (*see* communion, Eucharist): 172

grace: 111–13, 210

historical character of human thought and faith: 77–79

hypostatic union/Eucharist: 86, 104

in persona Christi: 148–49, 151, 170–71

in persona Christi/*in persona ecclesiae*: 134, 149–51, 153–56

institution narrative: 127 (*see* supper narrative)

"institutum ut sumatur" (Trent): 89

intercommunion: 185–207

Israel's cult, function of: 1–7

Jesus: as new cult/realization of old cult, 20; everything in salvation history assumed, 18–20; heavenly priest and liturgy, 18, 23, 27; his cult as ours, 20–26; historical, 25–26; light of the world, 179–80; mysteries of earthly economy, 21–22, 25–26; our archetype, 25–26; personalization of salvation history and cult, 18–20, 24–25; presence of, 22–26; risen, contemporary, 22–26; transformation, conversion into, 24–25; *Ursakrament*, 24

Last Supper account (*see* supper narrative)

life in Christ, death to self to live for others: 20

liturgy: basis, meaning, purpose, characteristics of, 18–21, 26, 173; (like NT), 20, 25; focused on present, 20–26; personalized in Jesus, 18–20

Liturgy of the Hours; sacrament of Christ, 176–77

local church: 191, 209–10, 214, 219–22

"Lord, I am not worthy": 47

Luther: 80, 94

Marriage: 188

Mass (*see* Eucharist, celebration): and confession, 48; as commutation of penances, 48; daily, 27, 49, 60, 160; development of rubrics, 49–50; frequency of, 32–33; intention,

168–69; multiplication of, 27–28, 33, 48, 160; only one papal Sunday mass in Rome, 176; *opus bonum*, 27; personal devotion, 30, 33; private (*see* private Mass); sacrament of the Church, 169–71; separation from communion, 58–59; small–group, 31–32, 159–60; stipend, 29, 48, 169; synchronized, 157–59; votive, 32; with exposition, 69

memorial (*see* anamnesis): 1–14, 16–17; actualization of the past/of tradition, 1–10; actualization theories, 7–10; encounter and participation, 8–10, 13–14, 37; Cranmer's understanding, 123; Late Medieval understanding, 123; of once-for-all, past, unrepeatable, salvific historical events, 7–11, 15–16

ministry in the Church: 227–29

miraculous hosts: 55, 66

monstrance/ostensorium: 68

mystagogy: 26

New Testament, compared to liturgy: 20–21, 25–26

offering: 20, 132–33, 153–55; prayer for acceptance of, 145–47, 153–55

once-for-all character of biblical/salvific events (*ephapax*): 8–10, 15–17, 225

ordination: 188, 218, 220, 227–29

Orthodoxy, Orthodox Church(es): concelebration in, 157–62; liturgical spirit of, 181–82

ostensorium (*see* monstrance)

pasch, paschal celebration: 26

Pauline view of liturgy: 19–20, 23–25; of salvation, 18–19, 24–25

presence of Christ in the Eucharist (*see* Real Presence)

priests: back to congregation, 49–50; separation from people, 44–46; special status of, 44–45

priest-monks: 48

private Mass: 160–61; development of, 27–35; divisive, 160, 169–70; not usual in antiquity, 160; prohibited on some occasions, 160

real change in Eucharist (*see* transformation, transsubstantiation)

Real Presence (*see* eucharistic controversies): 42–45, 47, 54, 61, 79–82, 85, 87–115, 127; catholic quality of, 91, 95; directed ultimately to sacramental communion, 89; —as sacramental presence: 42–44, 82; Augustine, 39; Thomas, 92; —theological views of: Cranmer, 117–28; Luther, 87, 94; Thomas Aquinas, 79, 92–93; Wycliffe, 98–100; Zwingli, 88, 94, 109–11, 117

Roman Canon: 35, 50, 124–26, 129–56; silent, 50

Rome: liturgically conservative, 168–69, 176; only papal mass on Sunday, 176; use of *fermentum*, 176

sacrament, symbolic nature of: 173–74

sacramental change: 82

sacrifice: 19–20, 150

sacrifice, interior, 18

sacrifice/offering, eucharistic: 122–24, 127–28, 132, 134, 140

salvation history: 15–18, 20–21, 22–26

Sanctus bell/candle: 63–64

stipend: 29, 48, 169

substance/species: 81–82, 84–86, 93, 96–98, 109